PENGUIN BOOKS

845

COLLECTED PLAYS

JOHN M. SYNGE

JOHN M. SYNGE

Collected Plays

PENGUIN BOOKS

HARMONDSWORTH · MIDDLESEX

FIRST PUBLICATION IN BOOK FORM:

The Shadow of the Glen and Riders to the Sea, 1905
The Well of the Saints, 1905
The Playboy of the Western World, 1907
The Tinker's Wedding, 1908
Deirdre of the Sorrows, 1910

FIRST PUBLISHED IN PENGUIN BOOKS 1952

MADE AND PRINTED IN GREAT BRITAIN
FOR PENGUIN BOOKS LTD
BY THE WHITEFRIARS PRESS LTD
LONDON AND TONBRIDGE

CONTENTS

Introduction   7

The Shadow of the Glen   15

Riders to the Sea   35

The Tinker's Wedding   51

The Well of the Saints   83

The Playboy of the Western World   137

Deirdre of the Sorrows   211

Note   267

Introduction

And that inquiring man John Synge comes next
That dying chose the living world for text,
And never could have rested in his tomb
But that, long-travelling, he had come
Towards nightfall upon certain set apart
In a most desolate stony place.
Towards nightfall upon a race
Passionate and simple as his heart.

W. B. YEATS

ONE wintry evening I had come out of a little shop on Aranmore; my friend, who was absentminded, followed me a few minutes later. Vaguely he noticed that I had left a bicycle behind, so, picking it up, he wheeled it after me. He had gone about a mile on the road when he heard footsteps walking softly behind him. He turned and waited. 'Would you be wanting that bicycle, sir?' said an islander, coming up to him. 'For if you do you are very welcome to it.'

It was this same dignified approach to life that drew J. M. Synge to the Aran Islands fifty years ago. It was here, on this stony striking edge of the Atlantic, that his imagination flared freely. Here he found, ready to his hand, a community as rounded as the belly of a pebble one would pick up on a shore, a people shaped by the sea's hardship, salty of speech, simple of heart, and touched extravagantly to life by the constant presence of death. It was Yeats who in 1898 told the wandering Synge to go to the Aran Islands – 'Live there as if you were one of the people themselves. Express a life that has never found expression.' Fifty years earlier, Synge's uncle had been Protestant curate on Aran; and, as a boy, hearing the story of that uncle's feud with the Galway fishermen and of how he armed his own boatmen to the teeth, Synge must have been impressed by the dramatic quality of life in the islands. And indeed that is what Aran at length gave to Synge, a heightened sense of human drama. Here were men and women who lived with the halter of hunger round their necks, who could be lifted sharply into high moments of gaiety or plunged into dark bottoms of anger; whose laughter had grief concealed in the sleeve, and whose tongue was forked for praise or blame. This balance and contrariness of mood was the very stuff of drama to Synge who, as against the nineties, felt that the airiest poetry and the most purple prose must have their roots in the soil, that the dove's foot must have dust on it. 'In these days,' he wrote, 'poetry is usually a flower of evil or good, but it is the timber of poetry that wears most surely, and there is no timber that has not strong roots among the clay and worms. Even if we grant that exalted poetry can be kept exalted by itself, the strong things in life are needed in poetry also, to show that what is exalted, or tender, is not made by feeble blood. It may almost be said that before verse can become human again it must learn to be brutal.'

It was Synge's 'hunger for harsh facts, for ugly surprising things, for all that defies our hope', his love for all that in speech of character was earthy, salty, and prickling to the springs of the mouth or mind, that roused the resentment of Dublin audiences. From *The Shadow of the Glen*, in which the farmer's wife goes off with the tramp, to *The Playboy of the Western World*, who kills his father, Synge's plays were bitterly attacked by Irish critics to whom the salty seemed the salacious, and the earthy was anathema, and the Rabelaisian element represented a 'Roman decadence'. Even Synge's choice of Irish phrase was, and still is, a point in dispute. George Moore praised Synge for having made a great literature out of that 'barbaric jargon', the peasant speech: St John Ervine denounced Synge as 'a faker of peasant speech'. Yet, protested Synge, 'I have used one or two words only that I have not heard among the country people of Ireland . . . . All art is a collaboration; and there is little doubt that in the happy ages of literature, striking and beautiful phrases were as ready to the storyteller's or the playwright's hand, as the rich cloaks and dresses of his time. . . . In a good play every speech should be as fully flavoured as a nut or an apple, and such speeches cannot be written by anyone who works among people who have shut their lips on poetry. In Ireland, for a few years more, we have a popular imagination that is fiery, and magnificent, and tender.'

Synge was a tireless collector of the imaginative speech of the Irish countryman, of what he called 'the living phrase'. An author, he held, should not be a phrase-coiner. He loved to walk the roads of Wicklow, Kerry, and the West; to talk to tinker, tailor, publican, and beggar, and to make notes. Sometimes he took a bicycle; for, being a shy man, he found it easier to get into conversation with passers-by if he pretended to have a breakdown. 'And how would I pay rent,' said a Wicklow tramp to Synge, 'and I only an old man living on his pocket.' 'That phrase,' remarked Synge to a friend afterwards, 'was worth tuppence.' He would chuckle over a letter from a Wexford tailor offering to make him a home-spun suit that 'would go round you and cover you like a curtain.' And his eye kindled in a Kerry pub when the landlord, talking about his two bachelor sisters, exclaimed – 'What are they to me anyway? No more than the button to the buttonhole.' Such phrases were part and parcel, thumb and thimble, of Synge's early life; and Wicklow was, and is still, rich in them. 'Will you look at the colour of that bullock!' said a Wicklow man admiringly. 'You'd think that the shadows of the clouds were passing on its back.' Often Synge would produce his own intuitive remark and note it afterwards. Once, resting with a woman friend in a Wicklow wood, she lay back in the grass, 'stretched back,' as Synge said, 'unto her necklace in the flowers of the earth.' The phrase went into *The Playboy*.

'Why do people think of eternity as a long, long thing?' said W. B. Yeats once to a friend. 'Eternity is the flash of light on a beetle's wing.' The Irish genius is an intuitive one; it can have sudden and dark insight and it can produce the flashing and long-illuminating phrase. But brilliant phrases and intuitive flashes, though they make an engaging folk-speech, do not make literature unless they are linked to a containing and over-all vision: the creative writer must have an outside to his inside, a unifying shape to his imaginings; he must be both divided and at one, involved and detached. Synge had no native detachment or unifying philosophy, and was little given to theory or reflection. 'All theory is bad for the artist,' he wrote, 'because it makes him live in the intelligence. . . .' Despite his cunningly selected store of phrase and folk-story, his rich and scattered knowledge of country people, Synge's life and work for years lacked direction, and his writing lacked distinction. It was in the narrow Western Islands that he found a convenient shape and ready framework that would hold and liberate his hiving and too-wandering imagination. 'It was only,' said Yeats, 'when he found Inishmaan and the Blaskets . . . that his writing lost its old morbid brooding, that he found his genius and peace.'

John Millington Synge was born in 1871 at Newtown Little, a village near Dublin, the youngest of a family of eight. A year later his father died. Being delicate – he suffered from asthma – Synge's schooling was desultory. He was a solitary lad who disliked games and companions and loved the loneliness of the Dublin hills. His mother's influence was certainly the most formative one in his life. She was a devout Protestant Ulster-woman, of strong character, pungent expression, and pronounced Evangelical views. And Synge, who was devoted to her, was suckled on 'the milk of the Word'. It grieved her when, on reading Darwin's *Origin of Species* at the age of fourteen, he began to doubt the story of the Garden of Eden. But the loss of Eden and of unity was the beginning of knowledge and self-assertion. And the estrangement from a strict Evangelical doctrine led to a widening of imagination. It made him a freeman and wanderer of the Wicklow glens and hills. Bird, insect, and flower, no one came to know them better than Synge. 'Out of the quarrel with ourselves,' said Yeats, 'we make poetry.' But, one way or another, Synge's Evangelical upbringing left its mark on him. To please his mother he refrained from riding his bicycle on Sundays. And when he first fell in love it was with a young woman, a member of the Plymouth Brethren, whose mother refused to countenance the affair because of Synge's 'unbelief'. His ascetic nature, his preoccupation with and insistence on 'the truth', 'the living phrase', the real as opposed to the fanciful – all this was partly a legacy from his Evangelical upbringing. When, in his early twenties, he escaped abroad to study music – he could play the fiddle, the flute, the piano – he lived meagrely on forty pounds a year; nor did he ever care for the Bohemian life of Paris. He preferred to wander alone through the outlying villages and countryside, for he was a student of men rather than books, and in his later years found it almost impossible to concentrate on reading. True, he earned an occasional guinea in Paris by reviewing books; but he would spend an inordinate time working out the rhythm and cadence of a single sentence. 'Don't buy a French encyclopedia,' he advised a friend. 'Get the *Encyclopedia Britannica* where the writer won't stop in the middle of an article to tell you "how fond one is of one's mother''. But, in the end, it was Synge's deep interest in clash of character, his study of French classical drama, and his choice of a sharply dramatic background, the Aran Islands, which contributed to his masterly sense of theatre. 'I have discovered,' said Yeats, 'on reading Synge's first two plays, *The Shadow of the Glen* and *Riders to the Sea*, for the Irish National Theatre Society, a man who has the qualities of Aeschylus and Sophocles combined.'

Synge knew the Irish glens and hills as Yeats never did. He talked to the travelling men and listened to the peasant story-tellers – those living libraries of a vanished Europe – at a time when the printed word had not yet taken away men's memories or the radio stolen their voices, and when pictures were still to be seen in the heart of a turf fire and not in a cinema. He did not belong to the Gaelic world, nor did he become one with the people. But he took their rich idiom and their living stories, and he used them as a theme on which he made his free variations: the real and the fanciful, the traditional and the individual, were the counterpoints of his drama. The story of a Connemara farmer, a married man with a family, who killed his father and then escaped into Aran – out of this Synge created the superb fantasy of *The Playboy*. It is irrelevant to object – as the demonstrators at the Abbey Theatre did in 1907 – that the result is untrue to Irish life. 'For a long time I have felt,' wrote Synge, 'that Poetry roughly is of two kinds, the poetry of real life . . . and the poetry of a land of fancy. . . . What is highest in poetry is always reached where the dreamer is leaning out to reality, or where the man of real life is lifted out of it, and in all the poets the greatest have both these elements, that is they are supremely engrossed with life, and yet with the wildness of their fancy they are always passing out of what is simple and plain.'

Synge wanted the best of both worlds. For he was born

between two worlds, of Anglo-Irish stock. He was reared between faith and doubt, torn between truth and fancy. He swayed between Paris and the Irish countryside. Like others of that divided Anglo-Irish race – from Sheridan to Shaw – he sought expression for, and found the resolution of, that conflict in the writing of drama. His unity is in his plays.

He died in 1909, the year after his mother died. 'I am certain,' wrote Yeats, 'that my friend's noble art is the victory of a man who in poverty and sickness created from the delight of expression.' Synge, a solitary man, made few friends in his lifetime. But it was noticed at his funeral that an old lady in black came forward and placed a single bunch of violets on the grave and went away. Nobody knew her. Was it, I wonder, the old lady whom, years before, Synge saw fast asleep in the Louvre, with a reticule hanging from satin ribbons: and stopping in front of her, fascinated, he gazed for some time and said to a friend – 'Would you not see all our mothers?'

W. R. RODGERS

The Shadow of the Glen

PERSONS IN THE PLAY

DAN BURKE, *Farmer and Herd*

NORA BURKE, *his Wife*

MICHAEL DARA, a *young Herd*

A TRAMP

SCENE – *The last cottage at the head of a long glen in County Wicklow*

Two chief aspects of Irish life in
Shadow & Riders.
Shadow = pastoral life
Riders = Sea-faring life.

The Shadow of the Glen

Cottage kitchen; turf-fire on the right; a bed near it against the wall, with a body lying on it covered with a sheet. A door is at the other end of the room, with a low table near it, and stools, or wooden chairs. There are a couple of glasses on the table, and a bottle of whisky, as if for a wake, with two cups, a teapot, and a home-made cake. There is another small door near the bed. NORA BURKE *is moving about the room, settling a few things, and lighting candles on the table, looking now and then at the bed with an uneasy look. Some one knocks softly at the door. She takes up a stocking with money from the table and puts it in her pocket. Then she opens the door.*

TRAMP [*outside*]. Good evening to you, lady of the house.

NORA. Good evening kindly, stranger; it's a wild night, God help you, to be out in the rain falling.

TRAMP. It is, surely, and I walking to Brittas from the Aughrim fair.

NORA. Is it walking on your feet, stranger?

TRAMP. On my two feet, lady of the house, and when I saw the light below I thought maybe if you'd a sup of new milk and a quiet, decent corner where a man could sleep . . . [*He looks in past her and sees the dead man.*] The Lord have mercy on us all!

NORA. It doesn't matter anyway, stranger; come in out of the rain.

TRAMP [*coming in slowly and going towards the bed*]. Is it departed he is?

NORA. It is, stranger. He's after dying on me, God forgive

him, and there I am now with a hundred sheep beyond on the hills, and no turf drawn for the winter.

TRAMP [*looking closely at the dead man*]. It's a queer look is on him for a man that's dead.

NORA [*half-humorously*]. He was always queer, stranger; and I suppose them that's queer and they living men will be queer bodies after.

TRAMP. Isn't it a great wonder you're letting him lie there, and he not tidied, or laid out itself?

NORA [*coming to the bed*]. I was afeard, stranger, for he put a black curse on me this morning if I'd touch his body the time he'd die sudden, or let anyone touch it except his sister only, and it's ten miles away she lives, in the big glen over the hill.

TRAMP [*looking at her and nodding slowly*]. It's a queer story he wouldn't let his own wife touch him, and he dying quiet in his bed.

NORA. He was an old man, and an odd man, stranger, and it's always upon the hills he was, thinking thoughts in the dark mist . . . [*She pulls back a bit of the sheet.*] Lay your hand on him now, and tell me if it's cold he is surely.

TRAMP. Is it getting the curse on me you'd be, woman of the house? I wouldn't lay my hand on him for the Lough Nahanagan and it filled with gold.

NORA [*looking uneasily at the body*]. Maybe cold would be no sign of death with the like of him, for he was always cold, every day since I knew him . . . and every night, stranger . . . [*she covers up his face and comes away from the bed*]; but I'm thinking it's dead he is surely, for he's complaining a while back of a pain in his heart, and this morning, the time he was going off to Brittas for three days or four, he was taken with a sharp turn. Then he went into his bed, and he was saying it was destroyed he was, the time the shadow was going up through the glen, and when the sun set on the bog beyond he made a great lep, and let a great cry out of him, and stiffened himself out the like of a dead sheep.

TRAMP [*crosses himself*]. God rest his soul.

NORA [*pouring him out a glass of whisky*]. Maybe that would do you better than the milk of the sweetest cow in County Wicklow.

TRAMP. The Almighty God reward you and may it be to your good health.

[*He drinks.*]

NORA [*giving him a pipe and tobacco*]. I've no pipes saving his own, stranger, but they're sweet pipes to smoke.

TRAMP. Thank you kindly, lady of the house.

NORA. Sit down now, stranger, and be taking your rest.

TRAMP [*filling a pipe and looking about the room*]. I've walked a great way through the world, lady of the house, and seen great wonders, but I never seen a wake till this day with fine spirits, and good tobacco, and the best of pipes, and no one to taste them but a woman only.

NORA. Didn't you hear me say it was only after dying on me he was when the sun went down, and how would I go out into the glen and tell the neighbours, and I a lone woman with no house near me?

TRAMP [*drinking*]. There's no offence, lady of the house?

NORA. No offence in life, stranger. How would the like of you, passing in the dark night, know the lonesome way I was with no house near me at all?

TRAMP [*sitting down*]. I knew rightly. [*He lights his pipe, so that there is a sharp light beneath his haggard face.*] And I was thinking, and I coming in through the door, that it's many a lone woman would be afeard of the like of me in the dark night, in a place wouldn't be as lonesome as this place, where there aren't two living souls would see the little light you have shining from the glass.

NORA [*slowly*]. I'm thinking many would be afeard, but I never knew what way I'd be afeard of beggar or bishop or any man of you at all . . . [*she looks towards the window and lowers her voice*]. It's other things than the like of you, stranger, would make a person afeard.

TRAMP [*looking round with a half-shudder*]. It is surely, God help us all!

NORA [*looking at him for a moment with curiosity*]. You're saying that, stranger, as if you were easy afeard.

TRAMP [*speaking mournfully*]. Is it myself, lady of the house, that does be walking round in the long nights, and crossing the hills when the fog is on them, the time a little stick would seem as big as your arm, and a rabbit as big as a bay horse, and a stack of turf as big as a towering church in the city of Dublin? If myself was easy afeard, I'm telling you, it's long ago I'd have been locked into the Richmond Asylum, or maybe have run up into the back hills with nothing on me but an old shirt, and been eaten by the crows the like of Patch Darcy – the Lord have mercy on him – in the year that's gone.

NORA [*with interest*]. You knew Darcy?

TRAMP. Wasn't I the last one heard his living voice in the whole world?

NORA. There were great stories of what was heard at that time, but would anyone believe the things they do be saying in the glen?

TRAMP. It was no lie, lady of the house. . . . I was passing below on a dark night the like of this night, and the sheep were lying under the ditch and every one of them coughing and choking like an old man, with the great rain and the fog. Then I heard a thing talking – queer talk, you wouldn't believe it at all, and you out of your dreams – and 'Merciful God,' says I, 'if I begin hearing the like of that voice out of the thick mist, I'm destroyed surely.' Then I run and I run till I was below in Rathvanna. I got drunk that night, I got drunk in the morning, and drunk the day after – I was coming from the races beyond – and the third day they found Darcy. . . . Then I knew it was himself I was after hearing, and I wasn't afeard any more.

NORA [*speaking sorrowfully and slowly*]. God spare Darcy; he'd always look in here and he passing up or passing down, and it's very lonesome I was after him a long while [*she looks over at the bed and lowers her voice, speaking very slowly*], and then I got happy again – if it's ever happy we are, stranger – for I got used to being lonesome.

[*A short pause; then she stands up.*]

NORA. Was there anyone on the last bit of the road, stranger, and you coming from Aughrim?

TRAMP. There was a young man with a drift of mountain ewes, and he running after them this way and that.

NORA [*with a half-smile*]. Far down, stranger?

TRAMP. A piece only.

[NORA *fills the kettle and puts it on the fire.*]

NORA. Maybe, if you're not easy afeard, you'd stay here a short while alone with himself.

TRAMP. I would surely. A man that's dead can do no hurt.

NORA [*speaking with a sort of constraint*]. I'm going a little back to the west, stranger, for himself would go there one night and another and whistle at that place, and then the young man you're after seeing – a kind of a farmer has come up from the sea to live in a cottage beyond – would walk round to see if there was a thing we'd have to be done, and I'm wanting him this night, the way he can go down into the glen when the sun goes up and tell the people that himself is dead.

TRAMP [*looking at the body in the sheet*]. It's myself will go for him, lady of the house, and let you not be destroying yourself with the great rain.

NORA. You wouldn't find your way, stranger, for there's a small path only, and it running up between two sluigs where an ass and cart would be drowned. [*She puts a shawl over her head.*] Let you be making yourself easy, and saying a prayer for his soul, and it's not long I'll be coming again.

TRAMP [*moving uneasily*]. Maybe if you'd a piece of a grey thread and a sharp needle – there's great safety in a needle, lady of the house – I'd be putting a little stitch here and there in my old coat, the time I'll be praying for his soul, and it going up naked to the saints of God.

NORA [*takes a needle and thread from the front of her dress and gives it to him*]. There's the needle, stranger, and I'm thinking you won't be lonesome, and you used to the back hills, for isn't a dead man itself more company than to be sitting alone, and hearing the winds crying, and you not knowing on what thing your mind would stay?

TRAMP [*slowly*]. It's true, surely, and the Lord have mercy on us all!

[NORA *goes out. The tramp begins stitching one of the tags in his coat, saying the 'De Profundis' under his breath. In an instant the sheet is drawn slowly down, and* DAN BURKE *looks out. The tramp moves uneasily, then looks up, and springs to his feet with a movement of terror.*]

DAN [*with a hoarse voice*]. Don't be afeard, stranger; a man that's dead can do no hurt.

TRAMP [*trembling*]. I meant no harm, your honour; and

won't you leave me easy to be saying a little prayer for your soul?

[*A long whistle is heard outside.*]

DAN [*sitting up in his bed and speaking fiercely*]. Ah, the devil mend her. . . . Do you hear that, stranger? Did ever you hear another woman could whistle the like of that with two fingers in her mouth? [*He looks at the table hurriedly.*] I'm destroyed with the drouth, and let you bring me a drop quickly before herself will come back.

TRAMP [*doubtfully*]. Is it not dead you are?

DAN. How would I be dead, and I as dry as a baked bone, stranger?

TRAMP [*pouring out the whisky*]. What will herself say if she smells the stuff on you, for I'm thinking it's not for nothing you're letting on to be dead?

DAN. It is not, stranger; but she won't be coming near me at all, and it's not long now I'll be letting on, for I've a cramp in my back, and my hip's asleep on me, and there's been the devil's own fly itching my nose. It's near dead I was wanting to sneeze, and you blathering about the rain, and Darcy [*bitterly*] – the devil choke him – and the towering church. [*Crying out impatiently.*] Give me that whisky. Would you have herself come back before I taste a drop at all?

[TRAMP *gives him the glass.*]

DAN [*after drinking*]. Go over now to that cupboard, and bring me a black stick you'll see in the west corner by the wall.

TRAMP [*taking a stick from the cupboard*]. Is it that, your honour?

DAN. It is, stranger; it's a long time I'm keeping that stick, for I've a bad wife in the house.

TRAMP [*with a queer look*]. Is it herself, master of the house, and she a grand woman to talk?

DAN. It's herself, surely, it's a bad wife she is – a bad wife for an old man, and I'm getting old, God help me, though I've an arm to me still. [*He takes the stick in his hand.*] Let you wait now a short while, and it's a great sight you'll see in this room in two hours or three. [*He stops to listen.*] Is that somebody above?

TRAMP [*listening*]. There's a voice speaking on the path.

DAN. Put that stick here in the bed and smooth the sheet the way it was lying. [*He covers himself up hastily.*] Be falling to sleep now, and don't let on you know anything, or I'll be having your life. I wouldn't have told you at all but it's destroyed with the drouth I was.

TRAMP [*covering his head*]. Have no fear, master of the house. What is it I know of the like of you that I'd be saying a word or putting out my hand to stay you at all?

[*He goes back to the fire, sits down on a stool with his back to the bed, and goes on stitching his coat.*]

DAN [*under the sheet, querulously*]. Stranger!

TRAMP [*quickly*]. Whisht! whisht! Be quiet, I'm telling you; they're coming now at the door.

[NORA *comes in with* MICHAEL DARA, *a tall, innocent young man, behind her.*]

NORA. I wasn't long at all, stranger, for I met himself on the path.

TRAMP. You were middling long, lady of the house.

NORA. There was no sign from himself?

TRAMP. No sign at all, lady of the house.

NORA [*to* MICHAEL]. Go over now and pull down the sheet, and look on himself, Michael Dara, and you'll see it's the truth I'm telling you.

MICHAEL. I will not, Nora; I do be afeard of the dead.

24

[*He sits down on a stool next the table, facing the tramp.*
NORA *puts the kettle on a lower hook of the pot-hooks, and piles
turf under it.*]

NORA [*turning to tramp*]. Will you drink a sup of tea with
myself and the young man, stranger, or [*speaking more
persuasively*] will you go into the little room and stretch
yourself a short while on the bed? I'm thinking it's
destroyed you are walking the length of that way in the
great rain.

TRAMP. Is it go away and leave you, and you having a
wake, lady of the house? I will not, surely. [*He takes a
drink from his glass, which he has beside him.*] And it's none
of your tea I'm asking either.

[*He goes on stitching.* NORA *makes the tea.*]

MICHAEL [*after looking at the tramp rather scornfully for a
moment*]. That's a poor coat you have, God help you, and
I'm thinking it's a poor tailor you are with it.

TRAMP. If it's a poor tailor I am, I'm thinking it's a poor
herd does be running backward and forward after a little
handful of ewes, the way I seen yourself running this day,
young fellow, and you coming from the fair.

[NORA *comes back to the table.*]

NORA [*to* MICHAEL, *in a low voice*]. Let you not mind him
at all, Michael Dara; he has a drop taken, and it's soon
he'll be falling asleep.

MICHAEL. It's no lie he's telling; I was destroyed, surely.
They were that wilful they were running off into one
man's bit of oats, and another man's bit of hay, and
tumbling into the red bog till it's more like a pack of old
goats than sheep they were. . . . Mountain ewes is a
queer breed, Nora Burke, and I not used to them at all.

NORA [*settling the tea-things*]. There's no one can drive
a mountain ewe but the men do be reared in the

Glenmalure, I've heard them say, and above by Rathvanna, and the Glen Imaal – men the like of Patch Darcy, God spare his soul, who would walk through five hundred sheep and miss one of them, and he not reckoning them at all.

MICHAEL [*uneasily*]. Is it the man went queer in his head the year that's gone ?

NORA. It is, surely.

TRAMP [*plaintively*]. That was a great man, young fellow – a great man, I'm telling you. There was never a lamb from his own ewes he wouldn't know before it was marked, and he'd run from this to the city of Dublin and never catch for his breath.

NORA [*turning round quickly*]. He was a great man surely, stranger; and isn't it a grand thing when you hear a living man saying a good word of a dead man, and he mad dying?

TRAMP. It's the truth I'm saying, God spare his soul.

[*He puts the needle under the collar of his coat, and settles himself to sleep in the chimney corner.* NORA *sits down at the table:* NORA *and* MICHAEL'*s backs are turned to the bed.*]

MICHAEL [*looking at her with a queer look*]. I heard tell this day, Nora Burke, that it was on the path below Patch Darcy would be passing up and passing down, and I heard them say he'd never pass it night or morning without speaking with yourself.

NORA [*in a low voice*]. It was no lie you heard, Michael Dara.

MICHAEL. I'm thinking it's a power of men you're after knowing if it's in a lonesome place you live itself.

NORA [*giving him his tea*]. It's in a lonesome place you do have to be talking with someone, and looking for someone, in the evening of the day, and if it's a power of men

I'm after knowing they were fine men, for I was a hard child to please, and a hard girl to please [*she looks at him a little sternly*], and it's a hard woman I am to please this day, Michael Dara, and it's no lie I'm telling you.

MICHAEL [*looking over to see that the tramp is asleep, and then pointing to the dead man*]. Was it a hard woman to please you were when you took himself for your man?

NORA. What way would I live, and I an old woman, if I didn't marry a man with a bit of a farm, and cows on it, and sheep on the back hills?

MICHAEL [*considering*]. That's true, Nora, and maybe it's no fool you were, for there's good grazing on it, if it is a lonesome place, and I'm thinking it's a good sum he's left behind.

NORA [*taking the stocking with the money from her pocket, and putting it on the table*]. I do be thinking in the long nights it was a big fool I was that time, Michael Dara; for what good is a bit of a farm with cows on it, and sheep on the back hills, when you do be sitting looking out from a door the like of that door, and seeing nothing but the mists rolling down the bog, and the mists again and they rolling up the bog, and hearing nothing but the wind crying out in the bits of broken trees were left from the great storm, and the streams roaring with the rain.

MICHAEL [*looking at her uneasily*]. What is it ails you this night, Nora Burke? I've never heard tell it's the like of that talk you do hear from men, and they after being a great while on the back hills.

NORA [*putting out the money on the table*]. It's a bad night, and a wild night, Michael Dara, and isn't it a great while I am at the foot of the back hills, sitting up here boiling food for himself, and food for the brood sow, and baking a cake when the night falls? [*She puts up the money listlessly in little piles on the table.*] Isn't it a long while I am sitting here in the winter and the summer, and the fine spring, with the young growing behind me and the old passing, saying to myself one time to look on Mary Brien, who wasn't that height [*holding out her hand*], and I a fine girl growing up, and there she is now with two children, and another coming on her in three months or four.

[*She pauses.*]

MICHAEL [*moving over three of the piles*]. That's three pounds we have now, Nora Burke.

NORA [*continuing in the same voice*]. And saying to myself another time, to look on Peggy Cavanagh, who had the lightest hand at milking a cow that wouldn't be easy, or turning a cake, and there she is now walking round on the roads, or sitting in a dirty old house, with no teeth in her mouth, and no sense, and no more hair than you'd see on a bit of hill and they after burning the furze from it.

MICHAEL. That's five pounds and ten notes, a good sum, surely! . . . It's not that way you'll be talking when you marry a young man, Nora Burke, and they were saying in the fair my lambs were the best lambs, and I got a grand price, for I'm no fool now at making a bargain when my lambs are good.

NORA. What was it you got?

MICHAEL. Twenty pounds for the lot, Nora Burke. . . . We'd do right to wait now till himself will be quiet awhile in the Seven Churches, and then you'll marry me in the chapel of Rathvanna, and I'll bring the sheep up on the bit of a hill you have on the back mountain, and we won't have anything we'd be afeard to let our minds on when the mist is down.

NORA [*pouring him out some whisky*]. Why would I marry you, Mike Dara? You'll be getting old and I'll be getting old, and in a little while, I'm telling you, you'll be sitting up in your bed – the way himself was sitting – with a shake in your face, and your teeth falling, and the white hair sticking out round you like an old bush where sheep do be leaping a gap.

[DAN BURKE *sits up noiselessly from under the sheet, with his hand to his face. His white hair is sticking out round his head.* NORA *goes on slowly without hearing him.*]

It's a pitiful thing to be getting old, but it's a queer thing surely. It's a queer thing to see an old man sitting up there in his bed with no teeth in him, and a rough word in his mouth, and his chin the way it would take the bark from the edge of an oak board you'd have building a door. . . . God forgive me, Michael Dara, we'll all be getting old, but it's a queer thing surely.

MICHAEL. It's too lonesome you are from living a long time with an old man, Nora, and you're talking again like a herd that would be coming down from the thick mist [*he puts his arm round her*], but it's a fine life you'll have now with a young man – a fine life, surely. . . .

[DAN *sneezes violently.* MICHAEL *tries to get to the door, but before he can do so* DAN *jumps out of the bed in queer white clothes, with the stick in his hand, and goes over and puts his back against it.*]

MICHAEL. Son of God deliver us!

[*Crosses himself, and goes backward across the room.*]

DAN [*holding up his hand at him*]. Now you'll not marry her the time I'm rotting below in the Seven Churches, and you'll see the thing I'll give you will follow you on the back mountains when the wind is high.

MICHAEL [*to* NORA]. Get me out of it, Nora, for the love

of God. He always did what you bid him, and I'm thinking he would do it now.

NORA [*looking at the tramp*]. Is it dead he is or living?

DAN [*turning towards her*]. It's little you care if it's dead or
living I am; but there'll be an end now of your fine times,
and all the talk you have of young men and old men, and
of the mist coming up or going down. [*He opens the door.*]
You'll walk out now from that door, Nora Burke; and
it's not to-morrow, or the next day, or any day of your
life, that you'll put in your foot through it again.

TRAMP [*standing up*]. It's a hard thing you're saying for an
old man, master of the house; and what would the like
of her do if you put her out on the roads?

DAN. Let her walk round the like of Peggy Cavanagh
below, and be begging money at the cross-roads, or
selling songs to the men. [*To* NORA.] Walk out now,
Nora Burke, and it's soon you'll be getting old with that
life, I'm telling you; it's soon your teeth'll be falling and
your head'll be the like of a bush where sheep do be
leaping a gap.

[*He pauses;* NORA *looks round at* MICHAEL.]

MICHAEL [*timidly*]. There's a fine Union below in Rath-
drum.

DAN. The like of her would never go there. . . . It's lonesome roads she'll be going and hiding herself away till the
end will come, and they find her stretched like a dead
sheep with the frost on her, or the big spiders maybe,
and they putting their webs on her, in the butt of a ditch.

NORA [*angrily*]. What way will yourself be that day, Daniel
Burke? What way will you be that day and you lying
down a long while in your grave? For it's bad you are
living, and it's bad you'll be when you're dead. [*She looks
at him a moment fiercely, then half turns away and speaks*

plaintively again.] Yet, if it is itself, Daniel Burke, who can help it at all, and let you be getting up into your bed, and not be taking your death with the wind blowing on you, and the rain with it, and you half in your skin.

DAN. It's proud and happy you'd be if I was getting my death the day I was shut of yourself. [*Pointing to the door.*] Let you walk out through that door, I'm telling you, and let you not be passing this way if it's hungry you are, or wanting a bed.

TRAMP [*pointing to* MICHAEL]. Maybe himself would take her.

NORA. What would he do with me now?

TRAMP. Give you the half of a dry bed, and good food in your mouth.

DAN. Is it a fool you think him, stranger, or is it a fool you were born yourself? Let her walk out of that door, and let you go along with her, stranger – if it's raining itself – for it's too much talk you have surely.

TRAMP [*going over to* NORA]. We'll be going now, lady of the house; the rain is falling, but the air is kind, and maybe it'll be a grand morning, by the grace of God.

NORA. What good is a grand morning when I'm destroyed surely, and I going out to get my death walking the roads?

TRAMP. You'll not be getting your death with myself, lady of the house, and I knowing all the ways a man can put food in his mouth. . . . We'll be going now, I'm telling you, and the time you'll be feeling the cold, and the frost, and the great rain, and the sun again, and the south wind blowing in the glens, you'll not be sitting up on a wet ditch, the way you're after sitting in this place, making yourself old with looking on each day, and it passing you by. You'll be saying one time, 'It's a grand

31

evening, by the grace of God,' and another time, 'It's a wild night, God help us; but it'll pass, surely.' You'll be saying. . . .

DAN [*goes over to them, crying out impatiently*]. Go out of that door, I'm telling you, and do your blathering below in the glen.

[NORA *gathers a few things into her shawl.*]

TRAMP [*at the door*]. Come along with me now, lady of the house, and it's not my blather you'll be hearing only, but you'll be hearing the herons crying out over the black lakes, and you'll be hearing the grouse and the owls with them, and the larks and the big thrushes when the days are warm; and it's not from the like of them you'll be hearing a tale of getting old like Peggy Cavanagh, and losing the hair off you, and the light of your eyes, but it's fine songs you'll be hearing when the sun goes up, and there'll be no old fellow wheezing, the like of a sick sheep, close to your ear.

NORA. I'm thinking it's myself will be wheezing that time with lying down under the Heavens when the night is cold; but you've a fine bit of talk, stranger, and it's with yourself I'll go. [*She goes towards the door, then turns to* DAN.] You think it's a grand thing you're after doing with your letting on to be dead, but what is it at all? What way would a woman live in a lonesome place the like of this place, and she not making a talk with the man passing? And what way will yourself live from this day, with none to care you? What is it you'll have now but a black life, Daniel Burke; and it's not long, I'm telling you, till you'll be lying again under that sheet, and you dead surely.

[*She goes out with the* TRAMP. MICHAEL *is slinking after them, but* DAN *stops him.*]

32

DAN. Sit down now and take a little taste of the stuff, Michael Dara. There's a great drouth on me, and the night is young.

MICHAEL [*coming back to the table*]. And it's very dry I am, surely, with the fear of death you put on me, and I after driving mountain ewes since the turn of the day.

DAN [*throwing away his stick*]. I was thinking to strike you, Michael Dara; but you're a quiet man, God help you, and I don't mind you at all. [*He pours out two glasses of whisky, and gives one to* MICHAEL.] Your good health, Michael Dara.

MICHAEL. God reward you, Daniel Burke, and may you have a long life and a quiet life, and good health with it.

[*They drink.*]

CURTAIN

Riders to the Sea

Synge's conception of Fate: Unpitiful
strife of humans with cosmic forces.
This raises chars. to heroic proportion
because nothing stands bet. them &
the Ocean (i.e. circumstances.)

PERSONS IN THE PLAY

MAURYA, *an old Woman*

BARTLEY, *her Son*

CATHLEEN, *her Daughter*

NORA, *a younger Daughter*

MEN AND WOMEN

SCENE – *An Island off the West of
Ireland*

Inevitableness of death of Bartley
∴ no suspense.
Homely details acquire a
premonitory significance.
e.g ominous gust of wind which
blows open the door, dropped
stitches etc. Yet Maurya's
disclosure comes as a shock.

Riders to the Sea

Cottage kitchen, with nets, oilskins, spinning-wheel, some new boards standing by the wall, etc. CATHLEEN, *a girl of about twenty, finishes kneading cake, and puts it down in the pot-oven by the fire; then wipes her hands, and begins to spin at the wheel.* NORA, *a young girl, puts her head in at the door.*

NORA [*in a low voice*]. Where is she?

CATHLEEN. She's lying down, God help her, and maybe sleeping, if she's able.

[NORA *comes in softly, and takes a bundle from under her shawl.*]

CATHLEEN [*spinning the wheel rapidly*]. What is it you have?

NORA. The young priest is after bringing them. It's a shirt and a plain stocking were got off a drowned man in Donegal.

[CATHLEEN *stops her wheel with a sudden movement, and leans out to listen.*]

NORA. We're to find out if it's Michael's they are, some time herself will be down looking by the sea.

CATHLEEN. How would they be Michael's, Nora? How would he go the length of that way to the far north?

NORA. The young priest says he's known the like of it. 'If it's Michael's they are,' says he, 'you can tell herself he's got a clean burial, by the grace of God; and if they're not his, let no one say a word about them, for she'll be getting her death,' says he, 'with crying and lamenting.'

[*The door which* NORA *half closed is blown open by a gust of wind.*]

CATHLEEN [*looking out anxiously*]. Did you ask him would he stop Bartley going this day with the horses to the Galway fair?

NORA. 'I won't stop him,' says he; 'but let you not be afraid. Herself does be saying prayers half through the night, and the Almighty God won't leave her destitute,' says he, 'with no son living.'

CATHLEEN. Is the sea bad by the white rocks, Nora?

NORA. Middling bad, God help us. There's a great roaring in the west, and it's worse it'll be getting when the tide's turned to the wind. [*She goes over to the table with the bundle.*] Shall I open it now?

CATHLEEN. Maybe she'd wake up on us, and come in before we'd done [*coming to the table*]. It's a long time we'll be, and the two of us crying.

NORA [*goes to the inner door and listens*]. She's moving about on the bed. She'll be coming in a minute.

CATHLEEN. Give me the ladder, and I'll put them up in the turf-loft, the way she won't know of them at all, and maybe when the tide turns she'll be going down to see would he be floating from the east.

[*They put the ladder against the gable of the chimney:* CATHLEEN *goes up a few steps and hides the bundle in the turf-loft.* MAURYA *comes from the inner room.*]

MAURYA [*looking up at* CATHLEEN *and speaking querulously*]. Isn't it turf enough you have for this day and evening?

CATHLEEN. There's a cake baking at the fire for a short space [*throwing down the turf*], and Bartley will want it when the tide turns if he goes to Connemara.

[NORA *picks up the turf and puts it round the pot-oven.*]

MAURYA [*sitting down on a stool at the fire*]. He won't go this day with the wind rising from the south and west. He won't go this day, for the young priest will stop him surely.

NORA. He'll not stop him, mother; and I heard Eamon Simon and Stephen Pheety and Colum Shawn saying he would go.

MAURYA. Where is he itself?

NORA. He went down to see would there be another boat sailing in the week, and I'm thinking it won't be long till he's here now, for the tide's turning at the green head, and the hooker's tacking from the east.

CATHLEEN. I hear some one passing the big stones.

NORA [*looking out*]. He's coming now, and he in a hurry.

BARTLEY [*comes in and looks round the room. Speaking sadly and quietly*]. Where is the bit of new rope, Cathleen, was bought in Connemara?

CATHLEEN [*coming down*]. Give it to him, Nora; it's on a nail by the white boards. I hung it up this morning, for the pig with the black feet was eating it.

NORA [*giving him a rope*]. Is that it, Bartley?

MAURYA. You'd do right to leave that rope, Bartley, hanging by the boards (BARTLEY *takes the rope*]. It will be wanting in this place, I'm telling you, if Michael is washed up to-morrow morning, or the next morning, or any morning in the week; for it's a deep grave we'll make him, by the grace of God.

BARTLEY [*beginning to work with the rope*]. I've no halter the way I can ride down on the mare, and I must go now quickly. This is the one boat going for two weeks or beyond it, and the fair will be a good fair for horses, I heard them saying below.

MAURYA. It's a hard thing they'll be saying below if the body is washed up and there's no man in it to make the coffin, and I after giving a big price for the finest white boards you'd find in Connemara.

[*She looks round at the boards.*]

BARTLEY. How would it be washed up, and we after looking each day for nine days, and a strong wind blowing a while back from the west and south ?

MAURYA. If it isn't found itself, that wind is raising the sea, and there was a star up against the moon, and it rising in the night. If it was a hundred horses, or a thousand horses, you had itself, what is the price of a thousand horses against a son where there is one son only ?

BARTLEY [*working at the halter, to* CATHLEEN]. Let you go down each day, and see the sheep aren't jumping in on the rye, and if the jobber comes you can sell the pig with the black feet if there is a good price going.

MAURYA. How would the like of her get a good price for a pig ?

BARTLEY [*to* CATHLEEN]. If the west wind holds with the last bit of the moon let you and Nora get up weed enough for another cock for the kelp. It's hard set we'll be from this day with no one in it but one man to work.

MAURYA. It's hard set we'll be surely the day you're drowned with the rest. What way will I live and the girls with me, and I an old woman looking for the grave ?

[BARTLEY *lays down the halter, takes off his old coat, and puts on a newer one of the same flannel.*]

BARTLEY [*to* NORA]. Is she coming to the pier ?

NORA [*looking out*]. She's passing the green head and letting fall her sails.

BARTLEY [*getting his purse and tobacco*]. I'll have half an hour to go down, and you'll see me coming again in two days, or in three days, or maybe in four days if the wind is bad.

MAURYA [*turning round to the fire, and putting her shawl over her head*]. Isn't it a hard and cruel man won't hear a word from an old woman, and she holding him from the sea?

CATHLEEN. It's the life of a young man to be going on the sea, and who would listen to an old woman with one thing and she saying it over?

BARTLEY [*taking the halter*]. I must go now quickly. I'll ride down on the red mare, and the grey pony 'ill run behind me. . . . The blessing of God on you.

[*He goes out.*]

MAURYA [*crying out as he is in the door*]. He's gone now, God spare us, and we'll not see him again. He's gone now, and when the black night is falling I'll have no son left me in the world.

CATHLEEN. Why wouldn't you give him your blessing and he looking round in the door? Isn't it sorrow enough is on every one in this house without your sending him out with an unlucky word behind him, and a hard word in his ear?

[MAURYA *takes up the tongs and begins raking the fire aimlessly without looking round.*]

NORA [*turning towards her*]. You're taking away the turf from the cake.

CATHLEEN [*crying out*]. The Son of God forgive us, Nora, we're after forgetting his bit of bread. [*She comes over to the fire.*]

NORA. And it's destroyed he'll be going till dark night, and he after eating nothing since the sun went up.

CATHLEEN [*turning the cake out of the oven*]. It's destroyed he'll be, surely. There's no sense left on any person in a house where an old woman will be talking for ever.

[MAURYA *sways herself on her stool.*]

CATHLEEN [*cutting off some of the bread and rolling it in a cloth; to* MAURYA]. Let you go down now to the spring well and give him this and he passing. You'll see him then and the dark word will be broken, and you can say 'God speed you,' the way he'll be easy in his mind.

MAURYA [*taking the bread*]. Will I be in it as soon as himself?

CATHLEEN. If you go now quickly.

MAURYA [*standing up unsteadily*]. It's hard set I am to walk.

CATHLEEN [*looking at her anxiously*]. Give her the stick, Nora, or maybe she'll slip on the big stones.

NORA. What stick?

CATHLEEN. The stick Michael brought from Connemara.

MAURYA [*taking a stick* NORA *gives her*]. In the big world the old people do be leaving things after them for their sons and children, but in this place it is the young men do be leaving things behind for them that do be old.

[*She goes out slowly.* NORA *goes over to the ladder.*]

CATHLEEN. Wait, Nora, maybe she'd turn back quickly. She's that sorry, God help her, you wouldn't know the thing she'd do.

NORA. Is she gone round by the bush?

CATHLEEN [*looking out*]. She's gone now. Throw it down quickly, for the Lord knows when she'll be out of it again.

NORA [*getting the bundle from the loft*]. The young priest said he'd be passing to-morrow, and we might go down and speak to him below if it's Michael's they are surely.

CATHLEEN [*taking the bundle*]. Did he say what way they were found?

NORA [*coming down*]. 'There were two men,' says he, 'and they rowing round with poteen before the cocks crowed, and the oar of one of them caught the body, and they passing the black cliffs of the north.'

CATHLEEN [*trying to open the bundle*]. Give me a knife,

Nora; the string's perished with the salt water, and there's a black knot on it you wouldn't loosen in a week.

NORA [*giving her a knife*]. I've heard tell it was a long way to Donegal.

CATHLEEN [*cutting the string*]. It is surely. There was a man in here a while ago – the man sold us that knife – and he said if you set off walking from the rocks beyond, it would be in seven days you'd be in Donegal.

NORA. And what time would a man take, and he floating?

[CATHLEEN *opens the bundle and takes out a bit of a shirt and a stocking. They look at them eagerly.*]

CATHLEEN [*in a low voice*]. The Lord spare us, Nora! isn't it a queer hard thing to say if it's his they are surely?

NORA. I'll get his shirt off the hook the way we can put the one flannel on the other. [*She looks through some clothes hanging in the corner.*] It's not with them, Cathleen, and where will it be?

CATHLEEN. I'm thinking Bartley put it on him in the morning, for his own shirt was heavy with the salt in it. [*Pointing to the corner.*] There's a bit of a sleeve was of the same stuff. Give me that and it will do.

[NORA *brings it to her and they compare the flannel.*]

CATHLEEN. It's the same stuff, Nora; but if it is itself, aren't there great rolls of it in the shops of Galway, and isn't it many another man may have a shirt of it as well as Michael himself?

NORA [*who has taken up the stocking and counted the stitches, crying out*]. It's Michael, Cathleen, it's Michael; God spare his soul, and what will herself say when she hears this story, and Bartley on the sea?

CATHLEEN [*taking the stocking*]. It's a plain stocking.

NORA. It's the second one of the third pair I knitted, and I put up three-score stitches, and I dropped four of them.

CATHLEEN [*counts the stitches*]. It's that number is in it [*crying out*]. Ah, Nora, isn't it a bitter thing to think of him floating that way to the far north, and no one to keen him but the black hags that do be flying on the sea?

NORA [*swinging herself half round, and throwing out her arms on the clothes*]. And isn't it a pitiful thing when there is nothing left of a man who was a great rower and fisher but a bit of an old shirt and a plain stocking?

CATHLEEN [*after an instant*]. Tell me is herself coming, Nora? I hear a little sound on the path.

NORA [*looking out*]. She is, Cathleen. She's coming up to the door.

CATHLEEN. Put these things away before she'll come in. Maybe it's easier she'll be after giving her blessing to Bartley, and we won't let on we've heard anything the time he's on the sea.

NORA [*helping* CATHLEEN *to close the bundle*]. We'll put them here in the corner.

[*They put them into a hole in the chimney corner.* CATHLEEN *goes back to the spinning-wheel.*]

NORA. Will she see it was crying I was?

CATHLEEN. Keep your back to the door the way the light 'll not be on you.

[NORA *sits down at the chimney corner, with her back to the door.* MAURYA *comes in very slowly, without looking at the girls, and goes over to her stool at the other side of the fire. The cloth with the bread is still in her hand. The girls look at each other, and* NORA *points to the bundle of bread.*]

CATHLEEN [*after spinning for a moment*]. You didn't give him his bit of bread?

[MAURYA *begins to keen softly, without turning round.*]

CATHLEEN. Did you see him riding down?

[MAURYA *goes on keening.*]

CATHLEEN [*a little impatiently*]. God forgive you; isn't it a better thing to raise your voice and tell what you seen, than to be making lamentation for a thing that's done? Did you see Bartley, I'm saying to you?

MAURYA [*with a weak voice*]. My heart's broken from this day.

CATHLEEN [*as before*]. Did you see Bartley?

MAURYA. I seen the fearfulest thing.

CATHLEEN [*leaves her wheel and looks out*]. God forgive you; he's riding the mare now over the green head, and the grey pony behind him.

MAURYA [*starts, so that her shawl falls back from her head and shows her white tossed hair. With a frightened voice*]. The grey pony behind him. . . .

CATHLEEN [*coming to the fire*]. What is it ails you at all?

MAURYA [*speaking very slowly*]. I've seen the fearfulest thing any person has seen since the day Bride Dara seen the dead man with the child in his arms.

CATHLEEN and NORA. Uah.

[*They crouch down in front of the old woman at the fire.*]

NORA. Tell us what it is you seen.

MAURYA. I went down to the spring well, and I stood there saying a prayer to myself. Then Bartley came along, and he riding on the red mare with the grey pony behind him [*she puts up her hands, as if to hide something from her eyes*]. The Son of God spare us, Nora!

CATHLEEN. What is it you seen?

MAURYA. I seen Michael himself.

CATHLEEN [*speaking softly*]. You did not, mother. It wasn't Michael you seen, for his body is after being found in the far north, and he's got a clean burial, by the grace of God.

45

MAURYA [*a little defiantly*]. I'm after seeing him this day, and he riding and galloping. Bartley came first on the red mare, and I tried to say 'God speed you,' but something choked the words in my throat. He went by quickly; and 'the blessing of God on you,' says he, and I could say nothing. I looked up then, and I crying, at the grey pony, and there was Michael upon it – with fine clothes on him, and new shoes on his feet.

CATHLEEN [*begins to keen*]. It's destroyed we are from this day. It's destroyed, surely.

NORA. Didn't the young priest say the Almighty God won't leave her destitute with no son living?

MAURYA [*in a low voice, but clearly*]. It's little the like of him knows of the sea. . . . Bartley will be lost now, and let you call in Eamon and make me a good coffin out of the white boards, for I won't live after them. I've had a husband, and a husband's father, and six sons in this house – six fine men, though it was a hard birth I had with every one of them and they coming to the world – and some of them were found and some of them were not found, but they're gone now the lot of them. . . . There were Stephen and Shawn were lost in the great wind, and found after in the Bay of Gregory of the Golden Mouth, and carried up the two of them on one plank, and in by that door.

[*She pauses for a moment, the girls start as if they heard something through the door that is half open behind them.*]

NORA [*in a whisper*]. Did you hear that, Cathleen? Did you hear a noise in the north-east?

CATHLEEN [*in a whisper*]. There's some one after crying out by the seashore.

MAURYA [*continues without hearing anything*]. There was Sheamus and his father, and his own father again, were

lost in a dark night, and not a stick or sign was seen of
them when the sun went up. There was Patch after was
drowned out of a curagh that turned over. I was sitting
here with Bartley, and he a baby lying on my two knees,
and I seen two women, and three women, and four
women coming in, and they crossing themselves and not
saying a word. I looked out then, and there were men
coming after them, and they holding a thing in the half
of a red sail, and water dripping out of it – it was a dry
day, Nora – and leaving a track to the door.

[*She pauses again with her hand stretched out towards the door.*
It opens softly and old women begin to come in, crossing them-
selves on the threshold, and kneeling down in front of the stage
with red petticoats over their heads.]

MAURYA [*half in a dream, to* CATHLEEN]. Is it Patch, or
Michael, or what is it at all ?

CATHLEEN. Michael is after being found in the far north,
and when he is found there how could he be here in this
place ?

MAURYA. There does be a power of young men floating
round in the sea, and what way would they know if it
was Michael they had, or another man like him, for
when a man is nine days in the sea, and the wind blowing,
it's hard set his own mother would be to say what man
was in it.

CATHLEEN. It's Michael, God spare him, for they're after
sending us a bit of his clothes from the far north.

[*She reaches out and hands* MAURYA *the clothes that belonged.*
to MICHAEL. MAURYA *stands up slowly, and takes them in*
her hands. NORA *looks out.*]

NORA. They're carrying a thing among them, and there's
water dripping out of it and leaving a track by the big
stones.

47

CATHLEEN [*in a whisper to the women who have come in*]. Is it Bartley it is?

ONE OF THE WOMEN. It is, surely, God rest his soul.

[*Two younger women come in and pull out the table. Then men carry in the body of* BARTLEY, *laid on a plank, with a bit of a sail over it, and lay it on the table.*]

CATHLEEN [*to the women as they are doing so*]. What way was he drowned?

ONE OF THE WOMEN. The grey pony knocked him over into the sea, and he was washed out where there is a great surf on the white rocks.

[MAURYA *has gone over and knelt down at the head of the table. The women are keening softly and swaying themselves with a slow movement.* CATHLEEN *and* NORA *kneel at the other end of the table. The men kneel near the door.*]

MAURYA [*raising her head and speaking as if she did not see the people around her*]. They're all gone now, and there isn't anything more the sea can do to me. . . . I'll have no call now to be up crying and praying when the wind breaks from the south, and you can hear the surf is in the east, and the surf is in the west, making a great stir with the two noises, and they hitting one on the other. I'll have no call now to be going down and getting Holy Water in the dark nights after Samhain, and I won't care what way the sea is when the other women will be keening. [*To* NORA.] Give me the Holy Water, Nora; there's a small sup still on the dresser.

[NORA *gives it to her.*]

MAURYA [*drops* MICHAEL'S *clothes across* BARTLEY'S *feet, and sprinkles the Holy Water over him*]. It isn't that I haven't prayed for you, Bartley, to the Almighty God. It isn't that I haven't said prayers in the dark night till you wouldn't know what I'd be saying; but it's a great

rest I'll have now, and it's time, surely. It's a great rest
I'll have now, and great sleeping in the long nights after
Samhain, if it's only a bit of wet flour we do have to eat,
and maybe a fish that would be stinking.

[*She kneels down again, crossing herself, and saying prayers
under her breath.*]

CATHLEEN [*to an old man*]. Maybe yourself and Eamon
would make a coffin when the sun rises. We have fine
white boards herself bought, God help her, thinking
Michael would be found, and I have a new cake you can
eat while you'll be working.

THE OLD MAN [*looking at the boards*]. Are there nails with
them?

CATHLEEN. There are not, Colum; we didn't think of
the nails.

ANOTHER MAN. It's a great wonder she wouldn't think
of the nails, and all the coffins she's seen made already.

CATHLEEN. It's getting old she is, and broken.

[MAURYA *stands up again very slowly and spreads out the
pieces of* MICHAEL'S *clothes beside the body, sprinkling them
with the last of the Holy Water.*]

NORA [*in a whisper to* CATHLEEN]. She's quiet now and
easy; but the day Michael was drowned you could hear
her crying out from this to the spring well. It's fonder
she was of Michael, and would anyone have thought
that?

CATHLEEN [*slowly and clearly*]. An old woman will be soon
tired with anything she will do, and isn't it nine days
herself is after crying and keening, and making great
sorrow in the house?

MAURYA [*puts the empty cup mouth downwards on the table,
and lays her hands together on* BARTLEY'S *feet*]. They're
all together this time, and the end is come. May the

Almighty God have mercy on Bartley's soul, and on Michael's soul, and on the souls of Sheamus and Patch, and Stephen and Shawn [*bending her head*]; and may He have mercy on my soul, Nora, and on the soul of every one is left living in the world.

[*She pauses, and the keen rises a little more loudly from the women, then sinks away.*]

MAURYA [*continuing*]. Michael has a clean burial in the far north, by the grace of the Almighty God. Bartley will have a fine coffin out of the white boards, and a deep grave surely. What more can we want than that? No man at all can be living for ever, and we must be satisfied.

[*She kneels down again and the curtain falls slowly.*]

lyrical fervour of the lament now gives way to a note of resignation

The Tinker's Wedding

PERSONS IN THE PLAY

MICHAEL BYRNE, a *Tinker*

MARY BYRNE, *an old Woman,
his Mother*

SARAH CASEY, *a young Tinker
Woman*

A PRIEST

SCENE – *A village roadside after
nightfall*

Preface

THE drama is made serious – in the French sense of the word – not by the degree in which it is taken up with problems that are serious in themselves, but by the degree in which it gives the nourishment, not very easy to define, on which our imaginations live. We should not go to the theatre as we go to a chemist's, or a dram-shop, but as we go to a dinner where the food we need is taken with pleasure and excitement. This was nearly always so in Spain and England and France when the drama was at its richest – the infancy and decay of the drama tend to be didactic – but in these days the playhouse is too often stocked with the drugs of many seedy problems, or with the absinthe or vermouth of the last musical comedy.

The drama, like the symphony, does not teach or prove anything. Analysts with their problems, and teachers with their systems, are soon as old-fashioned as the pharmacopoeia of Galen – look at Ibsen and the Germans – but the best plays of Ben Jonson and Molière can no more go out of fashion than the blackberries on the hedges.

Of the things which nourish the imagination humour is one of the most needful, and it is dangerous to limit or destroy it. Baudelaire calls laughter the greatest sign of the Satanic element in man; and where a country loses its humour, as some towns in Ireland are doing, there will be morbidity of mind, as Baudelaire's mind was morbid.

In the greater part of Ireland, however, the whole people, from the tinkers to the clergy, have still a life, and view of life, that are rich and genial and humorous. I do not think that these country people, who have so much humour themselves, will mind being laughed at without malice, as the people in every country have been laughed at in their own comedies.

2 December, 1907   J. M. S.

NOTE – *The Tinker's Wedding* was first written a few years ago, about the time I was working at *Riders to the Sea* and *In the Shadow of the Glen*. I have re-written it since.

Illustrative of Synge's non-religious attitude.
Contrast of 2 types of Irish civilisation – Kealteen & Xtian.
Tinkers in Ireland ≡ gypsies of England or gitanos of Spain.

The Tinker's Wedding *(Farce?)*

ACT ONE

A village roadside after nightfall. A fire of sticks is burning near the ditch a little to the right. MICHAEL *is working beside it. In the background, on the left, a sort of tent and ragged clothes drying on the hedge. On the right a chapel-gate.*

SARAH CASEY [*coming in on right, eagerly*]. We'll see his reverence this place, Michael Byrne, and he passing backward to his house to-night.

MICHAEL [*grimly*]. That'll be a sacred and a sainted joy!

SARAH [*sharply*]. It'll be small joy for yourself if you aren't ready with my wedding ring. [*She goes over to him*]. Is it near done this time, or what way is it at all?

MICHAEL. A poor way only, Sarah Casey, for it's the divil's job making a ring, and you'll be having my hands destroyed in a short while the way I'll not be able to make a tin can at all maybe at the dawn of day.

SARAH [*sitting down beside him and throwing sticks on the fire*]. If it's the divil's job, let you mind it, and leave your speeches that would choke a fool.

MICHAEL [*slowly and glumly*]. And it's you'll go talking of fools, Sarah Casey, when no man did ever hear a lying story even of your like unto this mortal day. You to be going beside me a great while, and rearing a lot of them, and then to be setting off with your talk of getting married, and your driving me to it, and I not asking it at all.

55

[SARAH *turns her back to him and arranges something in the ditch.*]

MICHAEL [*angrily*]. Can't you speak a word when I'm asking what is it ails you since the moon did change?

SARAH [*musingly*]. I'm thinking there isn't anything ails me, Michael Byrne; but the spring-time is a queer time, and it's queer thoughts maybe I do think at whiles.

MICHAEL. It's hard set you'd be to think queerer than welcome, Sarah Casey; but what will you gain dragging me to the priest this night, I'm saying, when it's new thoughts you'll be thinking at the dawn of day?

SARAH [*teasingly*]. It's at the dawn of day I do be thinking I'd have a right to be going off to the rich tinkers do be travelling from Tibradden to the Tara Hill; for it'd be a fine life to be driving with young Jaunting Jim, where there wouldn't be any big hills to break the back of you, with walking up and walking down.

MICHAEL [*with dismay*]. It's the like of that you do be thinking!

SARAH. The like of that, Michael Byrne, when there is a bit of sun in it, and a kind air, and a great smell coming from the thorn trees is above your head.

MICHAEL [*looks at her for a moment with horror, and then hands her the ring*]. Will that fit you now?

SARAH [*trying it on*]. It's making it tight you are, and the edges sharp on the tin.

MICHAEL [*looking at it carefully*]. It's the fat of your own finger, Sarah Casey; and isn't it a mad thing I'm saying again that you'd be asking marriage of me, or making a talk of going away from me, and you thriving and getting your good health by the grace of the Almighty God?

SARAH [*giving it back to him*]. Fix it now, and it'll do, if you're wary you don't squeeze it again.

MICHAEL [*moodily, working again*]. It's easy saying be wary; there's many things easy said, Sarah Casey, you'd wonder a fool even would be saying at all. [*He starts violently.*] The divil mend you, I'm scalded again!

SARAH [*scornfully*]. If you are, it's a clumsy man you are this night, Michael Byrne [*raising her voice*]; and let you make haste now, or herself will be coming with the porter.

MICHAEL [*defiantly, raising his voice*]. Let me make haste? I'll be making haste maybe to hit you a great clout; for I'm thinking it's the like of that you want. I'm thinking on the day I got you above at Rathvanna, and the way you began crying out and we coming down off the hill, crying out and saying 'I'll go back to my ma'; and I'm thinking on the way I came behind you that time, and hit you a great clout in the lug, and how quiet and easy it was you came along with me from that hour to this present day.

SARAH [*standing up and throwing all her sticks into the fire*]. And a big fool I was, too, maybe; but we'll be seeing Jaunting Jim to-morrow in Ballinaclash, and he after getting a great price for his white foal in the horse-fair of Wicklow, the way it'll be a great sight to see him squandering his share of gold, and he with a grand eye for a fine horse, and a grand eye for a woman.

MICHAEL [*working again with impatience*]. The divil do him good with the two of them.

SARAH [*kicking up the ashes with her foot*]. Ah, he's a great lad, I'm telling you, and it's proud and happy I'll be to see him, and he the first one called me the Beauty of Ballinacree, a fine name for a woman.

MICHAEL [*with contempt*]. It's the like of that name they do be putting on the horses they have below racing in

Arklow. It's easy pleased you are, Sarah Casey, easy pleased with a big word, or the liar speaks it.

SARAH. Liar!

MICHAEL. Liar, surely.

SARAH [*indignantly*]. Liar, is it? Didn't you ever hear tell of the peelers followed me ten miles along the Glen Malure, and they talking love to me in the dark night; or of the children you'll meet coming from school and they saying one to the other: 'It's this day we seen Sarah Casey, the Beauty of Ballinacree, a great sight, surely.'

MICHAEL. God help the lot of them.

SARAH. It's yourself you'll be calling God to help, in two weeks or three, when you'll be waking up in the dark night and thinking you see me coming with the sun on me, and I driving a high cart with Jaunting Jim going behind. It's lonesome and cold you'll be feeling the ditch where you'll be lying down that night, I'm telling you, and you hearing the old woman making a great noise in her sleep, and the bats squeaking in the trees.

MICHAEL. Whisht. I hear some one coming the road.

SARAH [*looking out right*]. It's some one coming forward from the doctor's door.

MICHAEL. It's often his reverence does be in there playing cards, or drinking a sup, or singing songs, until the dawn of day.

SARAH. It's a big boast of a man with a long step on him and a trumpeting voice. It's his reverence, surely; and if you have the ring done, it's a great bargain we'll make now and he after drinking his glass.

MICHAEL [*going to her and giving her the ring*]. There's your ring, Sarah Casey; but I'm thinking he'll walk by and not stop to speak with the like of us at all.

SARAH [*tidying herself, in great excitement*]. Let you be sitting

here and keeping a great blaze, the way he can look on
my face; and let you seem to be working, for it's great
love the like of him have to talk of work.

MICHAEL [*moodily, sitting down and beginning to work at a
tin can*]. Great love, surely.

SARAH [*eagerly*]. Make a great blaze now, Michael Byrne.

[*The* PRIEST *comes in on right; she comes forward in front
of him.*]

SARAH [*in a very plausible voice*]. Good evening, your reverence. It's a grand fine night, by the grace of God.

PRIEST. The Lord have mercy on us! What kind of a living
woman is it that you are at all?

SARAH. It's Sarah Casey I am, your reverence, the Beauty
of Ballinacree, and it's Michael Byrne is below in the
ditch.

PRIEST. A holy pair, surely! Let you get out of my way.

[*He tries to pass by.*]

SARAH [*keeping in front of him*]. We are wanting a little
word with your reverence.

PRIEST. I haven't a halfpenny at all. Leave the road, I'm
saying.

SARAH. It isn't a halfpenny we're asking, holy father; but
we were thinking maybe we'd have a right to be getting
married; and we were thinking it's yourself would marry
us for not a halfpenny at all; for you're a kind man, your
reverence, a kind man with the poor.

PRIEST [*with astonishment*]. Is it marry you for nothing at all?

SARAH. It is, your reverence; and we were thinking maybe
you'd give us a little small bit of silver to pay for the ring.

PRIEST [*loudly*]. Let you hold your tongue; let you be
quiet, Sarah Casey. I've no silver at all for the like of
you; and if you want to be married, let you pay your
pound. I'd do it for a pound only, and that's making it a

59

sight cheaper than I'd make it for one of my own pairs is
living here in the place.

SARAH. Where would the like of us get a pound, your
reverence?

PRIEST. Wouldn't you easy get it with your selling asses,
and making cans, and your stealing east and west in
Wicklow and Wexford and the county Meath? [*He tries
to pass her.*] Let you leave the road, and not be plaguing
me more.

SARAH [*pleadingly, taking money from her pocket*]. Wouldn't
you have a little mercy on us, your reverence? [*Holding
out money.*] Wouldn't you marry us for a half a sovereign,
and it a nice shiny one with a view on it of the living
king's mamma?

PRIEST. If it's ten shillings you have, let you get ten more
the same way, and I'll marry you then.

SARAH [*whining*]. It's two years we are getting that bit,
your reverence, with our pence and our halfpence and an
odd threepenny-bit; and if you don't marry us now,
himself and the old woman, who has a great drouth, will
be drinking it to-morrow in the fair [*she puts her apron to
her eyes, half sobbing*], and then I won't be married any
time, and I'll be saying till I'm an old woman: 'It's a
cruel and a wicked thing to be bred poor.'

PRIEST [*turning up towards the fire*]. Let you not be crying,
Sarah Casey. It's a queer woman you are to be crying at
the like of that, and you your whole life walking the
roads.

SARAH [*sobbing*]. It's two years we are getting the gold,
your reverence, and now you won't marry us for that
bit, and we hard-working poor people do be making
cans in the dark night, and blinding our eyes with the
black smoke from the bits of twigs we do be burning.

[*An old woman is heard singing tipsily on the left.*]

PRIEST [*looking at the can* MICHAEL *is making*]. When will you have that can done, Michael Byrne?

MICHAEL. In a short space only, your reverence, for I'm putting the last dab of solder on the rim.

PRIEST. Let you get a crown along with the ten shillings and the gallon can, Sarah Casey, and I will wed you so.

MARY [*suddenly shouting behind, tipsily*]. Larry was a fine lad, I'm saying; Larry was a fine lad, Sarah Casey —

MICHAEL. Whisht, now, the two of you. There's my mother coming, and she'd have us destroyed if she heard the like of that talk the time she's been drinking her fill.

MARY [*comes in singing*]:

> And when he asked him what way he'd die,
> And he hanging unrepented,
> 'Begob,' says Larry, 'that's all in my eye,
> By the clergy first invented.'

SARAH. Give me the jug now, or you'll have it spilt in the ditch.

MARY [*holding the jug with both her hands, in a stilted voice*]. Let you leave me easy, Sarah Casey. I won't spill it, I'm saying. God help you; are you thinking it's frothing full to the brim it is at this hour of the night, and I after carrying it in my two hands a long step from Jemmy Neill's?

MICHAEL [*anxiously*]. Is there a sup left at all?

SARAH [*looking into the jug*]. A little small sup only, I'm thinking.

MARY [*sees the* PRIEST, *and holds out jug towards him*]. God save your reverence. I'm after bringing down a smart drop; and let you drink it up now, for it's a middling drouthy man you are at all times, God forgive you, and this night is cruel dry.

[*She tries to go towards him.* SARAH *holds her back.*]

PRIEST [*waving her away*]. Let you not be falling to the flames. Keep off, I'm saying.

MARY [*persuasively*]. Let you not be shy of us, your reverence. Aren't we all sinners, God help us! Drink a sup now, I'm telling you; and we won't let on a word about it till the Judgment Day.

[*She takes up a tin mug, pours some porter into it, and gives it to him.*]

MARY [*singing, and holding the jug in her hand*]:

> A lonesome ditch in Ballygan
> The day you're beating a tenpenny can;
> A lonesome bank in Ballyduff
> The time . . .

[*She breaks off.*]

It's a bad, wicked song, Sarah Casey; and let you put me down now in the ditch, and I won't sing it till himself will be gone; for it's bad enough he is, I'm thinking, without ourselves making him worse.

SARAH [*putting her down, to the* PRIEST, *half laughing*]. Don't mind her at all, your reverence. She's no shame the time she's a drop taken; and if it was the Holy Father from Rome was in it, she'd give him a little sup out of her mug, and say the same as she'd say to yourself.

MARY [*to the* PRIEST]. Let you drink it up, holy father. Let you drink it up, I'm saying, and not be letting on you wouldn't do the like of it, and you with a stack of pint bottles above reaching the sky.

PRIEST [*with resignation*]. Well, here's to your good health, and God forgive us all.

[*He drinks.*]

MARY. That's right now, your reverence, and the blessing of God be on you. Isn't it a grand thing to see you sitting down, with no pride in you, and drinking a sup with the like of us, and we the poorest, wretched, starving creatures you'd see any place on the earth?

PRIEST. If it's starving you are itself, I'm thinking it's well for the like of you that do be drinking when there's drouth on you, and lying down to sleep when your legs are stiff. [*He sighs gloomily.*] What would you do if it was the like of myself you were, saying Mass with your mouth dry, and running east and west for a sick call maybe, and hearing the rural people again and they saying their sins?

MARY [*with compassion*]. It's destroyed you must be hearing the sins of the rural people on a fine spring.

PRIEST [*with despondency*]. It's a hard life, I'm telling you, a hard life, Mary Byrne; and there's the bishop coming in the morning, and he an old man, would have you destroyed if he seen a thing at all.

MARY [*with great sympathy*]. It'd break my heart to hear you talking and sighing the like of that, your reverence. [*She pats him on the knee.*] Let you rouse up now, if it's a poor, single man you are itself, and I'll be singing you songs unto the dawn of day.

PRIEST [*interrupting her*]. What is it I want with your songs when it'd be better for the like of you, that'll soon die, to be down on your two knees saying prayers to the Almighty God?

MARY. If it's prayers I want, you'd have a right to say one yourself, holy father; for we don't have them at all, and I've heard tell a power of times it's that you're for. Say one now, your reverence; for I've heard a power of

queer things and I walking the world, but there's one
thing I never heard any time, and that's a real priest
saying a prayer.

PRIEST. The Lord protect us!

MARY. It's no lie, holy father. I often heard the rural
people making a queer noise and they going to rest; but
who'd mind the like of them? And I'm thinking it should
be great game to hear a scholar, the like of you, speaking
Latin to the Saints above.

PRIEST [*scandalized*]. Stop your talking, Mary Byrne; you're
an old, flagrant heathen, and I'll stay no more with the
lot of you.

[*He rises.*]

MARY [*catching hold of him*]. Stop till you say a prayer, your
reverence; stop till you say a little prayer, I'm telling
you, and I'll give you my blessing and the last sup from
the jug.

PRIEST [*breaking away*]. Leave me go, Mary Byrne; for I
never met your like for hard abominations the score and
two years I'm living in the place.

MARY [*innocently*]. Is that the truth?

PRIEST. It is, then, and God have mercy on your soul.

[*The* PRIEST *goes towards the left, and* SARAH *follows him.*]

SARAH [*in a low voice*]. And what time will you do the thing
I'm asking, holy father? for I'm thinking you'll do it
surely, and not have me growing into an old, wicked
heathen like herself.

MARY [*calling out shrilly*]. Let you be walking back here,
Sarah Casey, and not be talking whisper-talk with the
like of him in the face of the Almighty God.

SARAH [*to the* PRIEST]. Do you hear her now, your reverence? Isn't it true, surely, she's an old, flagrant heathen,
would destroy the world.

PRIEST [*to* SARAH, *moving off*]. Well, I'll be coming down early to the chapel, and let you come to me a while after you see me passing, and bring the bit of gold along with you, and the tin can. I'll marry you for them two, though it's a pitiful small sum; for I wouldn't be easy in my soul if I left you growing into an old, wicked heathen the like of her.

SARAH [*following him out*]. The blessing of the Almighty God be on you, holy father, and that He may reward and watch you from this present day.

MARY [*nudging* MICHAEL]. Did you see that, Michael Byrne? Didn't you hear me telling you she's flighty a while back since the change of the moon? With her fussing for marriage, and she making whisper-talk with one man or another man along by the road.

MICHAEL. Whisht now, or she'll knock the head of you the time she comes back.

MARY. Ah, it's a bad, wicked way the world is this night, if there's a fine air in it itself. You'd never have seen me, and I a young woman, making whisper-talk with the like of him, and he the fearfullest old fellow you'd see any place walking the world.

[SARAH *comes back quickly*.]

MARY [*calling out to her*]. What is it you're after whispering above with himself?

SARAH [*exultingly*]. Lie down, and leave us in peace. [*She whispers with* MICHAEL.]

MARY [*poking out her pipe with a straw, sings*]:

She'd whisper with one, and she'd whisper with two –

[*She breaks off coughing*.] My singing voice is gone for this night, Sarah Casey. [*She lights her pipe*.] But if it's flighty you are itself, you're a grand, handsome woman, the glory of tinkers, the pride of Wicklow, the Beauty of Ballinacree. I wouldn't have you lying down and you lonesome to sleep this night in a dark ditch when the spring is coming in the trees; so let you sit down there by the big bough, and I'll be telling you the finest story you'd hear any place from Dundalk to Ballinacree, with great queens in it, making themselves matches from the start to the end, and they with shiny silks on them the length of the day, and white shifts for the night.

MICHAEL [*standing up with the tin can in his hand*]. Let you go asleep, and not have us destroyed.

MARY [*lying back sleepily*]. Don't mind him, Sarah Casey. Sit down now, and I'll be telling you a story would be fit to tell a woman the like of you in the spring-time of the year.

SARAH [*taking the can from* MICHAEL, *and tying it up in a piece of sacking*]. That'll not be rusting now in the dews of night. I'll put it up in the ditch the way it will be handy in the morning; and now we've that done, Michael Byrne, I'll go along with you and welcome for Tim Flaherty's hens.

[*She puts the can in the ditch.*]

MARY [*sleepily*]. I've a grand story of the great queens of Ireland, with white necks on them the like of Sarah Casey, and fine arms would hit you a slap the way Sarah Casey would hit you.

SARAH [*beckoning on the left*]. Come along now, Michael, while she's falling asleep.

[*He goes towards left.* MARY *sees that they are going, starts up suddenly, and turns over on her hands and knees.*]

MARY [*piteously*]. Where is it you're going? Let you walk back here, and not be leaving me lonesome when the night is fine.

SARAH. Don't be waking the world with your talk when we're going up through the back wood to get two of Tim Flaherty's hens are roosting in the ash-tree above at the well.

MARY. And it's leaving me lone you are? Come back here, Sarah Casey. Come back here, I'm saying; or if it's off you must go, leave me the two little coppers you have, the way I can walk up in a short while, and get another pint for my sleep.

SARAH. It's too much you have taken. Let you stretch yourself out and take a long sleep; for isn't that the best thing any woman can do, and she an old drinking heathen like yourself.

[*She and* MICHAEL *go out left.*]

MARY [*standing up slowly*]. It's gone they are and I with my feet that weak under me you'd knock me down with a rush; and my head with a noise in it the like of what you'd hear in a stream and it running between two rocks and rain falling. [*She goes over to the ditch where the can is tied in sacking, and takes it down.*] What good am I this night, God help me? What good are the grand stories I have when it's few would listen to an old woman, few but a girl maybe would be in great fear the time her hour was come, or a little child wouldn't be sleeping with the hunger on a cold night? [*She takes the can from the sacking, and fits in three empty bottles and straw in its place, and ties them up.*] Maybe the two of them have a good right to be walking out the little short while they'd be young; but if they have itself, they'll not keep Mary Byrne from her full pint when the night's fine, and there's a dry moon in the sky. [*She takes up the can, and puts the package back in the ditch.*] Jemmy Neill's a decent lad; and he'll give me a good drop for the can; and maybe if I keep near the peelers to-morrow for the first bit of the fair, herself won't strike me at all; and if she does itself, what's a little stroke on your head beside sitting lonesome on a fine night, hearing the dogs barking, and the bats squeaking, and you saying over, it's a short while only till you die.

[*She goes out singing* '*The night before Larry was stretched.*']

CURTAIN

ACT TWO

The same scene as before. Early morning. SARAH *is washing her face in an old bucket; then plaits her hair.* MICHAEL *is tidying himself also.* MARY BYRNE *is asleep against the ditch.*

SARAH [*to* MICHAEL, *with pleased excitement*]. Go over, now, to the bundle beyond, and you'll find a kind of a red handkerchief to put upon your neck, and a green one for myself.

MICHAEL [*getting them*]. You're after spending more money on the like of them. Well, it's a power we're losing this time, and we not gaining a thing at all. [*With the handkerchief.*] Is it them two?

SARAH. It is, Michael. [*She takes one of them.*] Let you tackle that one round under your chin; and let you not forget to take your hat from your head when we go up into the church. I asked Biddy Flynn below, that's after marrying her second man, and she told me it's the like of that they do.

[MARY *yawns, and turns over in her sleep.*]

SARAH [*with anxiety*]. There she is waking up on us, and I thinking we'd have the job done before she'd know of it at all.

MICHAEL. She'll be crying out now, and making game of us, and saying it's fools we are surely.

SARAH. I'll send her to her sleep again, or get her out of it one way or another; for it'd be a bad case to have a divil's scholar the like of her turning the priest against us maybe with her godless talk.

MARY [*waking up, and looking at them with curiosity, blandly*].

69

That's fine things you have on you, Sarah Casey; and it's a great stir you're making this day, washing your face. I'm that used to the hammer, I wouldn't hear it at all; but washing is a rare thing, and you're after waking me up, and I having a great sleep in the sun.

[*She looks around cautiously at the bundle in which she has hidden the bottles.*]

SARAH [*coaxingly*]. Let you stretch out again for a sleep, Mary Byrne; for it'll be a middling time yet before we go to the fair.

MARY [*with suspicion*]. That's a sweet tongue you have, Sarah Casey; but if sleep's a grand thing, it's a grand thing to be waking up a day the like of this, when there's a warm sun in it, and a kind air, and you'll hear the cuckoos singing and crying out on the top of the hills.

SARAH. If it's that gay you are, you'd have a right to walk down and see would you get a few halfpence from the rich men do be driving early to the fair.

MARY. When rich men do be driving early it's queer tempers they have, the Lord forgive them; the way it's little but bad words and swearing out you'd get from them all.

SARAH [*losing her temper and breaking out fiercely*]. Then if you'll neither beg nor sleep, let you walk off from this place where you're not wanted, and not have us waiting for you maybe at the turn of day.

MARY [*rather uneasy, turning to* MICHAEL]. God help our spirits, Michael; there she is again rousing cranky from the break of dawn. Oh! isn't she a terror since the moon did change? [*She gets up slowly.*] And I'd best be going forward to sell the gallon can.

[*She goes over and takes up the bundle.*]

SARAH [*crying out angrily*]. Leave that down, Mary Byrne. Oh! aren't you the scorn of women to think that you'd have that drouth and roguery on you that you'd go drinking the can and the dew not dried from the grass?

MARY [*in a feigned tone of pacification with the bundle still in her hand*]. It's not a drouth but a heartburn I have this day, Sarah Casey, so I'm going down to cool my gullet at the blessed well; and I'll sell the can to the parson's daughter below, a harmless poor creature would fill your hand with shillings for a brace of lies.

SARAH. Leave down the tin can, Mary Byrne, for I hear the drouth upon your tongue to-day.

MARY. There's not a drink-house from this place to the fair, Sarah Casey; the way you'll find me below with the full price, and not a farthing gone. [*She turns to go off left.*]

SARAH [*jumping up, and picking up the hammer threateningly*]. Put down that can, I'm saying.

MARY [*looking at her for a moment in terror, and putting down the bundle in the ditch*]. Is it raving mad you're going, Sarah Casey, and you the pride of women to destroy the world?

SARAH [*going up to her, and giving her a push off left*]. I'll show you if it's raving mad I am. Go on from this place, I'm saying, and be wary now.

MARY [*turning back after her*]. If I go, I'll be telling old and young you're a weathered heathen savage, Sarah Casey, the one did put down a head of the parson's cabbage to boil in the pot with your clothes [*the PRIEST comes in behind her, on the left, and listens*], and quenched the flaming candles on the throne of God the time your shadow fell within the pillars of the chapel door.

[SARAH *turns on her, and she springs round nearly into the* PRIEST'S *arms. When she sees him, she claps her shawl over her mouth, and goes up towards the ditch, laughing to herself.*]

PRIEST [*going to* SARAH, *half terrified at the language that he has heard*]. Well, aren't you a fearful lot? I'm thinking it's only humbug you were making at the fall of night, and you won't need me at all.

SARAH [*with anger still in her voice*]. Humbug is it! Would you be turning back upon your spoken promise in the face of God?

PRIEST [*dubiously*]. I'm thinking you were never christened, Sarah Casey; and it would be a queer job to go dealing Christian sacraments unto the like of you. [*Persuasively, feeling in his pocket.*] So it would be best, maybe, I'd give you a shilling for to drink my health, and let you walk on, and not trouble me at all.

SARAH. That's your talking, is it? If you don't stand to your spoken word, holy father, I'll make my own complaint to the mitred bishop in the face of all.

PRIEST. You'd do that!

SARAH. I would surely, holy father, if I walked to the city of Dublin with blood and blisters on my naked feet.

PRIEST [*uneasily scratching his ear*]. I wish this day was done, Sarah Casey; for I'm thinking it's a risky thing getting mixed in any matters with the like of you.

SARAH. Be hasty then, and you'll have us done with before you'd think at all.

PRIEST [*giving in*]. Well, maybe it's right you are, and let you come up to the chapel when you see me looking from the door.

[*He goes up into the chapel.*]

SARAH [*calling after him*]. We will, and God preserve you, holy father.

MARY [*coming down to them, speaking with amazement and consternation, but without anger*]. Going to the chapel! It's at marriage you're fooling again, maybe? [SARAH *turns her back on her.*] It was for that you were washing your face, and you after sending me for porter at the fall of night the way I'd drink a good half from the jug? [*Going round in front of* SARAH.] Is it at marriage you're fooling again?

SARAH [*triumphantly*]. It is, Mary Byrne. I'll be married now in a short while; and from this day there will no one have a right to call me a dirty name, and I selling cans in Wicklow or Wexford or the city of Dublin itself.

MARY [*turning to* MICHAEL]. And it's yourself is wedding her, Michael Byrne?

MICHAEL [*gloomily*]. It is, God spare us.

MARY [*looks at* SARAH *for a moment, and then bursts out into a laugh of derision*]. Well, she's a tight, hardy girl, and it's no lie; but I never knew till this day it was a black born fool I had for a son. You'll breed asses, I've heard them say, and poaching dogs, and horses'd go licking the wind, but it's a hard thing, God help me, to breed sense in a son.

MICHAEL [*gloomily*]. If I didn't marry her, she'd be walking off to Jaunting Jim maybe at the fall of night; and it's well yourself knows there isn't the like of her for getting money and selling songs to the men.

MARY. And you're thinking it's paying gold to his reverence would make a woman stop when she's a mind to go?

SARAH [*angrily*]. Let you not be destroying us with your talk when I've as good a right to a decent marriage as any speckled female does be sleeping in the black hovels above, would choke a mule.

MARY [*soothingly*]. It's as good a right you have, surely, Sarah Casey, but what good will it do? Is it putting that ring on your finger will keep you from getting an aged woman and losing the fine face you have, or be easing your pains; when it's the grand ladies do be married in silk dresses, with rings of gold, that do pass any woman with their share of torment in the hour of birth, and do be paying the doctors in the city of Dublin a great price at that time, the like of what you'd pay for a good ass and a cart ? [*She sits down.*]

SARAH [*puzzled*]. Is that the truth ?

MARY [*pleased with the point she has made*]. Wouldn't any know it's the truth ? Ah, it's few short years you are yet in the world, Sarah Casey, and it's little or nothing at all maybe you know about it.

SARAH [*vehement but uneasy*]. What is it yourself knows of the fine ladies when they wouldn't let the like of you go near to them at all ?

MARY. If you do be drinking a little sup in one town and another town, it's soon you get great knowledge and a great sight into the world. You'll see men there, and women there, sitting up on the ends of barrels in the dark night, and they making great talk would soon have the like of you, Sarah Casey, as wise as a March hare.

MICHAEL [*to* SARAH]. That's the truth she's saying, and maybe, if you've sense in you at all you'd have a right still to leave your fooling, and not be wasting our gold.

SARAH [*decisively*]. If it's wise or fool I am, I've made a good bargain, and I'll stand to it now.

MARY. What is it he's making you give ?

MICHAEL. The ten shillings in gold, and the tin can is above tied in the sack.

MARY [*looking at the bundle with surprise and dread*]. The bit of gold and the tin can, is it ?

MICHAEL. The half a sovereign and the gallon can.

MARY [*scrambling to her feet quickly*]. Well, I think I'll be walking off the road to the fair the way you won't be destroying me going too fast on the hills. [*She goes a few steps towards the left, then turns and speaks to* SARAH *very persuasively*.] Let you not take the can from the sack, Sarah Casey; for the people is coming above would be making game of you, and pointing their fingers if they seen you do the like of that. Let you leave it safe in the bag, I'm saying, Sarah darling. It's that way will be best. [*She goes towards left, and pauses for a moment, looking about her with embarrassment.*]

MICHAEL [*in a low voice*]. What ails her at all?

SARAH [*anxiously*]. It's real wicked she does be when you hear her speaking as easy as that.

MARY [*to herself*]. I'd be safer in the chapel, I'm thinking; for if she caught me after on the road, maybe she would kill me then.

[*She comes hobbling back towards the right.*]

SARAH. Where is it you're going? It isn't that way we'll be walking to the fair.

MARY. I'm going up into the chapel to give you my blessing and hear the priest saying his prayers. It's a lonesome road is running below to Grianan, and a woman would never know the things might happen her and she walking single in a lonesome place.

[*As she reaches the chapel-gate, the* PRIEST *comes to it in his surplice.*]

PRIEST [*crying out*]. Come along now. Is it the whole day you'd keep me here saying my prayers, and I getting my death with not a bit in my stomach, and my breakfast in ruins, and the Lord Bishop maybe driving on the road to-day?

SARAH. We're coming now, holy father.

PRIEST. Give me the bit of gold into my hand.

SARAH. It's here, holy father.

[*She gives it to him.* MICHAEL *takes the bundle from the ditch and brings it over, standing a little behind* SARAH. *He feels the bundle and looks at* MARY *with a meaning look.*]

PRIEST [*looking at the gold*]. It's a good one, I'm thinking, wherever you got it. And where is the can?

SARAH [*taking the bundle*]. We have it here in a bit of clean sack, your reverence. We tied it up in the inside of that to keep it from rusting in the dews of night, and let you not open it now or you'll have the people making game of us and telling the story on us, east and west to the butt of the hills.

PRIEST [*taking the bundle*]. Give it here into my hand, Sarah Casey. What is it any person would think of a tinker making a can?

[*He begins opening the bundle.*]

SARAH. It's a fine can, your reverence; for if it's poor, simple people we are, it's fine cans we can make, and himself, God help him, is a great man surely at the trade.

[PRIEST *opens the bundle; the three empty bottles fall out.*]

SARAH. Glory to the saints of joy!

PRIEST. Did ever any man see the like of that? To think you'd be putting deceit on me, and telling lies to me, and I going to marry you for a little sum wouldn't marry a child.

SARAH [*crestfallen and astonished*]. It's the divil did it, your reverence, and I wouldn't tell you a lie. [*Raising her hands.*] May the Lord Almighty strike me dead if the divil isn't after hooshing the tin can from the bag.

PRIEST [*vehemently*]. Go along now, and don't be swearing your lies. Go along now, and let you not be thinking I'm

big fool enough to believe the like of that when it's
after selling it you are, or making a swap for drink of it,
maybe, in the darkness of the night.

MARY [*in a peacemaking voice, putting her hand on the*
PRIEST's *left arm*]. She wouldn't do the like of that,
your reverence, when she hasn't a decent standing
drouth on her at all; and she setting great store on her
marriage the way you'd have a right to be taking her
easy, and not minding the can. What differ would an
empty can make with a fine, rich, hardy man the like of
you?

SARAH [*imploringly*]. Marry us, your reverence, for the ten
shillings in gold, and we'll make you a grand can in the
evening – a can would be fit to carry water for the holy
man of God. Marry us now and I'll be saying fine prayers
for you, morning and night, if it'd be raining itself, and
it'd be in two black pools I'd be setting my knees.

PRIEST [*loudly*]. It's a wicked, thieving, lying, scheming lot
you are, the pack of you. Let you walk off now and take
every stinking rag you have there from the ditch.

MARY [*putting her shawl over her head*]. Marry her, your
reverence, for the love of God, for there'll be queer
doings below if you send her off the like of that and she
swearing crazy on the road.

SARAH [*angrily*]. It's the truth she's saying; for it's herself,
I'm thinking, is after swapping the tin can for a pint, the
time she was raging mad with the drouth, and ourselves
above walking the hill.

MARY [*crying out with indignation*]. Have you no shame,
Sarah Casey, to tell lies unto a holy man?

SARAH [*to* MARY, *working herself into a rage*]. It's making
game of me you'd be, and putting a fool's head on me in
the face of the world; but if you were thinking to be

mighty cute walking off, or going up to hide in the church, I've got you this time, and you'll not run from me now.

[*She seizes one of the bottles.*]

MARY [*hiding behind the priest*]. Keep her off, your reverence; keep her off, for the love of the Almighty God. What at all would the Lord Bishop say if he found me here lying with my head broken across, or the two of yous maybe digging a bloody grave for me at the door of the church?

PRIEST [*waving SARAH off*]. Go along, Sarah Casey. Would you be doing murder at my feet? Go along from me now, and wasn't I a big fool to have to do with you when it's nothing but distraction and torment I get from the kindness of my heart?

SARAH [*shouting*]. I've bet a power of strong lads east and west through the world, and are you thinking I'd turn back from a priest? Leave the road now, or maybe I would strike yourself.

PRIEST. You would not, Sarah Casey. I've no fear for the lot of you; but let you walk off, I'm saying, and not be coming where you've no business, and screeching tumult and murder at the doorway of the church.

SARAH. I'll not go a step till I have her head broke, or till I'm wed with himself. If you want to get shut of us, let you marry us now, for I'm thinking the ten shillings in gold is a good price for the like of you, and you near burst with the fat.

PRIEST. I wouldn't have you coming in on me and soiling my church; for there's nothing at all, I'm thinking, would keep the like of you from hell. [*He throws down the ten shillings on the ground.*] Gather up your gold now, and begone from my sight, for if ever I set an eye on you

78

again you'll hear me telling the peelers who it was stole
the black ass belonging to Philly O'Cullen, and whose
hay it is the grey ass does be eating.

SARAH. You'd do that?

PRIEST. I would, surely.

SARAH. If you do, you'll be getting all the tinkers from
Wicklow and Wexford, and the county Meath, to put up
block tin in the place of glass to shield your windows
where you do be looking out and blinking at the girls.
It's hard set you'll be that time, I'm telling you, to fill
the depth of your belly the long days of Lent; for we
wouldn't leave a laying pullet in your yard at all.

PRIEST [*losing his temper finally*]. Go on, now, or I'll send
the Lords of Justice a dated story of your villainies –
burning, stealing, robbing, raping to this mortal day. Go
on now, I'm saying, if you'd run from Kilmainham or
the rope itself. '

MICHAEL [*taking off his coat*]. Is it run from the like of you,
holy father? Go up to your own shanty, or I'll beat you
with the ass's reins till the world would hear you roaring
from this place to the coast of Clare.

PRIEST. Is it lift your hand upon myself when the Lord
would blight your members if you'd touch me now? Go
on from this.

[*He gives him a shove.*]

MICHAEL. Blight me, is it? Take it then, your reverence,
and God help you so.

[*He runs at him with the reins.*]

PRIEST [*runs up to ditch, crying out*]. There are the peelers
passing, by the grace of God. Hey, below!

MARY [*clapping her hand over his mouth*]. Knock him down
on the road; they didn't hear him at all.

[MICHAEL *pulls him down.*]

SARAH. Gag his jaws.

MARY. Stuff the sacking in his teeth.

[*They gag him with the sack that had the can in it.*]

SARAH. Tie the bag around his head, and if the peelers come, we'll put him headfirst in the boghole is beyond the ditch.

[*They tie him up in some sacking.*]

MICHAEL [*to* MARY]. Keep him quiet, and the rags tight on him for fear he'd screech. [*He goes back to their camp.*] Hurry with the things, Sarah Casey. The peelers aren't coming this way, and maybe we'll get off from them now.

[*They bundle the things together in wild haste, the* PRIEST *wriggling and struggling about on the ground, with old* MARY *trying to keep him quiet.*]

MARY [*patting his head*]. Be quiet, your reverence. What is it ails you, with your wrigglings now? Is it choking maybe? [*She puts her hand under the sack, and feels his mouth, patting him on the back.*] It's only letting on you are, holy father, for your nose is blowing back and forward as easy as an east wind on an April day. [*In a soothing voice.*] There now, holy father, let you stay easy, I'm telling you, and learn a little sense and patience, the way you'll not be so airy again going to rob poor sinners of their scraps of gold. [*He gets quieter.*] That's a good boy you are now, your reverence, and let you not be uneasy, for we wouldn't hurt you at all. It's sick and sorry we are to tease you; but what did you want meddling with the like of us, when it's a long time we are going our own ways – father and son, and his son after him, or mother and daughter, and her own daughter again; and it's little need we ever had of going up into a church and swearing – I'm told there's swearing with it – a word no man would believe, or with drawing rings on our fingers, would be cutting our skins maybe when we'd be taking the ass from the shafts, and pulling the straps the time they'd be slippy with going around beneath the heavens in rains falling.

MICHAEL [*who has finished bundling up the things, comes over with* SARAH]. We're fixed now; and I have a mind to run him in a boghole the way he'll not be tattling to the peelers of our games to-day.

SARAH. You'd have a right too, I'm thinking.

MARY [*soothingly*]. Let you not be rough with him, Sarah Casey, and he after drinking his sup of porter with us at the fall of night. Maybe he'd swear a mighty oath he wouldn't harm us, and then we'd safer loose him; for if we went to drown him, they'd maybe hang the batch of us, man and child and woman, and the ass itself.

MICHAEL. What would he care for an oath?

MARY. Don't you know his like do live in terror of the wrath of God? [*Putting her mouth to the* PRIEST'S *ear in the sacking.*] Would you swear an oath, holy father, to leave us in our freedom, and not talk at all? [PRIEST *nods in sacking.*] Didn't I tell you? Look at the poor fellow nodding his head off in the bias of the sacks. Strip them off from him, and he'll be easy now.

MICHAEL [*as if speaking to a horse*]. Hold up, holy father. [*He pulls the sacking off, and shows the* PRIEST *with his hair on end. They free his mouth.*]

MARY. Hold him till he swears.

PRIEST [*in a faint voice*]. I swear, surely. If you let me go in peace, I'll not inform against you or say a thing at all, and may God forgive me for giving heed unto your like to-day.

SARAH [*puts the ring on his finger*]. There's the ring, holy father, to keep you minding of your oath until the end of time; for my heart's scalded with your fooling; and it'll be a long day till I go making talk of marriage or the like of that.

MARY [*complacently, standing up slowly*]. She's vexed now, your reverence; and let you not mind her at all, for she's right, surely, and it's little need we ever had of the like of you to get us our bit to eat, and our bit to drink, and our time of love when we were young men and women, and were fine to look at.

MICHAEL. Hurry on now. He's a great man to have kept us from fooling our gold; and we'll have a great time drinking that bit with the trampers on the green of Clash.

[*They gather up their things. The* PRIEST *stands up.*]

PRIEST [*lifting up his hand*]. I've sworn not to call the hand of man upon your crimes to-day; but I haven't sworn I wouldn't call the fire of heaven from the hand of the Almighty God.

[*He begins saying a Latin malediction in a loud ecclesiastical voice.*]

MARY. There's an old villain.

ALL [*together*]. Run, run. Run for your lives.

[*They rush out, leaving the* PRIEST *master of the situation.*]

CURTAIN

The Well of the Saints

PERSONS IN THE PLAY

MARTIN DOUL, *weather-beaten, blind Beggar*

MARY DOUL, *his Wife, weather-beaten, ugly woman, blind also, nearly fifty*

TIMMY, *a middle-aged, almost elderly, but vigorous Smith*

MOLLY BYRNE, *fine-looking Girl with fair hair*

BRIDE, *another handsome Girl*

MAT SIMON

PATCH

THE SAINT, *a wandering Friar*

OTHER GIRLS AND MEN

SCENE – *Some lonely mountainous district in the east of Ireland one or more centuries ago*

The Well of the Saints

*Roadside with big stones, etc., on the right; low loose wall at back
with gap near centre; at left, ruined doorway of church with
bushes beside it.* MARTIN DOUL *and* MARY DOUL *grope
in on left and pass over to stones on right, where they sit.*

MARY DOUL. What place are we now, Martin Doul?

MARTIN DOUL. Passing the gap.

MARY DOUL [*raising her head*]. The length of that! Well,
the sun's coming warm this day if it's late autumn itself.

MARTIN DOUL [*putting out his hands in sun*]. What way
wouldn't it be warm and it getting high up in the south?
You were that length plaiting your yellow hair you have
the morning lost on us, and the people are after passing
to the fair of Clash.

MARY DOUL. It isn't going to the fair, the time they do
be driving their cattle and they with a litter of pigs
maybe squealing in their carts, they'd give us a thing at
all. [*She sits down.*] It's well you know that, but you must
be talking.

MARTIN DOUL [*sitting down beside her and beginning to
shred rushes she gives him*]. If I didn't talk I'd be destroyed
in a short while listening to the clack you do be making,
for you've a queer cracked voice, the Lord have mercy
on you, if it's fine to look on you are itself.

MARY DOUL. Who wouldn't have a cracked voice sitting
out all the year in the rain falling? It's a bad life for the
voice, Martin Doul, though I've heard tell there isn't

85

anything like the wet south wind does be blowing upon us for keeping a white beautiful skin -- the like of my skin -- on your neck and on your brows, and there isn't anything at all like a fine skin for putting splendour on a woman.

MARTIN DOUL [*teasingly, but with good humour*]. I do be thinking odd times we don't know rightly what way you have your splendour, or asking myself, maybe, if you have it at all, for the time I was a young lad, and had fine sight, it was the ones with sweet voices were the best in face.

MARY DOUL. Let you not be making the like of that talk when you've heard Timmy the smith, and Mat Simon, and Patch Ruadh and a power besides saying fine things of my face, and you know rightly it was 'the beautiful dark woman' they did call me in Ballinatone.

MARTIN DOUL [*as before*]. If it was itself I heard Molly Byrne saying at the fall of night it was little more than a fright you were.

MARY DOUL [*sharply*]. She was jealous, God forgive her, because Timmy the smith was after praising my hair --

MARTIN DOUL [*with mock irony*]. Jealous!

MARY DOUL. Ay, jealous, Martin Doul; and if she wasn't itself, the young and silly do be always making game of them that's dark, and they'd think it a fine thing if they had us deceived, the way we wouldn't know we were so fine-looking at all.

[*She puts her hand to her face with a complacent gesture.*]

MARTIN DOUL [*a little plaintively*]. I do be thinking in the long nights it'd be a grand thing if we could see ourselves for one hour, or a minute itself, the way we'd know surely we were the finest man and the finest woman of the seven counties of the east -- [*bitterly*] and then the

seeing rabble below might be destroying their souls telling bad lies, and we'd never heed a thing they'd say.

MARY DOUL. If you weren't a big fool you wouldn't heed
them this hour, Martin Doul, for they're a bad lot those
that have their sight, and they do have great joy, the time
they do be seeing a grand thing, to let on they don't see
it at all, and to be telling fool's lies, the like of what
Molly Byrne was telling to yourself.

MARTIN DOUL. If it's lies she does be telling she's a
sweet, beautiful voice you'd never tire to be hearing, if
it was only the pig she'd be calling, or crying out in the
long grass, maybe, after her hens. [*Speaking pensively.*] It
should be a fine, soft, rounded woman, I'm thinking,
would have a voice the like of that.

MARY DOUL [*sharply again, scandalized*]. Let you not be
minding if it's flat or rounded she is; for she's a flighty,
foolish woman you'll hear when you're off a long
way, and she making a great noise and laughing at the
well.

MARTIN DOUL. Isn't laughing a nice thing the time a
woman's young?

MARY DOUL [*bitterly*]. A nice thing is it? A nice thing to
hear a woman making a loud braying laugh the like of
that? Ah, she's a great one for drawing the men, and
you'll hear Timmy himself, the time he does be sitting
in his forge, getting mighty fussy if she'll come walking
from Grianan, the way you'll hear his breath going, and
he wringing his hands.

MARTIN DOUL [*slightly piqued*]. I've heard him say a power
of times it's nothing at all she is when you see her at the
side of you, and yet I never heard any man's breath getting
uneasy the time he'd be looking on yourself.

MARY DOUL. I'm not the like of the girls do be running

round on the roads, swinging their legs, and they with their necks out looking on the men. . . . Ah, there's a power of villainy walking the world, Martin Doul, among them that do be gadding around, with their gaping eyes, and their sweet words, and they with no sense in them at all.

MARTIN DOUL [*sadly*]. It's the truth, maybe, and yet I'm told it's a grand thing to see a young girl walking the road.

MARY DOUL. You'd be as bad as the rest of them if you had your sight, and I did well, surely, not to marry a seeing man – it's scores would have had me and welcome – for the seeing is a queer lot, and you'd never know the thing they'd do.

[*A moment's pause.*]

MARTIN DOUL [*listening*]. There's some one coming on the road.

MARY DOUL. Let you put the pith away out of their sight, or they'll be picking it out with the spying eyes they have, and saying it's rich we are, and not sparing us a thing at all.

[*They bundle away the rushes.* TIMMY *the smith comes in on left.*]

MARTIN DOUL [*with a begging voice*]. Leave a bit of silver for blind Martin, your honour. Leave a bit of silver, or a penny copper itself, and we'll be praying the Lord to bless you and you going the way.

TIMMY [*stopping before them*]. And you letting on a while back you knew my step!

[*He sits down.*]

MARTIN [*with his natural voice*]. I know it when Molly Byrne's walking in front, or when she's two perches, maybe, lagging behind; but it's few times I've heard you

walking up the like of that, as if you'd met a thing wasn't
right and you coming on the road.

TIMMY [*hot and breathless, wiping his face*]. You've good ears,
God bless you, if you're a liar itself; for I'm after walking
up in great haste from hearing wonders in the fair.

MARTIN DOUL [*rather contemptuously*]. You're always hearing queer wonderful things, and the lot of them nothing
at all; but I'm thinking, this time, it's a strange thing
surely you'd be walking up before the turn of day, and
not waiting below to look on them lepping, or dancing,
or playing shows on the green of Clash.

TIMMY [*huffed*]. I was coming to tell you it's in this place
there'd be a bigger wonder done in a short while
[MARTIN DOUL *stops working*] than was ever done on
the green of Clash, or the width of Leinster itself; but
you're thinking, maybe, you're too cute a little fellow
to be minding me at all.

MARTIN DOUL [*amused, but incredulous*]. There'll be wonders in this place, is it?

TIMMY. Here at the crossing of the roads.

MARTIN DOUL. I never heard tell of anything to happen
in this place since the night they killed the old fellow
going home with his gold, the Lord have mercy on him,
and threw down his corpse into the bog. Let them not
be doing the like of that this night, for it's ourselves have
a right to the crossing roads, and we don't want any of
your bad tricks, or your wonders either, for it's wonder
enough we are ourselves.

TIMMY. If I'd a mind I'd be telling you of a real wonder
this day, and the way you'll be having a great joy, maybe,
you're not thinking on at all.

MARTIN DOUL [*interested*]. Are they putting up a still behind in the rocks? It'd be a grand thing if I'd a sup handy

the way I wouldn't be destroying myself groping up across the bogs in the rain falling.

TIMMY [*still moodily*]. It's not a still they're bringing, or the like of it either.

MARY DOUL [*persuasively, to* TIMMY]. Maybe they're hanging a thief, above at the bit of a tree. I'm told it's a great sight to see a man hanging by his neck; but what joy would that be to ourselves, and we not seeing it at all?

TIMMY [*more pleasantly*]. They're hanging no one this day, Mary Doul, and yet, with the help of God, you'll see a power hanged before you die.

MARY DOUL. Well, you've queer humbugging talk. . . . What way would I see a power hanged, and I a dark woman since the seventh year of my age?

TIMMY. Did ever you hear tell of a place across a bit of the sea, where there is an island, and the grave of the four beautiful saints?

MARY DOUL. I've heard people have walked round from the west and they speaking of that.

TIMMY [*impressively*]. There's a green ferny well, I'm told, behind that place, and if you put a drop of the water out of it on the eyes of a blind man, you'll make him see as well as any person is walking the world.

MARTIN DOUL [*with excitement*]. Is that the truth, Timmy? I'm thinking you're telling a lie.

TIMMY [*gruffly*]. That's the truth, Martin Doul, and you may believe it now, for you're after believing a power of things weren't as likely at all.

MARY DOUL. Maybe we could send a young lad to bring us the water. I could wash a naggin bottle in the morning, and I'm thinking Patch Ruadh would go for it, if we gave him a good drink, and the bit of money we have hid in the thatch.

TIMMY. It'd be no good to be sending a sinful man the like of ourselves, for I'm told the holiness of the water does be getting soiled with the villainy of your heart, the time you'd be carrying it, and you looking round on the girls, maybe, or drinking a small sup at a still.

MARTIN DOUL [*with disappointment*]. It'd be a long terrible way to be walking ourselves, and I'm thinking that's a wonder will bring small joy to us at all.

TIMMY [*turning on him impatiently*]. What is it you want with your walking? It's as deaf as blind you're growing if you're not after hearing me say it's in this place the wonder could be done.

MARTIN DOUL [*with a flash of anger*]. If it is, can't you open the big slobbering mouth you have and say what way it'll be done, and not be making blather till the fall of night.

TIMMY [*jumping up*]. I'll be going on now [MARY DOUL *rises*], and not wasting time talking civil talk with the like of you.

MARY DOUL [*standing up, disguising her impatience*]. Let you come here to me, Timmy, and not be minding him at all. [TIMMY *stops, and she gropes up to him and takes him by the coat.*] You're not huffy with myself, and let you tell me the whole story and don't be fooling me more. . . . Is it yourself has brought us the water?

TIMMY. It is not, surely.

MARY DOUL. Then tell us your wonder, Timmy. . . . What person'll bring it at all?

TIMMY [*relenting*]. It's a fine holy man will bring it, a saint of the Almighty God.

MARY DOUL [*overawed*]. A saint is it?

TIMMY. Ay, a fine saint, who's going round through the churches of Ireland, with a long cloak on him, and naked feet, for he's brought a sup of the water slung at his side, and, with the like of him, any little drop is enough to cure the dying, or to make the blind see as clear as the grey hawks do be high up, on a still day, sailing the sky.

MARTIN DOUL [*feeling for his stick*]. What place is he, Timmy? I'll be walking to him now.

TIMMY. Let you stay quiet, Martin. He's straying around saying prayers at the churches and high crosses, between this place and the hills, and he with a great crowd going behind – for it's fine prayers he does be saying, and fasting with it, till he's as thin as one of the empty rushes you have there on your knee; then he'll be coming after to this place to cure the two of you – we're after telling him the way you are – and to say his prayers in the church.

MARTIN DOUL [*turning suddenly to* MARY DOUL]. And we'll be seeing ourselves this day. Oh, glory be to God, is it true surely?

MARY DOUL [*very pleased, to* TIMMY]. Maybe I'd have time to walk down and get the big shawl I have below, for I do look my best, I've heard them say, when I'm dressed up with that thing on my head.

TIMMY. You'd have time surely –

MARTIN DOUL [*listening*]. Whisht now. . . . I hear people again coming by the stream.

TIMMY [*looking out left, puzzled*]. It's the young girls I left walking after the Saint. . . . They're coming now [*goes up to entrance*] carrying things in their hands, and they walking as easy as you'd see a child walk who'd have a dozen eggs hid in her bib.

MARTIN DOUL [*listening*]. That's Molly Byrne, I'm thinking.

[MOLLY BYRNE *and* BRIDE *come on left and cross to*

MARTIN DOUL, *carrying water-can, Saint's bell, and cloak.*]

MOLLY [*volubly*]. God bless you, Martin. I've holy water here, from the grave of the four saints of the west, will have you cured in a short while and seeing like ourselves –

TIMMY [*crosses to* MOLLY, *interrupting her*]. He's heard that. God help you. But where at all is the Saint, and what way is he after trusting the holy water with the likes of you?

MOLLY BYRNE. He was afeard to go a far way with the clouds is coming beyond, so he's gone up now through the thick woods to say a prayer at the crosses of Grianan, and he's coming on this road to the church.

TIMMY [*still astonished*]. And he's after leaving the holy water with the two of you? It's a wonder, surely.

[*Comes down left a little.*]

MOLLY BYRNE. The lads told him no person could carry them things through the briars and steep, slippy-feeling rocks he'll be climbing above, so he looked round then, and gave the water, and his big cloak, and his bell to the two of us, for young girls, says he, are the cleanest holy people you'd see walking the world.

[MARY DOUL *goes near seat.*]

MARY DOUL [*sits down, laughing to herself*]. Well, the Saint's a simple fellow, and it's no lie.

MARTIN DOUL [*leaning forward, holding out his hands*]. Let you give me the water in my hand, Molly Byrne, the way I'll know you have it surely.

MOLLY BYRNE [*giving it to him*]. Wonders is queer things, and maybe it'd cure you, and you holding it alone.

MARTIN DOUL [*looking round*]. It does not, Molly. I'm not seeing at all. [*He shakes the can.*] There's a small sup only. Well, isn't it a great wonder the little trifling thing would bring seeing to the blind, and be showing us the big women and the young girls, and all the fine things is walking the world.

[*He feels for* MARY DOUL *and gives her the can.*]

MARY DOUL [*shaking it*]. Well, glory be to God —

MARTIN DOUL [*pointing to* BRIDE]. And what is it herself has, making sounds in her hand?

BRIDE [*crossing to* MARTIN DOUL]. It's the Saint's bell; you'll hear him ringing out the time he'll be going up some place, to be saying his prayers.

[MARTIN DOUL *holds out his hands; she gives it to him.*]

MARTIN DOUL [*ringing it*]. It's a sweet, beautiful sound.

MARY DOUL. You'd know, I'm thinking, by the little silvery voice of it, a fasting holy man was after carrying it a great way at his side.

[BRIDE *crosses a little right behind* MARTIN DOUL.]

MOLLY BYRNE [*unfolding* SAINT'S *cloak*]. Let you stand up now, Martin Doul, till I put his big cloak on you. [MARTIN DOUL *rises, comes forward, centre a little.*] The way we'd see how you'd look, and you a saint of the Almighty God.

MARTIN DOUL [*standing up, a little diffidently*]. I've heard the priests a power of times making great talk and praises of the beauty of the saints.

[MOLLY BYRNE *slips cloak round him.*]

TIMMY [*uneasily*]. You'd have a right to be leaving him alone, Molly. What would the Saint say if he seen you making game with his cloak?

MOLLY BYRNE [*recklessly*]. How would he see us, and he saying prayers in the wood? [*She turns* MARTIN DOUL *round.*] Isn't that a fine, holy-looking saint, Timmy the smith? [*Laughing foolishly.*] There's a grand, handsome fellow, Mary Doul; and if you seen him now you'd be as proud, I'm thinking, as the archangels below, fell out with the Almighty God.

MARY DOUL [*with quiet confidence going to* MARTIN DOUL *and feeling his cloak*]. It's proud we'll be this day, surely.

[MARTIN DOUL *is still ringing.*]

MOLLY BYRNE [*to* MARTIN DOUL]. Would you think well to be all your life walking round the like of that, Martin Doul, and you bell-ringing with the saints of God?

MARY DOUL [*turning on her, fiercely*]. How would he be bell-ringing with the saints of God and he wedded with myself?

MARTIN DOUL. It's the truth she's saying, and if bell-ringing is a fine life, yet I'm thinking maybe, it's better I am wedded with the beautiful dark woman of Ballina-tone.

MOLLY BYRNE [*scornfully*]. You're thinking that, God help you; but it's little you know of her at all.

MARTIN DOUL. It's little surely, and I'm destroyed this day waiting to look upon her face.

TIMMY [*awkwardly*]. It's well you know the way she is; for the like of you do have great knowledge in the feeling of your hands.

MARTIN DOUL [*still feeling the cloak*]. We do, maybe. Yet it's little I know of faces, or of fine beautiful cloaks, for it's few cloaks I've had my hand to, and few faces [*plaintively*]; for the young girls is mighty shy, Timmy the smith, and it isn't much they heed me, though they do be saying I'm a handsome man.

MARY DOUL [*mockingly, with good humour*]. Isn't it a queer thing the voice he puts on him, when you hear him talking of the skinny-looking girls, and he married with a woman he's heard called the wonder of the western world?

TIMMY [*pityingly*]. The two of you will see a great wonder this day, and it's no lie.

MARTIN DOUL. I've heard tell her yellow hair, and her white skin, and her big eyes are a wonder, surely –

BRIDE [*who has looked out left*]. Here's the Saint coming from the selvage of the wood. . . . Strip the cloak from him, Molly, or he'll be seeing it now.

MOLLY BYRNE [*hastily to* BRIDE]. Take the bell and put herself by the stones. [*To* MARTIN DOUL.] Will you hold your head up till I loosen the cloak? [*She pulls off the cloak and throws it over her arm. Then she pushes* MARTIN DOUL *over and stands beside* MARY DOUL.] Stand there now, quiet, and let you not be saying a word.

[*She and* BRIDE *stand a little on their left, demurely, with bell, etc., in their hands.*]

MARTIN DOUL [*nervously arranging his clothes*]. Will he mind the way we are, and not tidied or washed cleanly at all?

MOLLY BYRNE. He'll not see what way you are. . . . He'd walk by the finest woman in Ireland, I'm thinking, and not trouble to raise his two eyes to look upon her face. . . . Whisht!

[*The* SAINT *comes left, with crowd.*]

SAINT. Are these the two poor people?

TIMMY [*officiously*]. They are, holy father; they do be always sitting here at the crossing of the roads, asking a bit of copper from them that do pass, or stripping rushes for lights, and they not mournful at all, but talking out straight with a full voice, and making game with them that likes it.

SAINT [*to* MARTIN DOUL *and* MARY DOUL]. It's a hard

life you've had not seeing sun or moon, or the holy priests itself praying to the Lord, but it's the like of you who are brave in a bad time will make a fine use of the gift of sight, the Almighty God will bring to you to-day. [*He takes his cloak and puts it about him.*] It's on a bare starving rock that there's the grave of the four beauties of God, the way it's little wonder, I'm thinking, if it's with bare starving people the water should be used. [*He takes the water and bell and slings them round his shoulders.*] So it's to the like of yourselves I do be going, who are wrinkled and poor, a thing rich men would hardly look at at all, but would throw a coin to or a crust of bread.

MARTIN DOUL [*moving uneasily*]. When they look on herself, who is a fine woman —

TIMMY [*shaking him*]. Whisht now, and be listening to the Saint.

SAINT [*looks at them a moment, continues*]. If it's raggy and dirty you are itself, I'm saying, the Almighty God isn't at all like the rich men of Ireland; and, with the power of the water I'm after bringing in a little curagh into Cashla Bay, He'll have pity on you, and put sight into your eyes.

MARTIN DOUL [*taking off his hat*]. I'm ready now, holy father —

SAINT [*taking him by the hand*]. I'll cure you first, and then I'll come for your wife. We'll go up now into the church, for I must say a prayer to the Lord. [*To MARY DOUL, as he moves off.*] And let you be making your mind still and saying praises in your heart, for it's a great wonderful thing when the power of the Lord of the world is brought down upon your like.

PEOPLE [*pressing after him*]. Come now till we watch.

BRIDE. Come, Timmy.

SAINT [*waving them back*]. Stay back where you are, for I'm
not wanting a big crowd making whispers in the church.
Stay back there, I'm saying, and you'd do well to be
thinking on the way sin has brought blindness to the
world, and to be saying a prayer for your own sakes
against false prophets and heathens, and the words of
women and smiths, and all knowledge that would soil
the soul or the body of a man.

[PEOPLE *shrink back. He goes into church.* MARY DOUL
gropes half-way towards the door and kneels near path. PEOPLE
form a group at right.]

TIMMY. Isn't it a fine, beautiful voice he has, and he a
fine, brave man if it wasn't for the fasting?

BRIDE. Did you watch him moving his hands?

MOLLY BYRNE. It'd be a fine thing if some one in this
place could pray the like of him, for I'm thinking the
water from our own blessed well would do rightly if a
man knew the way to be saying prayers, and then there'd
be no call to be bringing water from that wild place,
where, I'm told, there are no decent houses, or fine-
looking people at all.

BRIDE [*who is looking in at door from right*]. Look at the
great trembling Martin has shaking him, and he on his
knees.

TIMMY [*anxiously*]. God help him. . . . What will he be
doing when he sees his wife this day? I'm thinking it was
bad work we did when we let on she was fine-looking,
and not a wrinkled, wizened hag the way she is.

MAT SIMON. Why would he be vexed, and we after giving
him great joy and pride, the time he was dark?

MOLLY BYRNE [*sitting down in* MARY DOUL'S *seat and
tidying her hair*]. If it's vexed he is itself, he'll have other
things now to think on as well as his wife; and what does

any man care for a wife, when it's two weeks, or three, he is looking on her face?

MAT SIMON. That's the truth now, Molly, and it's more joy dark Martin got from the lies we told of that hag is kneeling by the path than your own man will get from you, day or night, and he living at your side.

MOLLY BYRNE [*defiantly*]. Let you not be talking, Mat Simon, for it's not yourself will be my man, though you'd be crowing and singing fine songs if you'd that hope in you at all.

TIMMY [*shocked, to* MOLLY BYRNE]. Let you not be raising your voice when the Saint's above at his prayers.

BRIDE [*crying out*]. Whisht. . . . Whisht. . . . I'm thinking he's cured.

MARTIN DOUL [*crying out in the church*]. Oh, glory be to God.

SAINT [*solemnly*]. Laus Patri sit et Filio cum Spiritu Paraclito Qui suae dono gratiae misertus est Hiberniae. . . .

MARTIN DOUL [*ecstatically*]. Oh, glory be to God, I see now surely. . . . I see the walls of the church, and the green bits of ferns in them, and yourself, holy father, and the great width of the sky.

[*He runs out half-foolish with joy, and comes past* MARY DOUL *as she scrambles to her feet, drawing a little away from her as he goes by.*]

TIMMY [*to the others*]. He doesn't know her at all.

[*The* SAINT *comes out behind* MARTIN DOUL, *and leads* MARY DOUL *into the church.* MARTIN DOUL *comes on to the* PEOPLE. *The men are between him and the* GIRLS; *he verifies his position with his stick.*]

MARTIN DOUL [*crying out joyfully*]. That's Timmy, I know Timmy by the black of his head. . . . That's Mat Simon, I know Mat by the length of his legs. . . . That should be

Patch Ruadh, with the gamey eyes in him, and the fiery hair. [*He sees* MOLLY BYRNE *on* MARY DOUL'S *seat, and his voice changes completely*.] Oh, it was no lie they told me, Mary Doul. Oh, glory to God and the seven saints I didn't die and not see you at all. The blessing of God on the water, and the feet carried it round through the land. The blessing of God on this day, and them that brought me the Saint, for it's grand hair you have [*she lowers her head a little confused*], and soft skin, and eyes would make the saints, if they were dark awhile and seeing again, fall down out of the sky. [*He goes nearer to her.*] Hold up your head, Mary, the way I'll see it's richer I am than the great kings of the east. Hold up your head, I'm saying, for it's soon you'll be seeing me, and I not a bad one at all.

[*He touches her and she starts up.*]

MOLLY BYRNE. Let you keep away from me, and not be soiling my chin.

[PEOPLE *laugh loudly*.]

MARTIN DOUL [*bewildered*]. It's Molly's voice you have.

MOLLY BYRNE. Why wouldn't I have my own voice? Do you think I'm a ghost?

MARTIN DOUL. Which of you all is herself? [*He goes up to* BRIDE.] Is it you is Mary Doul? I'm thinking you're more the like of what they said [*peering at her*]. For you've yellow hair, and white skin, and it's the smell of my own turf is rising from your shawl.

[*He catches her shawl.*]

BRIDE [*pulling away her shawl*]. I'm not your wife, and let you get out of my way.

[*The* PEOPLE *laugh again*.]

MARTIN DOUL [*with misgiving, to another* GIRL]. Is it yourself it is? You're not so fine looking, but I'm thinking you'd do, with the grand nose you have, and your nice hands and your feet.

GIRL [*scornfully*]. I never seen any person that took me for blind, and a seeing woman, I'm thinking, would never wed the like of you.

[*She turns away, and the* PEOPLE *laugh once more, drawing back a little and leaving him on their left.*]

PEOPLE [*jeeringly*]. Try again, Martin, try again, and you'll be finding her yet.

MARTIN DOUL [*passionately*]. Where is it you have her hidden away ? Isn't it a black shame for a drove of pitiful beasts the like of you to be making game of me, and putting a fool's head on me the grand day of my life ? Ah, you're thinking you're a fine lot, with you're giggling, weeping eyes, a fine lot to be making game of myself and the woman I've heard called the great wonder of the west.

[*During this speech, which he gives with his back towards the church,* MARY DOUL *has come out with her sight cured, and come down towards the right with a silly simpering smile, till she is a little behind* MARTIN DOUL.]

MARY DOUL [*when he pauses*]. Which of you is Martin Doul ?

MARTIN DOUL [*wheeling round*]. It's her voice, surely.

[*They stare at each other blankly.*]

MOLLY BYRNE [*to* MARTIN DOUL]. Go up now and take her under the chin and be speaking the way you spoke to myself.

MARTIN DOUL [*in a low voice, with intensity*]. If I speak now, I'll speak hard to the two of you –

MOLLY BYRNE [*to* MARY DOUL]. You're not saying a word, Mary. What is it you think of himself, with the fat legs on him, and the little neck like a ram ?

MARY DOUL. I'm thinking it's a poor thing when the Lord God gives you sight and puts the like of that man in your way.

MARTIN DOUL. It's on your two knees you should be thanking the Lord God you're not looking on yourself, for if it was yourself you seen you'd be running round in a short while like the old screeching madwoman is running round in the glen.

MARY DOUL [*beginning to realize herself*]. If I'm not so fine as some of them said, I have my hair, and big eyes, and my white skin —

MARTIN DOUL [*breaking out into a passionate cry*]. Your hair, and your big eyes, is it? . . . I'm telling you there isn't a wisp on any grey mare on the ridge of the world isn't finer than the dirty twist on your head. There isn't two eyes in any starving sow isn't finer than the eyes you were calling blue like the sea.

MARY DOUL [*interrupting him*]. It's the devil cured you this day with your talking of sows; it's the devil cured you this day, I'm saying, and drove you crazy with lies.

MARTIN DOUL. Isn't it yourself is after playing lies on me, ten years, in the day and in the night; but what is that to you now the Lord God has given eyes to me, the way I see you an old, wizendy hag, was never fit to rear a child to me itself.

MARY DOUL. I wouldn't rear a crumpled whelp the like of you. It's many a woman is married with finer than yourself should be praising God if she's no child, and isn't loading the earth with things would make the heavens lonesome above, and they scaring the larks, and the crows, and the angels passing in the sky.

MARTIN DOUL. Go on now to be seeking a lonesome place where the earth can hide you away; go on now,

I'm saying, or you'll be having men and women with their knees bled, and they screaming to God for a holy water would darken their sight, for there's no man but would liefer be blind a hundred years, or a thousand itself, than to be looking on your like.

MARY DOUL [*raising her stick*]. Maybe if I hit you a strong blow you'd be blind again, and having what you want –

[*The* SAINT *is seen in church door with his head bent in prayer.*]

MARTIN DOUL [*raising his stick and driving* MARY DOUL *back towards left*]. Let you keep off from me now if you wouldn't have me strike out the little handful of brains you have about on the road.

[*He is going to strike her, but* TIMMY *catches him by the arm.*]

TIMMY. Have you no shame to be making a great row, and the Saint above saying his prayers?

MARTIN DOUL. What is it I care for the like of him? [*Struggling to free himself.*] Let me hit her one good one, for the love of the Almighty God, and I'll be quiet after till I die.

TIMMY [*shaking him*]. Will you whisht, I'm saying.

SAINT [*coming forward, centre*]. Are their minds troubled with joy, or is their sight uncertain, the way it does often be the day a person is restored?

TIMMY. It's too certain their sight is, holy father; and they're after making a great fight, because they're a pair of pitiful shows.

SAINT [*coming between them*]. May the Lord who has given you sight send a little sense into your heads, the way it won't be on your two selves you'll be looking – on two pitiful sinners of the earth – but on the splendour of the Spirit of God, you'll see an odd time shining out through the big hills, and steep streams falling to the sea. For if it's on the like of that you do be thinking, you'll not be minding the faces of men, but you'll be saying prayers and great praises, till you'll be living the way the great saints do be living, with little but old sacks, and skin covering their bones. [*To* TIMMY.] Leave him go now, you're seeing he's quiet again. [*He frees* MARTIN DOUL.] And let you [*he turns to* MARY DOUL] not be raising your voice, a bad thing in a woman; but let the lot of you, who have seen the power of the Lord, be thinking on it in the dark night, and be saying to yourselves it's great pity and love He has for the poor, starving people of Ireland. [*He gathers his cloak about him.*] And now the Lord send blessing to you all, for I am going on to Annagolan, where there is a deaf woman, and to Laragh, where there are two men without sense, and to Glenassil, where there are children blind from their birth; and then I'm going to sleep this night in the bed of the holy Kevin, and to be praising God, and asking great blessing on you all.

[*He bends his head.*]

CURTAIN

ACT TWO

Village roadside, on left the door of a forge, with broken wheels, etc., lying about. A well near centre, with board above it, and room to pass behind it. MARTIN DOUL *is sitting near forge, cutting sticks.*

TIMMY [*heard hammering inside forge, then calls*]. Let you make haste out there. . . . I'll be putting up new fires at the turn of day, and you haven't the half of them cut yet.

MARTIN DOUL [*gloomily*]. It's destroyed I'll be whacking your old thorns till the turn of day, and I with no food in my stomach would keep the life in a pig. [*He turns towards the door.*] Let you come out here and cut them yourself if you want them cut, for there's an hour every day when a man has a right to his rest.

TIMMY [*coming out, with a hammer, impatiently*]. Do you want me to be driving you off again to be walking the roads? There you are now, and I giving you your food, and a corner to sleep, and money with it; and, to hear the talk of you, you'd think I was after beating you, or stealing your gold.

MARTIN DOUL. You'd do it handy, maybe, if I'd gold to steal.

TIMMY [*throws down hammer; picks up some of the sticks already cut, and throws them into door*]. There's no fear of your having gold — a lazy, basking fool the like of you.

MARTIN DOUL. No fear, maybe, and I here with yourself, for it's more I got a while since, and I sitting blinded in Grianan, than I get in this place, working hard, and destroying myself, the length of the day.

TIMMY [*stopping with amazement*]. Working hard? [*He goes over to him.*] I'll teach you to work hard, Martin Doul. Strip off your coat now, and put a tuck in your sleeves, and cut the lot of them, while I'd rake the ashes from the forge, or I'll not put up with you another hour itself.

MARTIN DOUL [*horrified*]. Would you have me getting my death sitting out in the black wintry air with no coat on me at all?

TIMMY [*with authority*]. Strip it off now, or walk down upon the road.

MARTIN DOUL [*bitterly*]. Oh, God help me! [*He begins taking off his coat.*] I've heard tell you stripped the sheet from your wife and you putting her down into the grave, and that there isn't the like of you for plucking your living ducks, the short days, and leaving them running round in their skins, in the great rains and the cold. [*He tucks up his sleeves.*] Ah. I've heard a power of queer things of yourself, and there isn't one of them I'll not believe from this day, and be telling to the boys.

TIMMY [*pulling over a big stick*]. Let you cut that now, and give me rest from your talk, for I'm not heeding you at all.

MARTIN DOUL [*taking stick*]. That's a hard, terrible stick, Timmy; and isn't it a poor thing to be cutting strong timber the like of that, when it's cold the bark is, and slippy with the frost of the air?

TIMMY [*gathering up another armful of sticks*]. What way wouldn't it be cold, and it freezing since the moon was changed?

[*He goes into forge*]

MARTIN DOUL [*querulously, as he cuts slowly*]. What way, indeed, Timmy? For it's a raw, beastly day we do have each day, till I do be thinking it's well for the blind don't be seeing them grey clouds driving on the hill, and don't be looking on people with their noses red, the like of your nose, and their eyes weeping and watering, the like of your eyes, God help you, Timmy the smith.

TIMMY [*seen blinking in doorway*]. Is it turning now you are against your sight?

MARTIN DOUL [*very miserably*]. It's a hard thing for a man to have his sight, and he living near to the like of you [*he cuts a stick and throws it away*], or wed with a wife [*cuts a stick*]; and I do be thinking it should be a hard thing for the Almighty God to be looking on the world, bad days, and on men the like of yourself walking around on it, and they slipping each way in the muck.

TIMMY [*with pot-hooks which he taps on anvil*]. You'd have a right to be minding, Martin Doul, for it's a power the Saint cured lose their sight after a while: Mary Doul's dimming again, I've heard them say; and I'm thinking the Lord, if He hears you making that talk, will have little pity left for you at all.

MARTIN DOUL. There's not a bit of fear of me losing my sight, and if it's a dark day itself it's too well I see every wicked wrinkle you have round by your eye.

TIMMY [*looking at him sharply*]. The day's not dark since the clouds broke in the east.

MARTIN DOUL. Let you not be tormenting yourself trying to make me afeard. You told me a power of bad lies the time I was blind, and it's right now for you to stop, and be taking your rest [MARY DOUL *comes in unnoticed on right with a sack filled with green stuff on her arm*], for it's little ease or quiet any person would get if the big fools of Ireland weren't weary at times. [*He looks up and sees* MARY DOUL.] Oh, glory be to God, she's coming again.

[*He begins to work busily with his back to her.*]

TIMMY [*amused, to* MARY DOUL, *as she is going by without looking at them*]. Look on him now, Mary Doul. You'd be a great one for keeping him steady at his work, for he's after idling and blathering to this hour from the dawn of day.

MARY DOUL [*stiffly*]. Of what is it you're speaking, Timmy the smith?

TIMMY [*laughing*]. Of himself, surely. Look on him there, and he with the shirt on him ripping from his back. You'd have a right to come round this night, I'm thinking, and put a stitch into his clothes, for it's long enough you are not speaking one to the other.

MARY DOUL. Let the two of you not torment me at all.

[*She goes out left, with her head in the air.*]

MARTIN DOUL [*stops work and looks after her*]. Well, isn't it a queer thing she can't keep herself two days without looking on my face?

TIMMY [*jeeringly*]. Looking on your face is it? And she after going by with her head turned the way you'd see a priest going where there'd be a drunken man in the side ditch talking with a girl. [MARTIN DOUL *gets up and goes to corner of forge, and looks out left.*] Come back here and don't mind her at all. Come back here, I'm saying, you've no call to be spying behind her since she went off and left you, in place of breaking her heart, trying to keep you in the decency of clothes and food.

MARTIN DOUL [*crying out indignantly*]. You know rightly, Timmy, it was myself drove her away.

TIMMY. That's a lie you're telling, yet it's little I care which one of you was driving the other, and let you walk back here, I'm saying, to your work.

MARTIN DOUL [*turning round*]. I'm coming, surely.

[*He stops and looks out right, going a step or two towards centre.*]

TIMMY. On what is it you're gaping, Martin Doul?

MARTIN DOUL. There's a person walking above. . . . It's Molly Byrne, I'm thinking, coming down with her can.

TIMMY. If she is itself let you not be idling this day, or minding her at all, and let you hurry with them sticks, for I'll want you in a short while to be blowing in the forge.

[*He throws down pot-hooks.*]

MARTIN DOUL [*crying out*]. Is it roasting me now you'd be? [*Turns back and sees pot-hooks; he takes them up.*] Pot-hooks? Is it over them you've been inside sneezing and sweating since the dawn of day?

TIMMY [*resting himself on anvil, with satisfaction*]. I'm making a power of things you do have when you're settling with a wife, Martin Doul; for I heard tell last night the Saint'll be passing again in a short while, and I'd have him wed Molly with myself. . . . He'd do it, I've heard them say, for not a penny at all.

MARTIN DOUL [*lays down hooks and looks at him steadily*]. Molly'll be saying great praises now to the Almighty God and He giving her a fine, stout, hardy man the like of you.

TIMMY [*uneasily*]. And why wouldn't she, if she's a fine woman itself?

MARTIN DOUL [*looking up right*]. Why wouldn't she, indeed, Timmy? . . . The Almighty God's made a fine match in the two of you, for if you went marrying a woman was the like of yourself you'd be having the fearfulest little children, I'm thinking, was ever seen in the world.

TIMMY [*seriously offended*]. God forgive you! if you're an

ugly man to be looking at, I'm thinking your tongue's worse than your view.

MARTIN DOUL [*hurt also*]. Isn't it destroyed with the cold I am, and if I'm ugly itself I never seen anyone the like of you for dreepiness this day, Timmy the smith, and I'm thinking now herself's coming above you'd have a right to step up into your old shanty, and give a rub to your face, and not be setting there with your bleary eyes, and your big nose, the like of an old scarecrow stuck down upon the road.

TIMMY [*looking up the road uneasily*]. She's no call to mind what way I look, and I after building a house with four rooms in it above on the hill. [*He stands up.*] But it's a queer thing the way yourself and Mary Doul are after setting every person in this place, and up beyond to Rathvanna, talking of nothing, and thinking of nothing, but the way they do be looking in the face. [*Going towards forge.*] It's the devil's work you're after doing with your talk of fine looks, and I'd do right, maybe, to step in and wash the blackness from my eyes.

[*He goes into forge.* MARTIN DOUL *rubs his face furiously with the tail of his coat.* MOLLY BYRNE *comes on right with a water-can, and begins to fill it at the well.*]

MARTIN DOUL. God save you, Molly Byrne.

MOLLY BYRNE [*indifferently*]. God save you.

MARTIN DOUL. That's a dark, gloomy day, and the Lord have mercy on us all.

MOLLY BYRNE. Middling dark.

MARTIN DOUL. It's a power of dirty days, and dark mornings, and shabby-looking fellows [*he makes a gesture over his shoulder*] we do have to be looking on when we have our sight, God help us, but there's one fine thing we have, to be looking on a grand, white, handsome girl, the like of you . . . and every time I set my eyes on you I do be blessing the saints, and the holy water, and the power of the Lord Almighty in the heavens above.

MOLLY BYRNE. I've heard the priests say it isn't looking on a young girl would teach many to be saying their prayers.

[*Bailing water into her can with a cup.*]

MARTIN DOUL. It isn't many have been the way I was, hearing your voice speaking, and not seeing you at all.

MOLLY BYRNE. That should have been a queer time for an old, wicked, coaxing fool to be sitting there with your eyes shut, and not seeing a sight of girl or woman passing the road.

MARTIN DOUL. If it was a queer time itself it was great joy and pride I had the time I'd hear your voice speaking and you passing to Grianan [*beginning to speak with plaintive intensity*], for it's of many a fine thing your voice would put a poor dark fellow in mind, and the day I'd hear it it's of little else at all I would be thinking.

MOLLY BYRNE. I'll tell your wife if you talk to me the like of that. . . . You've heard, maybe, she's below picking nettles for the widow O'Flynn, who took great pity on her when she seen the two of you fighting, and yourself putting shame on her at the crossing of the roads.

MARTIN DOUL [*impatiently*]. Is there no living person can speak a score of words to me, or say 'God speed you', itself, without putting me in mind of the old woman, or that day either at Grianan?

MOLLY BYRNE [*maliciously*]. I was thinking it should be a fine thing to put you in mind of the day you called the grand day of your life.

MARTIN DOUL. Grand day, is it? [*Plaintively again, throwing aside his work, and leaning towards her.*] Or a bad black day when I was roused up and found I was the like of the little children do be listening to the stories of an old woman, and do be dreaming after in the dark night that it's in grand houses of gold they are, with speckled horses to ride, and do be waking again, in a short while, and they destroyed with the cold, and the thatch dripping, maybe, and the starved ass braying in the yard?

MOLLY BYRNE [*working indifferently*]. You've great romancing this day, Martin Doul. Was it up at the still you were at the fall of night?

MARTIN DOUL [*stands up, comes towards her, but stands at far (right) side of well*]. It was not, Molly Byrne, but lying down in a little rickety shed. . . . Lying down across a sop of straw, and I thinking I was seeing you walk, and hearing the sound of your step on a dry road, and hearing you again, and you laughing and making great talk in a high room with dry timber lining the roof. For it's a fine sound your voice has that time, and it's better I am, I'm thinking, lying down, the way a blind man does be lying, than to be sitting here in the grey light taking hard words of Timmy the smith.

MOLLY BYRNE [*looking at him with interest*]. It's queer talk you have if it's a little, old, shabby stump of a man you are itself.

MARTIN DOUL. I'm not so old as you do hear them say.

MOLLY BYRNE. You're old, I'm thinking, to be talking that talk with a girl.

MARTIN DOUL [*despondingly*]. It's not a lie you're telling maybe, for it's long years I'm after losing from the world, feeling love and talking love, with the old woman, and I fooled the whole while with the lies of Timmy the smith.

MOLLY BYRNE [*half invitingly*]. It's a fine way you're want-

ing to pay Timmy the smith. . . . And it's not his *lies*
you're making love to this day, Martin Doul.

MARTIN DOUL. It is not, Molly, and the Lord forgive us
all. [*He passes behind her and comes near her left.*] For I've
heard tell there are lands beyond in Cahir Iveraghig and
the Reeks of Cork with warm sun in them, and fine light
in the sky. [*Bending towards her.*] And light's a grand thing
for a man ever was blind, or a woman, with a fine neck,
and a skin on her the like of you, the way we'd have a
right to go off this day till we'd have a fine life passing
abroad through them towns of the south, and we telling
stories, maybe, or singing songs at the fairs.

MOLLY BYRNE [*turning round half amused, and looking him
over from head to foot*]. Well, isn't it a queer thing when
your own wife's after leaving you because you're a pitiful
show, you'd talk the like of that to me?

MARTIN DOUL [*drawing back a little, hurt, but indignant*].
It's a queer thing, maybe, for all things is queer in the
world. [*In a low voice with peculiar emphasis.*] But there's
one thing I'm telling you, if she walked off away from me,
it wasn't because of seeing me, and I no more than I am,
but because I was looking on her with my two eyes, and
she getting up, and eating her food, and combing her
hair, and lying down for her sleep.

MOLLY BYRNE [*interested, off her guard*]. Wouldn't any
married man you'd have be doing the like of that?

MARTIN DOUL [*seizing the moment that he has her attention*].
I'm thinking by the mercy of God it's few sees anything
but them is blind for a space [*with excitement*]. It's a few
sees the old women rotting for the grave, and it's few
sees the like of yourself. [*He bends over her.*] Though it's
shining you are, like a high lamp would drag in the ships
out of the sea.

MOLLY BYRNE [*shrinking away from him*]. Keep off from me, Martin Doul.

MARTIN DOUL [*quickly, with low, furious intensity*]. It's the truth I'm telling you. [*He puts his hand on her shoulder and shakes her.*] And you'd do right not to marry a man is after looking out a long while on the bad days of the world; for what way would the like of him have fit eyes to look on yourself, when you rise up in the morning and come out of the little door you have above in the lane, the time it'd be a fine thing if a man would be seeing, and losing his sight, the way he'd have your two eyes facing him, and he going the roads, and shining above him, and he looking in the sky, and springing up from the earth, the time he'd lower his head, in place of the muck that seeing men do meet all roads spread on the world.

MOLLY BYRNE [*who has listened half mesmerized, starting away*]. It's the like of that talk you'd hear from a man would be losing his mind.

MARTIN DOUL [*going after her, passing to her right*]. It'd be little wonder if a man near the like of you would be losing his mind. Put down your can now, and come along with myself, for I'm seeing you this day, seeing you, maybe, the way no man has seen you in the world. [*He takes her by the arm and tries to pull her away softly to the right.*] Let you come on now, I'm saying, to the lands of Iveragh and the Reeks of Cork, where you won't set down the width of your two feet and not be crushing fine flowers, and making sweet smells in the air.

MOLLY BYRNE [*laying down can; trying to free herself*]. Leave me go, Martin Doul! Leave me go, I'm saying!

MARTIN DOUL. Let you not be fooling. Come along now the little path through the trees.

MOLLY BYRNE [*crying out towards forge*]. Timmy – Timmy
the smith. [TIMMY *comes out of forge, and* MARTIN
DOUL *lets her go.* MOLLY BYRNE, *excited and breathless,
pointing to* MARTIN DOUL.] Did ever you hear that
them that loses their sight loses their senses along with
it, Timmy the smith!

TIMMY [*suspicious, but uncertain*]. He's no sense, surely, and
he'll be having himself driven off this day from where
he's good sleeping, and feeding, and wages for his
work.

MOLLY BYRNE [*as before*]. He's a bigger fool than that,
Timmy. Look on him now, and tell me if that isn't a
grand fellow to think he's only to open his mouth to have
a fine woman, the like of me, running along by his heels.

[MARTIN DOUL *recoils towards centre, with his hand to his
eyes;* MARY DOUL *is seen on left coming forward softly*.]

TIMMY [*with blank amazement*]. Oh, the blind is wicked
people, and it's no lie. But he'll walk off this day and not
be troubling us more.

[*Turns back left and picks up* MARTIN DOUL'S *coat and
stick; some things fall out of coat pocket, which he gathers up
again*.]

MARTIN DOUL [*turns round, sees* MARY DOUL, *whispers
to* MOLLY BYRNE *with imploring agony*]. Let you not put
shame on me, Molly, before herself and the smith. Let
you not put shame on me and I after saying fine words to
you, and dreaming . . . dreams . . . in the night. [*He
hesitates, and looks round the sky*.] Is it a storm of thunder
is coming, or the last end of the world? [*He staggers
towards* MARY DOUL, *tripping slightly over tin can*.] The
heavens is closing, I'm thinking, with darkness and great
trouble passing in the sky. [*He reaches* MARY DOUL,
and seizes her left arm with both his hands – with a frantic cry.]

Is it the darkness of thunder is coming, Mary Doul! Do you see me clearly with your eyes?

MARY DOUL [*snatches her arm away, and hits him with empty sack across the face*]. I see you a sight too clearly, and let you keep off from me now.

MOLLY BYRNE [*clapping her hands*]. That's right, Mary. That's the way to treat the like of him is after standing there at my feet and asking me to go off with him, till I'd grow an old wretched road-woman the like of yourself.

MARY DOUL [*defiantly*]. When the skin shrinks on your chin, Molly Byrne, there won't be the like of you for a shrunk hag in the four quarters of Ireland. . . . It's a fine pair, you'd be, surely!

[MARTIN DOUL *is standing at back right centre, with his back to the audience.*]

TIMMY [*coming over to* MARY DOUL]. Is it no shame you have to let on she'd ever be the like of you?

MARY DOUL. It's them that's fat and flabby do be wrinkled young, and that whitish yellowy hair she has does be soon turning the like of a handful of thin grass you'd see rotting, where the wet lies, at the north of a sty. [*Turning to go out on right.*] Ah, it's a better thing to have a simple, seemly face, the like of my face, for two-score years, or fifty itself, than to be setting fools mad a short while, and then to be turning a thing would drive off the little children from your feet.

[*She goes out;* MARTIN DOUL *has come forward again, mastering himself, but uncertain.*]

TIMMY. Oh, God protect us, Molly, from the words of the blind. [*He throws down* MARTIN DOUL'S *coat and stick.*] There's your old rubbish now, Martin Doul, and let you take it up, for it's all you have, and walk off through the world, for if ever I meet you coming again, if it's seeing or blind you are itself, I'll bring out the big hammer and hit you a welt with it will leave you easy till the judgement day.

MARTIN DOUL [*rousing himself with an effort*]. What call have you to talk the like of that with myself?

TIMMY [*pointing to* MOLLY BYRNE]. It's well you know what call I have. It's well you know a decent girl, I'm thinking to wed, has no right to have her heart scalded with hearing talk – and queer, bad talk, I'm thinking – from a raggy-looking fool the like of you.

MARTIN DOUL [*raising his voice*]. It's making game of you she is, for what seeing girl would marry with yourself? Look on him, Molly, look on him, I'm saying, for I'm seeing him still, and let you raise your voice, for the time is come, and bid him go up into his forge, and be sitting there by himself, sneezing and sweating, and he beating pot-hooks till the judgement day.

[*He seizes her arm again.*]

MOLLY BYRNE. Keep him off from me, Timmy!

TIMMY [*pushing* MARTIN DOUL *aside*]. Would you have me strike you, Martin Doul? Go along now after your wife, who's a fit match for you, and leave Molly with myself.

MARTIN DOUL [*despairingly*]. Won't you raise your voice, Molly, and lay hell's long curse on his tongue?

MOLLY BYRNE [*on* TIMMY'S *left*]. I'll be telling him it's destroyed I am with the sight of you and the sound of your voice. Go off now after your wife, and if she beats you again, let you go after the tinker girls is above running the hills, or down among the sluts of the town, and you'll learn one day, maybe, the way a man should speak with a well-reared, civil girl the like of me. [*She takes* TIMMY *by the arm.*] Come up now into the forge till he'll be gone down a bit on the road, for it's near afeard I am of the wild look he has come in his eyes.

[*She goes into the forge.* TIMMY *stops in the doorway.*]

TIMMY. Let me not find you out here again, Martin Doul. [*He bares his arm.*] It's well you know Timmy the smith has great strength in his arm, and it's a power of things it has broken a sight harder than the old bone of your skull.

[*He goes into the forge and pulls the door after him.*]

MARTIN DOUL [*stands a moment with his hand to his eyes*]. And that's the last thing I'm to set my sight on in the life of the world — the villainy of a woman and the bloody strength of a man. Oh, God, pity a poor blind fellow, the way I am this day with no strength in me to do hurt to them at all. [*He begins groping about for a moment, then stops.*] Yet if I've no strength in me I've a voice left for my prayers, and may God blight them this day, and my own soul the same hour with them, the way I'll see them after, Molly Byrne and Timmy the smith, the two of them on a high bed, and they screeching in hell. . . . It'll be a grand thing that time to look on the two of them; and they twisting and roaring out, and twisting and roaring again, one day and the next day, and each day always and ever. It's not blind I'll be that time, and it won't be hell to me, I'm thinking, but the like of heaven itself; and it's fine care I'll be taking the Lord Almighty doesn't know.

[*He turns to grope out.*]

CURTAIN

ACT THREE

The same Scene as in first Act, but gap in centre has been filled with briars, or branches of some sort. MARY DOUL, *blind again, gropes her way in on left, and sits as before. She has a few rushes with her. It is an early spring day.*

MARY DOUL [*mournfully*]. Ah, God help me . . . God help me; the blackness wasn't so black at all the other time as it is this time, and it's destroyed I'll be now, and hard set to get my living working alone, when it's few are passing and the winds are cold. [*She begins shredding rushes.*] I'm thinking short days will be long days to me from this time, and I sitting here, not seeing a blink, or hearing a word, and no thought in my mind but long prayers that Martin Doul'll get his reward in a short while for the villainy of his heart. It's great jokes the people'll be making now, I'm thinking, and they passing me by, pointing their fingers maybe, and asking what place is himself, the way it's no quiet or decency I'll have from this day till I'm an old woman with long white hair and it twisting from my brow. [*She fumbles with her hair, and then seems to hear something. Listens for a moment.*] There's a queer, slouching step coming on the road. . . . God help me, he's coming surely.

[*She stays perfectly quiet.* MARTIN DOUL *gropes in on right, blind also.*]

MARTIN DOUL [*gloomily*]. The devil mend Mary Doul for putting lies on me, and letting on she was grand. The devil mend the old Saint for letting me see it was lies. [*He sits down near her.*] The devil mend Timmy the smith for killing me with hard work, and keeping me with an empty, windy stomach in me, in the day and in the night. Ten thousand devils mend the soul of Molly Byrne – [MARY DOUL *nods her head with approval*] – and the bad, wicked souls is hidden in all the women of the world. [*He rocks himself, with his hand over his face.*] It's lonesome I'll be from this day, and if living people is a bad lot, yet Mary Doul, herself, and she a dirty, wrinkled-looking hag, was better maybe to be sitting along with than no one at all. I'll be getting my death now, I'm thinking, sitting alone in the cold air, hearing the night coming, and the blackbirds flying round in the briars crying to themselves, the time you'll hear one cart getting off a long way in the east, and another cart getting off a long way in the west, and a dog barking maybe, and a little wind turning the sticks. [*He listens and sighs heavily.*] I'll be destroyed sitting alone and losing my senses this time the way I'm after losing my sight, for it'd make any person afeard to be sitting up hearing the sound of his breath – [*he moves his feet on the stones*] – and the noise of his feet, when it's a power of queer things do be stirring, little sticks breaking, and the grass moving – [MARY DOUL *half sighs, and he turns on her in horror*] – till you'd take your dying oath on sun and moon a thing was breathing on the stones. [*He listens towards her for a moment, then starts up nervously, and gropes about for his stick.*] I'll be going now, I'm thinking, but I'm not sure what place my stick's in, and I'm destroyed with terror and dread. [*He touches her face as he is groping about and cries out.*] There's a thing with a cold, living face on it sitting up at my side. [*He turns to run away, but misses his path and stumbles in against the wall.*] My road is lost on me now! Oh, merciful God, set my foot on the path this day, and I'll be saying prayers morning and night, and not straining

my ear after young girls, or doing any bad thing till I
die –

MARY DOUL [*indignantly*]. Let you not be telling lies to
the Almighty God.

MARTIN DOUL. Mary Doul, is it? [*Recovering himself with
immense relief.*] Is it Mary Doul, I'm saying?

MARY DOUL. There's a sweet tone in your voice I've not
heard for a space. You're taking me for Molly Byrne, I'm
thinking.

MARTIN DOUL [*coming towards her, wiping sweat from his
face*]. Well, sight's a queer thing for upsetting a man. It's
a queer thing to think I'd live to this day to be fearing the
like of you; but if it's shaken I am for a short while, I'll
soon be coming to myself.

MARY DOUL. You'll be grand then, and it's no lie.

MARTIN DOUL [*sitting down shyly, some way off*]. You've no
call to be talking, for I've heard tell you're as blind as
myself.

MARY DOUL. If I am I'm bearing in mind I'm married to
a little dark stump of a fellow looks the fool of the world,
and I'll be bearing in mind from this day the great hulla-
baloo he's after making from hearing a poor woman
breathing quiet in her place.

MARTIN DOUL. And you'll be bearing in mind, I'm
thinking, what you seen a while back when you looked
down into a well, or a clear pool, maybe, when there
was no wind stirring and a good light in the sky.

MARY DOUL. I'm minding that surely, for if I'm not the
way the liars were saying below I seen a thing in them
pools put joy and blessing in my heart.

[*She puts her hand to her hair again.*]

MARTIN DOUL [*laughing ironically*]. Well, they were saying below I was losing my senses, but I never went any

day the length of that. . . . God help you, Mary Doul, if you're not a wonder for looks, you're the maddest female woman is walking the counties of the east.

MARY DOUL [*scornfully*]. You were saying all times you'd a great ear for hearing the lies in a word. A great ear, God help you, and you think you're using it now.

MARTIN DOUL. If it's not lies you're telling, would you have me think you're not a wrinkled poor woman is looking like three scores, maybe, or two scores and a half!

MARY DOUL. I would not, Martin. [*She leans forward earnestly.*] For when I seen myself in them pools, I seen my hair would be grey or white, maybe, in a short while, and I seen with it that I'd a face would be a great wonder when it'll have soft white hair falling around it, the way when I'm an old woman there won't be the like of me surely in the seven counties of the east.

MARTIN DOUL [*with real admiration*]. You're a cute thinking woman, Mary Doul, and it's no lie.

MARY DOUL [*triumphantly*]. I am, surely, and I'm telling you a beautiful white-haired woman is a grand thing to see, for I'm told when Kitty Bawn was selling poteen below, the young men itself would never tire to be looking in her face.

MARTIN DOUL [*taking off his hat and feeling his head, speaking with hesitation*]. Did you think to look, Mary Doul, would there be a whiteness the like of that coming upon me?

MARY DOUL [*with extreme contempt*]. On you, God help you! . . . In a short while you'll have a head on you as bald as an old turnip you'd see rolling round in the muck. You need never talk again of your fine looks, Martin Doul, for the day of that talk's gone for ever.

MARTIN DOUL. That's a hard word to be saying, for I was thinking if I'd a bit of comfort, the like of yourself, it's not far off we'd be from the good days went before, and that'd be a wonder surely. But I'll never rest easy, thinking you're a grey, beautiful woman, and myself a pitiful show.

MARY DOUL. I can't help your looks, Martin Doul. It wasn't myself made you with your rat's eyes, and your big ears, and your griseldy chin.

MARTIN DOUL [*rubs his chin ruefully, then beams with delight*]. There's one thing you've forgot, if you're a cute thinking woman itself.

MARY DOUL. Your slouching feet, is it? Or your hooky neck, or your two knees is black with knocking one on the other?

MARTIN DOUL [*with delighted scorn*]. There's talking for a cute woman. There's talking surely!

MARY DOUL [*puzzled at joy of his voice*]. If you'd anything but lies to say you'd be talking yourself.

MARTIN DOUL [*bursting with excitement*]. I've this to say, Mary Doul. I'll be letting my beard grow in a short while, a beautiful, long, white, silken, streamy beard, you wouldn't see the like of in the eastern world. . . . Ah, a white beard's a grand thing on an old man, a grand thing for making the quality stop and be stretching out their hands with good silver or gold, and a beard's a thing you'll never have, so you may be holding your tongue.

MARY DOUL [*laughing cheerfully*]. Well, we're a great pair, surely, and it's great times we'll have yet, maybe, and great talking before we die.

MARTIN DOUL. Great times from this day, with the help of the Almighty God, for a priest itself would believe the lies of an old man would have a fine white beard growing on his chin.

MARY DOUL. There's the sound of one of them twittering yellow birds do be coming in the spring-time from beyond the sea, and there'll be a fine warmth now in the sun, and a sweetness in the air, the way it'll be a grand thing to be sitting here quiet and easy, smelling the things growing up, and budding from the earth.

MARTIN DOUL. I'm smelling the furze a while back sprouting on the hill, and if you'd hold your tongue you'd hear the lambs of Grianan, though it's near drowned their crying is with the full river making noises in the glen.

MARY DOUL [*listens*]. The lambs is bleating, surely, and there's cocks and laying hens making a fine stir a mile off on the face of the hill. [*She starts.*]

MARTIN DOUL. What's that is sounding in the west?
[*A faint sound of a bell is heard.*]

MARY DOUL. It's not the churches, for the wind's blowing from the sea.

MARTIN DOUL [*with dismay*]. It's the old Saint, I'm thinking, ringing his bell.

MARY DOUL. The Lord protect us from the saints of God! [*They listen.*] He's coming this road, surely.

MARTIN DOUL [*tentatively*]. Will we be running off, Mary Doul?

MARY DOUL. What place would we run?

MARTIN DOUL. There's the little path going up through the sloughs. . . . If we reached the bank above, where the elders do be growing, no person would see a sight of us, if it was a hundred yeomen were passing itself; but I'm afeard after the time we were with our sight we'll not find our way to it at all.

MARY DOUL [*standing up*]. You'd find the way, surely. You're a grand man the world knows at finding your way winter or summer, if there was deep snow in it itself, or thick grass and leaves, maybe, growing from the earth.

MARTIN DOUL [*taking her hand*]. Come a bit this way; it's here it begins. [*They grope about gap.*] There's a tree pulled into the gap, or a strange thing happened, since I was passing it before.

MARY DOUL. Would we have a right to be crawling in below under the sticks?

MARTIN DOUL. It's hard set I am to know what would be right. And isn't it a poor thing to be blind when you can't run off itself, and you fearing to see?

MARY DOUL [*nearly in tears*]. It's a poor thing, God help us, and what good'll our grey hairs be itself, if we have our sight, the way we'll see them falling each day, and turning dirty in the rain?

[*The bell sounds near by.*]

MARTIN DOUL [*in despair*]. He's coming now, and we won't get off from him at all.

MARY DOUL. Could we hide in the bit of a briar is growing at the west butt of the church?

MARTIN DOUL. We'll try that, surely. [*He listens a moment.*] Let you make haste; I hear them trampling in the wood.

[*They grope over to church.*]

MARY DOUL. It's the words of the young girls making a great stir in the trees. [*They find the bush.*] Here's the briar on my left, Martin; I'll go in first, I'm the big one, and I'm easy to see.

MARTIN DOUL [*turning his head anxiously*]. It's easy heard you are; and will you be holding your tongue?

MARY DOUL [*partly behind bush*]. Come in now beside of me. [*They kneel down, still clearly visible.*] Do you think can they see us now, Martin Doul?

MARTIN DOUL. I'm thinking they can't, but I'm hard set to know; for the lot of them young girls, the devil save them, have sharp, terrible eyes, would pick out a poor man, I'm thinking, and he lying below hid in his grave.

MARY DOUL. Let you not be whispering sin, Martin Doul, or maybe it's the finger of God they'd see pointing to ourselves.

MARTIN DOUL. It's yourself is speaking madness, Mary Doul; haven't you heard the Saint say it's the wicked do be blind?

MARY DOUL. If it is you'd have a right to speak a big, terrible word would make the water not cure us at all.

MARTIN DOUL. What way would I find a big, terrible word, and I shook with the fear; and if I did itself, who'd know rightly if it's good words or bad would save us this day from himself?

MARY DOUL. They're coming. I hear their feet on the stones.

[*The* SAINT *comes in on right, with* TIMMY *and* MOLLY BYRNE *in holiday clothes, the others as before.*]

TIMMY. I've heard tell Martin Doul and Mary Doul were seen this day about on the road, holy father, and we were thinking you'd have pity on them and cure them again.

SAINT. I would, maybe, but where are they at all? I'll have little time left when I have the two of you wed in the church.

MAT SIMON [*at their seat*]. There are the rushes they do have lying round on the stones. It's not far off they'll be, surely.

MOLLY BYRNE [*pointing with astonishment*]. Look beyond, Timmy.

[*They all look over and see* MARTIN DOUL.]

TIMMY. Well, Martin's a lazy fellow to be lying in there at the height of the day. [*He goes over shouting.*] Let you get up out of that. You were near losing a great chance by your sleepiness this day, Martin Doul. . . . The two of them's in it, God help us all!

MARTIN DOUL [*scrambling up with* MARY DOUL]. What is it you want, Timmy, that you can't leave us in peace?

TIMMY. The Saint's come to marry the two of us, and I'm after speaking a word for yourselves, the way he'll be curing you now; for if you're a foolish man itself, I do be pitying you, for I've a kind heart, when I think of you sitting dark again, and you after seeing a while, and working for your bread.

[MARTIN DOUL *takes* MARY DOUL's *hand and tries to grope his way off right; he has lost his hat, and they are both covered with dust and grass seeds.*]

PEOPLE. You're going wrong. It's this way, Martin Doul.

[*They push him over in front of the* SAINT, *near centre.* MARTIN DOUL *and* MARY DOUL *stand with piteous hang-dog dejection.*]

SAINT. Let you not be afeard, for there's great pity with the Lord.

MARTIN DOUL. We aren't afeard, holy father.

SAINT. It's many a time those that are cured with the well of the four beauties of God lose their sight when a time is gone, but those I cure a second time go on seeing till the hour of death. [*He takes the cover from his can.*] I've a few drops only left of the water, but, with the help of God, it'll be enough for the two of you, and let you kneel down now upon the road.

[MARTIN DOUL *wheels round with* MARY DOUL *and tries to get away.*]

SAINT. You can kneel down here, I'm saying, we'll not trouble this time going to the church.

TIMMY [*turning* MARTIN DOUL *round, angrily*]. Are you going mad in your head, Martin Doul? It's here you're to kneel. Did you not hear his reverence, and he speaking to you now?

SAINT. Kneel down, I'm saying, the ground's dry at your feet.

MARTIN DOUL [*with distress*]. Let you go on your own way, holy father. We're not calling you at all.

SAINT. I'm not saying a word of penance, or fasting itself, for I'm thinking the Lord has brought you great teaching in the blinding of your eyes; so you've no call now to be fearing me, let you kneel down till I give you your sight.

MARTIN DOUL. We're not asking our sight, holy father, and let you be walking on and leaving us in our peace at the crossing roads, for it's best we are this way, and we're not asking to see.

SAINT [*to the* PEOPLE]. Is his mind gone that he's no wish to be cured this day, and looking out on the wonders of the world?

MARTIN DOUL. It's wonders enough I seen in a short space, holy father, for the life of one man only.

TIMMY. Is it he see wonders?

PATCH. He's making game.

MAT SIMON. He's may be drunk, holy father.

SAINT [*puzzled*]. I never heard tell of any person wouldn't have great joy to be looking on the earth, and the image of the Lord is thrown upon men.

MARTIN [*raising his voice, by degrees*]. That's great sights, holy father. . . . What was it I seen my first day, but your own bleeding feet and they cut with the stones, and my last day, but the villainy of herself you're wedding, God forgive you, Timmy the smith. . . . That was great sights maybe. . . . And wasn't it great sights seeing the roads when the north winds would be driving and the skies would be harsh and you'd see the horses, and the asses, and the dogs itself, maybe, with their heads hanging, and they closing their eyes –

TIMMY. There's talking.

MAT SIMON. He's maybe right, it's lonesome living when the days are dark.

MOLLY BYRNE. He's not right. Let you speak up, holy father, and confound him now.

SAINT [*coming close to* MARTIN DOUL *and putting his hand on his shoulder*]. Did you never hear tell of the summer and the fine spring in places where the holy men of Ireland have built up churches to the Lord, that you'd wish to be closed up and seeing no sight of the glittering seas, and the furze is opening above, will soon have the hills shining as if it was fine creels of gold they were, rising to the sky?

PATCH. That's it, holy father.

MAT SIMON. What will you say now, Martin Doul?

MARTIN DOUL [*fiercely*]. I'll say it's ourselves have finer sight than the lot of you, and we sitting abroad in the sweetness of the warmth of night [*the* SAINT *draws back from him*], hearing a late thrush, maybe, and the swift crying things do be racing in the air, till we do be looking up in our own minds into a grand sky, and seeing lakes, and broadening rivers, and hills are waiting for the spade and plough.

MAT SIMON [*roaring laughing*]. It's songs he's making now, holy father.

PATCH. It's mad he is.

MOLLY BYRNE. It's not, but lazy, holy father, and not wishing to work; for, awhile since, he was all times longing and screeching for the light of day.

MARTIN DOUL [*with vehement bitterness*]. If I was, I seen my fill in a short while with the look of my wife, and the look of your own wicked grin, the time you do be making game with a man.

MOLLY BYRNE. There's talking. . . . Let you not mind him more, holy father, but leave him in darkness, if it's that is best fitting the blackness of his heart.

TIMMY. Cure Mary Doul, your reverence, who is a quiet poor woman, never said a hard word but when she'd be vexed with himself, or with the young girls do be making game of her below.

MAT SIMON. That's it. Cure Mary Doul, your reverence.

SAINT. There's little use, I'm thinking, talking to the like of him, but if you've any sense, Mary Doul, let you kneel down at my feet, and I'll bring sight into your eyes.

MARTIN DOUL [*more defiantly*]. You will not, holy father. . . . Would you have her looking on me, and saying hard words to me till the hour of death?

SAINT [*severely*]. If she's wanting her sight, I wouldn't have the like of you stop her at all. [*To* MARY DOUL.] Kneel down, I'm saying.

MARY DOUL [*confused*]. Let us be as we are, holy father, and then we'll be known again, in a short while, as the people is happy and blind, and we'll be having an easy time with no trouble to live, and we getting half-pence on the road.

MOLLY BYRNE. Let you not be raving. Kneel down and get your sight, and let himself be taking half-pence if he likes it best.

TIMMY. If it's choosing a wilful blindness you are, there isn't anyone will give you a half'orth of meal, or be doing the little things you do need to keep you living in the world at all.

MAT SIMON. If you had your sight you could be keeping a watch on him that no other woman came near him in the night or day.

MARY DOUL [*partly convinced*]. That's true, maybe.

SAINT. Kneel down, for I must be hastening with the marriage, and going my own way before the fall of night.

ALL [*together*]. Kneel down, Mary, kneel down when you're bid by the Saint.

MARY DOUL [*looking uneasily towards* MARTIN DOUL]. Maybe it's right they are, and I will if you wish it, holy father.

[*She kneels down. The* SAINT *takes off his hat and gives it to someone near him. All the men take off their hats. He goes forward a step to take* MARTIN DOUL'S *hand away from* MARY DOUL.]

SAINT [*to* MARTIN DOUL]. Go aside now. We're not wanting you here.

[MARTIN DOUL *pushes him away roughly, and stands with his left hand on* MARY DOUL'S *shoulder.*]

MARTIN DOUL. Keep off yourself, holy father, and let you not be taking my rest from me in the darkness of my wife. . . . What call has the likes of you coming where you're not wanted, and making a great mess with the holy water you have, and the length of your prayers? [*Defiantly.*] Go on, I'm saying, and leave us this place on the road.

SAINT. If it was a seeing man I heard talking the like of that I'd put a black curse on him would weigh down his soul, till it'd be falling to hell, but you're a poor blind sinner,

God forgive you, and I don't mind you, at all. [*He raises his can.*] Go aside now till I give the blessing to your wife, and if you won't go of your own will, there are those standing by will make you surely.

MARTIN DOUL. Well, there's bitter hardness in the pity of your like, and what is it you want coming for to break our happiness and hour of ease. Let you rise up, Mary, and not heed them more. [*He pulls* MARY DOUL.]

SAINT [*imperiously*]. Let you take that man and drive him down upon the road.

MAT SIMON. Come on, now.

PATCH. Come on from talking badness to the holy saint.

[*They seize* MARTIN DOUL.]

MARTIN DOUL [*throwing himself down on the ground*]. I'll not come, I'm saying, and let you take his holy water to cure the blackness of your souls to-day.

MARY DOUL. Leave him easy, holy father, when I'd liefer live dark all times beside him, than be getting eyesight and new torments now.

SAINT. You have taken your choice. Drag him off from her, I'm saying.

PEOPLE. That's it. That's it. Come forward till we drop him in the pool beyond.

MARTIN DOUL [*screaming*]. Make them leave me go, holy father. Make them leave me go, I'm saying, and let you not think badly of my heathen talk, but cure her this day, or do anything you will.

SAINT [*to* PEOPLE]. Let him be. . . . Let him be, if his sense has come to him at all.

MARTIN DOUL [*shakes himself loose, feels for* MARY DOUL, *sinking his voice to a plausible whine*]. You may cure herself, surely, holy father; I wouldn't stop you at all – and it's great joy she'll have looking on your face – but let you cure myself along with her, the way I'll see when it's lies she's telling, and be looking out day and night upon the holy men of God.

[*He kneels down a little before* MARY DOUL.]

SAINT [*speaking half to the* PEOPLE]. Men who are dark a long while and thinking over queer thoughts in their heads, aren't the like of simple men, who do be working every day, and praying, and living like ourselves; so if he has found a right mind at the last minute itself, I'll cure him, if the Lord will, and not be thinking of the hard, foolish words he's after saying this day to us all.

MARTIN DOUL [*listening eagerly*]. I'm waiting now, holy father.

SAINT [*with can in his hand, close to* MARTIN DOUL]. With the power of the water from the grave of the four beauties of God, with the power of this water, I'm saying, that I put upon your eyes —

[*He raises can.* MARTIN DOUL *with a sudden movement strikes the can from the* SAINT'S *hand and sends it rocketing across stage.*]

PEOPLE [*with a terrified murmur*]. Will you look what he's done. Oh, glory be to God.

MARTIN DOUL [*stands up triumphantly, and pulls* MARY DOUL *up*]. If I'm a poor dark sinner I've sharp ears, God help me, and it's well I heard the little splash of the water you had there in the can. Go on now, holy father, for if you're a fine Saint itself, it's more sense is in a blind man, and more power maybe than you're thinking at all. Let you walk on now with your worn feet, and your welted knees, and your fasting, holy ways have left you with a big head on you and a thin pitiful arm. For if it's a right some of you have to be working and sweating the like of Timmy the smith, and a right some of you have to be fasting and praying and talking holy talk the like of yourself, I'm thinking it's a good right ourselves have to be sitting blind, hearing a soft wind turning round the little leaves of the spring and feeling the sun, and we not tormenting our souls with the sight of the grey days, and the holy men, and the dirty feet is trampling the world.

[*He gropes towards his stone with* MARY DOUL.]

MAT SIMON. It'd be an unlucky fearful thing, I'm thinking, to have the like of that man living near us at all in the townland of Grianan. Wouldn't he bring down a curse upon us, holy father, from the heavens of God?

SAINT [*tying his girdle*]. God has great mercy, but great wrath for them that sin.

THE PEOPLE. Go on now, Martin Doul. Go on from this place. Let you not be bringing great storms or droughts on us maybe from the power of the Lord.

[*Some of them throw things at him.*]

MARTIN DOUL [*turning round defiantly and picking up a stone*]. Keep off now, the yelping lot of you, or it's more than one maybe will get a bloody head on him with the pitch of my stone. Keep off now, and let you not be afeard; for we're going on the two of us to the towns of the south, where the people will have kind voices maybe, and we won't know their bad looks or their villainy at all. [*He takes* MARY DOUL'S *hand again.*] Come along now and we'll be walking to the south, for we've seen too much of every one in this place, and it's small joy we'd have living near them, or hearing the lies they do be telling from the grey of dawn till the night.

MARY DOUL [*despondingly*]. That's the truth, surely; and we'd have a right to be gone, if it's a long way itself, as I've heard them say, where you do have to be walking with a slough of wet on the one side and a slough of wet on the other, and you going a stony path with a north wind blowing behind. [*They go out.*]

TIMMY. There's a power of deep rivers with floods in them where you do have to be lepping the stones and you going to the south, so I'm thinking the two of them will be drowned together in a short while, surely.

SAINT. They have chosen their lot, and the Lord have mercy on their souls. [*He rings his bell.*] And let the two of you come up now into the church, Molly Byrne and Timmy the smith, till I make your marriage and put my blessing on you all.

[*He turns to the church; procession forms, and the curtain comes down, as they go slowly into the church.*]

The Playboy of the Western World

cp: Under Milk Wood.

PERSONS IN THE PLAY

CHRISTOPHER MAHON

OLD MAHON, *his Father, a Squatter*

MICHAEL JAMES FLAHERTY (called MICHAEL JAMES), *a Publican*

MARGARET FLAHERTY (called PEGEEN MIKE), *his Daughter*

WIDOW QUIN, *a Woman of about thirty*

SHAWN KEOGH, *her Cousin, a young Farmer*

PHILLY CULLEN and JIMMY FARRELL, *small Farmers*

SARA TANSEY, SUSAN BRADY and HONOR BLAKE, *Village Girls*

A BELLMAN

SOME PEASANTS

The action takes place near a village, on a wild coast of Mayo. The first Act passes on an evening of autumn, the other two Acts on the following day.

Preface

In writing *The Playboy of the Western World*, as in my other plays, I have used one or two words only that I have not heard among the country people of Ireland, or spoken in my own nursery before I could read the newspapers. A certain number of the phrases I employ I have heard also from herds and fishermen along the coast from Kerry to Mayo or from beggar-women and ballad-singers nearer Dublin; and I am glad to acknowledge how much I owe to the folk-imagination of these fine people. Anyone who has lived in real intimacy with the Irish peasantry will know that the wildest sayings and ideas in this play are tame indeed, compared with the fancies one may hear in any little hillside cabin in Geesala, or Carraroe, or Dingle Bay. All art is a collaboration; and there is little doubt that in the happy ages of literature, striking and beautiful phrases were as ready to the story-teller's or the play-wright's hand, as the rich cloaks and dresses of his time. It is probable that when the Elizabethan dramatist took his ink-horn and sat down to his work he used many phrases that he had just heard, as he sat at dinner, from his mother or his children. In Ireland, those of us who know the people have the same privilege. When I was writing *The Shadow of the Glen*, some years ago, I got more aid than any learning could have given me from a chink in the floor of the old Wicklow house where I was staying, that let me hear what was being said by the servant girls in the kitchen. This matter, I think, is of importance, for in countries where the imagination of the people, and the language they use, is rich and living, it is possible for a writer to be rich and copious in his words, and at the same time to give the reality, which is the root of all poetry, in a comprehensive and natural form. In the modern literature of towns, however, richness is found only in sonnets, or prose poems, or in one or two elaborate books that are far away from the profound and common interests of life. One has, on one side, Mallarmé and Huysmans producing this literature; and on the other, Ibsen and Zola dealing with the reality of life in joyless and pallid words. On the stage one must have reality, and one must have joy; and that is why the intellectual modern drama has failed, and people have grown sick of the false joy of the musical comedy, that has been given them in place of the rich joy found only in what is superb and wild in reality. In a good play every speech should be as fully flavoured as a nut or apple, and such speeches cannot be written by anyone who works among people who have shut their lips on poetry. In Ireland, for a few years more, we have a popular imagination that is fiery, and magnificent, and tender; so that those of us who wish to write start with a chance that is not given to writers in places where the spring-time of the local life has been forgotten, and the harvest is a memory only, and the straw has been turned into bricks.

21 *January* 1907   J. M. S.

No inter connecting their but. the lowest social scale and Goy Almighty. The two groups face to face with each other - juxtaposed.
Type of Romantic drama.
Criminal always likely to be a saint in this context.

The Playboy of the Western World

ACT ONE

Country public-house or shebeen, very rough and untidy. There is a sort of counter on the right with shelves, holding many bottles and jugs, just seen above it. Empty barrels stand near the counter. At back, a little to left of counter, there is a door into the open air, then, more to the left, there is a settle with shelves above it, with more jugs, and a table beneath a window. At the left there is a large open fireplace, with turf fire, and a small door into inner room. PEGEEN, a wild-looking but fine girl, of about twenty, is writing at table. She is dressed in the usual peasant dress.

PEGEEN [*slowly as she writes*]. Six yards of stuff for to make a yellow gown. A pair of lace boots with lengthy heels on them and brassy eyes. A hat is suited for a wedding-day. A fine-tooth comb. To be sent with three barrels of porter in Jimmy Farrell's creel cart on the evening of the coming Fair to Mister Michael James Flaherty. With the best compliments of this season. Margaret Flaherty.

SHAWN KEOGH [*a fat and fair young man comes in as she signs, looks round awkwardly, when he sees she is alone*]. Where's himself?

PEGEEN [*without looking at him*]. He's coming. [*She directs letter.*] To Mister Sheamus Mulroy, Wine and Spirit Dealer, Castlebar.

SHAWN [*uneasily*]. I didn't see him on the road.

PEGEEN. How would you see him [*licks stamp and puts it on letter*] and it dark night this half-hour gone by?

SHAWN [*turning towards door again*]. I stood a while outside
wondering would I have a right to pass on or to walk in
and see you, Pegeen Mike [*comes to fire*], and I could hear
the cows breathing and sighing in the stillness of the air,
and not a step moving any place from this gate to the
bridge.

PEGEEN [*putting letter in envelope*]. It's above at the cross-
roads he is, meeting Philly Cullen and a couple more are
going along with him to Kate Cassidy's wake.

SHAWN [*looking at her blankly*]. And he's going that length
in the dark night.

PEGEEN [*impatiently*]. He is surely, and leaving me lonesome on the scruff of the hill. [*She gets up and puts envelope
on dresser, then winds clock.*] Isn't it long the nights are now,
Shawn Keogh, to be leaving a poor girl with her own self
counting the hours to the dawn of day?

SHAWN [*with awkward humour*]. If it is, when we're wedded
in a short while you'll have no call to complain, for I've
little will to be walking off to wakes or weddings in the
darkness of the night.

PEGEEN [*with rather scornful good-humour*]. You're making
mighty certain, Shaneen, that I'll wed you now.

SHAWN. Aren't we after making a good bargain, the way
we're only waiting these days on Father Reilly's dispensation from the bishops, or the Court of Rome.

PEGEEN [*looking at him teasingly, washing up at dresser*]. It's a
wonder, Shaneen, the Holy Father'd be taking notice of
the likes of you; for if I was him I wouldn't bother with
this place where you'll meet none but Red Linahan, has
a squint in his eye, and Patcheen is lame in his heel, or
the mad Mulrannies were driven from California and
they lost in their wits. We're a queer lot these times to
go troubling the Holy Father on his sacred seat.

SHAWN [*scandalized*]. If we are, we're as good this place as another, maybe, and as good these times as we were for ever.

PEGEEN [*with scorn*]. As good, is it? Where now will you meet the like of Daneen Sullivan knocked the eye from a peeler; or Marcus Quin, God rest him, got six months for maiming ewes, and he a great warrant to tell stories of holy Ireland till he'd have the old women shedding down tears about their feet. Where will you find the like of them, I'm saying?

SHAWN [*timidly*]. If you don't, it's a good job, maybe; for [*with peculiar emphasis on the words*] Father Reilly has small conceit to have that kind walking around and talking to the girls.

PEGEEN [*impatiently throwing water from basin out of the door*]. Stop tormenting me with Father Reilly [*imitating his voice*] when I'm asking only what way I'll pass these twelve hours of dark, and not take my death with the fear. [*Looking out of door.*]

SHAWN [*timidly*]. Would I fetch you the Widow Quin, maybe?

PEGEEN. Is it the like of that murderer? You'll not, surely.

SHAWN [*going to her, soothingly*]. Then I'm thinking himself will stop along with you when he sees you taking on; for it'll be a long night-time with great darkness, and I'm after feeling a kind of fellow above in the furzy ditch, groaning wicked like a maddening dog, the way it's good cause you have, maybe, to be fearing now.

PEGEEN [*turning on him sharply*]. What's that? Is it a man you seen?

SHAWN [*retreating*]. I couldn't see him at all; but I heard him groaning out, and breaking his heart. It should have been a young man from his words speaking.

PEGEEN [*going after him*]. And you never went near to see
was he hurted or what ailed him at all ?

SHAWN. I did not, Pegeen Mike. It was a dark, lonesome
place to be hearing the like of him.

PEGEEN. Well, you're a daring fellow, and if they find his
corpse stretched above in the dews of dawn, what'll you
say then to the peelers, or the Justice of the Peace ?

SHAWN [*thunderstruck*]. I wasn't thinking of that. For the
love of God, Pegeen Mike, don't let on I was speaking of
him. Don't tell your father and the men is coming above ;
for if they heard that story they'd have great blabbing this
night at the wake.

PEGEEN. I'll maybe tell them, and I'll maybe not.

SHAWN. They are coming at the door. Will you whisht,
I'm saying ?

PEGEEN. Whisht yourself.

[*She goes behind counter.* MICHAEL JAMES, *fat jovial publican, comes in followed by* PHILLY CULLEN, *who is thin and
mistrusting, and* JIMMY FARRELL, *who is fat and amorous,
about forty-five.*]

MEN [*together*]. God bless you! The blessing of God on this
place!

PEGEEN. God bless you kindly.

MICHAEL [*to men, who go to the counter*]. Sit down now, and
take your rest. [*Crosses to* SHAWN *at the fire.*] And how
is it you are, Shawn Keogh ? Are you coming over the
sands to Kate Cassidy's wake ?

SHAWN. I am not, Michael James. I'm going home the
short cut to my bed.

PEGEEN [*speaking across the counter*]. He's right, too, and
have you no shame, Michael James, to be quitting off for
the whole night, and leaving myself lonesome in the
shop ?

they do not really mind which is which.

MICHAEL [*good-humouredly*]. Isn't it the same whether I go for the whole night or a part only? and I'm thinking it's a queer daughter you are if you'd have me crossing backward through the Stooks of the Dead Women, with a drop taken.

PEGEEN. If I am a queer daughter, it's a queer father'd be leaving me lonesome these twelve hours of dark, and I piling the turf with the dogs barking, and the calves mooing, and my own teeth rattling with the fear.

JIMMY [*flatteringly*]. What is there to hurt you, and you a fine, hardy girl would knock the head of any two men in the place?

PEGEEN [*working herself up*]. Isn't there the harvest boys with their tongues red for drink, and the ten tinkers is camped in the east glen, and the thousand militia — bad cess to them! — walking idle through the land. There's lots surely to hurt me, and I won't stop alone in it, let himself do what he will.

MICHAEL. If you're that afeard, let Shawn Keogh stop along with you. It's the will of God, I'm thinking, himself should be seeing to you now.

[*They all turn on* SHAWN.]

SHAWN [*in horrified confusion*]. I would and welcome, Michael James, but I'm afeard of Father Reilly; and what at all would the Holy Father and the Cardinals of Rome be saying if they heard I did the like of that?

MICHAEL [*with contempt*]. God help you! Can't you sit in by the hearth with the light lit and herself beyond in the room? You'll do that surely, for I've heard tell there's a queer fellow above, going mad or getting his death, maybe, in the gripe of the ditch, so she'd be safer this night with a person here.

SHAWN [*with plaintive despair*]. I'm afeard of Father Reilly,

145

Accepted without question.
A naturally outlaw community.
absorb saints & sinners equally

I'm saying. Let you not be tempting me, and we near married itself.

PHILLY [*with cold contempt*]. Lock him in the west room. He'll stay then and have no sin to be telling to the priest.

MICHAEL [*to* SHAWN, *getting between him and the door*]. Go up now.

SHAWN [*at the top of his voice*]. Don't stop me, Michael James. Let me out of the door, I'm saying, for the love of the Almighty God. Let me out [*trying to dodge past him*]. Let me out of it, and may God grant you His indulgence in the hour of need.

MICHAEL [*loudly*]. Stop your noising, and sit down by the hearth.

[*Gives him a push and goes to counter laughing.*]

SHAWN [*turning back, wringing his hands*]. Oh, Father Reilly, and the saints of God, where will I hide myself to-day? Oh, St Joseph and St Patrick and St Brigid and St James, have mercy on me now!

[SHAWN *turns round, sees door clear, and makes a rush for it.*]

MICHAEL [*catching him by the coat-tail*]. You'd be going, is it?

SHAWN [*screaming*]. Leave me go, Michael James, leave me go, you old Pagan, leave me go, or I'll get the curse of the priests on you, and of the scarlet-coated bishops of the Courts of Rome.

[*With a sudden movement he pulls himself out of his coat, and disappears out of the door, leaving his coat in* MICHAEL'S *hands.*]

MICHAEL [*turning round, and holding up coat*]. Well, there's the coat of a Christian man. Oh, there's sainted glory this day in the lonesome west; and by the will of God I've got you a decent man, Pegeen, you'll have no call to be spying after if you've a score of young girls, maybe, weeding in your fields.

PEGEEN [*taking up the defence of her property*]. What right have you to be making game of a poor fellow for minding the priest, when it's your own the fault is, not paying a penny pot-boy to stand along with me and give me courage in the doing of my work?

[*She snaps the coat away from him, and goes behind counter with it.*]

MICHAEL [*taken aback*]. Where would I get a pot-boy? Would you have me send the bell-man screaming in the streets of Castlebar?

SHAWN [*opening the door a chink and putting in his head, in a small voice*]. Michael James!

MICHAEL [*imitating him*]. What ails you?

SHAWN. The queer dying fellow's beyond looking over the ditch. He's come up, I'm thinking, stealing your hens. [*Looks over his shoulder.*] God help me, he's following me now [*he runs into room*], and if he's heard what I said, he'll be having my life, and I going home lonesome in the darkness of the night.

[*For a perceptible moment they watch the door with curiosity. Some one coughs outside. Then* CHRISTY MAHON, *a slight young man, comes in very tired and frightened and dirty.*]

CHRISTY [*in a small voice*]. God save all here!

MEN. God save you kindly!

CHRISTY [*going to the counter*]. I'd trouble you for a glass of porter, woman of the house.

[*He puts down coin.*]

PEGEEN [*serving him*]. You're one of the tinkers, young fellow, is beyond camped in the glen?

CHRISTY. I am not; but I'm destroyed walking.

MICHAEL [*patronizingly*]. Let you come up then to the fire. You're looking famished with the cold.

CHRISTY. God reward you. [*He takes up his glass and goes a little way across to the left, then stops and looks about him.*] Is it often the polis do be coming into this place, master of the house?

MICHAEL. If you'd come in better hours, you'd have seen 'Licensed for the Sale of Beer and Spirits, to be Consumed on the Premises,' written in white letters above the door, and what would the polis want spying on me, and not a decent house within four miles, the way every living Christian is a bona fide, saving one widow alone?

CHRISTY [*with relief*]. It's a safe house, so.

[*He goes over to the fire, sighing and moaning. Then he sits down, putting his glass beside him, and begins gnawing a turnip, too miserable to feel the others staring at him with curiosity.*]

MICHAEL [*going after him*]. Is it yourself is fearing the polis? You're wanting, maybe?

CHRISTY. There's many wanting.

MICHAEL. Many, surely, with the broken harvest and the ended wars. [*He picks up some stockings, etc., that are near the fire, and carries them away furtively.*] It should be larceny, I'm thinking?

CHRISTY [*dolefully*]. I had it in my mind it was a different word and a bigger.

PEGEEN. There's a queer lad. Were you never slapped in school, young fellow, that you don't know the name of your deed?

CHRISTY [*bashfully*]. I'm slow at learning, a middling scholar only.

MICHAEL. If you're a dunce itself, you'd have a right to know that larceny's robbing and stealing. Is it for the like of that you're wanting?

CHRISTY [*with a flash of family pride*]. And I the son of a strong farmer [*with a sudden qualm*], God rest his soul, could have bought up the whole of your old house a while since, from the butt of his tail-pocket, and not have missed the weight of it gone.

MICHAEL [*impressed*]. If it's not stealing, it's maybe something big.

CHRISTY [*flattered*]. Aye; it's maybe something big.

JIMMY. He's a wicked-looking young fellow. Maybe he followed after a young woman on a lonesome night.

CHRISTY [*shocked*]. Oh, the saints forbid, mister; I was all times a decent lad.

PHILLY [*turning on* JIMMY]. You're a silly man, Jimmy Farrell. He said his father was a farmer a while since, and there's himself now in a poor state. Maybe the land was grabbed from him, and he did what any decent man would do.

MICHAEL [*to* CHRISTY, *mysteriously*]. Was it bailiffs?

CHRISTY. The divil a one.

MICHAEL. Agents?

CHRISTY. The divil a one.

MICHAEL. Landlords?

CHRISTY [*peevishly*]. Ah, not at all, I'm saying. You'd see the like of them stories on any little paper of a Munster town. But I'm not calling to mind any person, gentle, simple, judge or jury, did the like of me.

[*They all draw nearer with delighted curiosity.*]

PHILLY. Well, that lad's a puzzle-the-world.

JIMMY. He'd beat Dan Davies' circus, or the holy missioners making sermons on the villainy of man. Try him again, Philly.

PHILLY. Did you strike golden guineas out of solder, young fellow, or shilling coins itself?

CHRISTY. I did not, mister, not sixpence nor a farthing coin.

JIMMY. Did you marry three wives maybe? I'm told there's a sprinkling have done that among the holy Luthers of the preaching north.

CHRISTY [*shyly*]. I never married with one, let alone with a couple or three.

PHILLY. Maybe he went fighting for the Boers, the like of the man beyond, was judged to be hanged, quartered, and drawn. Were you off east, young fellow, fighting bloody wars for Kruger and the freedom of the Boers?

CHRISTY. I never left my own parish till Tuesday was a week.

PEGEEN [*coming from counter*]. He's done nothing, so. [*To* CHRISTY.] If you didn't commit murder or a bad, nasty thing; or false coining, or robbery, or butchery, or the like of them, there isn't anything that would be worth your troubling for to run from now. You did nothing at all.

CHRISTY [*his feelings hurt*]. That's an unkindly thing to be saying to a poor orphaned traveller, has a prison behind him, and hanging before, and hell's gap gaping below.

PEGEEN [*with a sign to the men to be quiet*]. You're only saying it. You did nothing at all. A soft lad the like of you wouldn't slit the windpipe of a screeching sow.

CHRISTY [*offended*]. You're not speaking the truth.

PEGEEN [*in mock rage*]. Not speaking the truth, is it? Would you have me knock the head of you with the butt of the broom?

CHRISTY [*twisting round on her with a sharp cry of horror*]. Don't strike me. I killed my poor father, Tuesday was a week, for doing the like of that.

PEGEEN [*with blank amazement*]. Is it killed your father?

CHRISTY [*subsiding*]. With the help of God I did, surely, and that the Holy Immaculate Mother may intercede for his soul.

PHILLY [*retreating with* JIMMY]. There's a daring fellow.

JIMMY. Oh, glory be to God!

MICHAEL [*with great respect*]. That was a hanging crime, mister honey. You should have good reason for doing the like of that.

CHRISTY [*in a very reasonable tone*]. He was a dirty man, God forgive him, and he getting old and crusty, the way I couldn't put up with him at all.

PEGEEN. And you shot him dead?

CHRISTY [*shaking his head*]. I never used weapons. I've no licence, and I'm a law-fearing man.

MICHAEL. It was with a hilted knife maybe? I'm told, in the big world, it's bloody knives they use.

CHRISTY [*loudly, scandalized*]. Do you take me for a slaughter-boy?

PEGEEN. You never hanged him, the way Jimmy Farrell hanged his dog from the licence, and had it screeching and wriggling three hours at the butt of a string, and himself swearing it was a dead dog, and the peelers swearing it had life?

CHRISTY. I did not, then. I just riz the loy and let fall the edge of it on the ridge of his skull, and he went down at my feet like an empty sack, and never let a grunt or groan from him at all.

MICHAEL [*making a sign to* PEGEEN *to fill* CHRISTY's *glass*]. And what way weren't you hanged, mister? Did you bury him then?

CHRISTY [*considering*]. Aye. I buried him then. Wasn't I digging spuds in the field?

MICHAEL. And the peelers never followed after you the eleven days that you're out?

CHRISTY [*shaking his head*]. Never a one of them, and I walking forward facing hog, dog, or divil on the highway of the road.

PHILLY [*nodding wisely*]. It's only with a common week-day kind of a murderer them lads would be trusting their carcase, and that man should be a great terror when his temper's roused.

MICHAEL. He should then. [*To* CHRISTY.] And where was it, mister honey, that you did the deed?

CHRISTY [*looking at him with suspicion*]. Oh, a distant place, master of the house, a windy corner of high, distant hills.

PHILLY [*nodding with approval*]. He's a close man, and he's right, surely.

PEGEEN. That'd be a lad with the sense of Solomon to have for a pot-boy, Michael James, if it's the truth you're seeking one at all.

PHILLY. The peelers is fearing him, and if you'd that lad in the house there isn't one of them would come smelling around if the dogs itself were lapping poteen from the dung-pit of the yard.

JIMMY. Bravery's a treasure in a lonesome place, and a lad would kill his father, I'm thinking, would face a foxy divil with a pitchpike on the flags of hell.

PEGEEN. It's the truth they're saying, and if I'd that lad in the house, I wouldn't be fearing the loosed kharki cut-throats, or the walking dead.

CHRISTY [*swelling with surprise and triumph*]. Well, glory be to God!

MICHAEL [*with deference*]. Would you think well to stop here and be pot-boy, mister honey, if we gave you good wages, and didn't destroy you with the weight of work?

SHAWN [*coming forward uneasily*]. That'd be a queer kind to bring into a decent, quiet household with the like of Pegeen Mike.

PEGEEN [*very sharply*]. Will you whisht? Who's speaking to you?

SHAWN [*retreating*]. A bloody-handed murderer the like of . . .

PEGEEN [*snapping at him*]. Whisht, I am saying; we'll take no fooling from your like at all. [*To* CHRISTY *with a honeyed voice.*] And you, young fellow, you'd have a right to stop, I'm thinking, for we'd do our all and utmost to content your needs.

CHRISTY [*overcome with wonder*]. And I'd be safe this place from the searching law?

MICHAEL. You would, surely. If they're not fearing you, itself, the peelers in this place is decent, drouthy poor fellows, wouldn't touch a cur dog and not give warning in the dead of night.

PEGEEN [*very kindly and persuasively*]. Let you stop a short while anyhow. Aren't you destroyed walking with your feet in bleeding blisters, and your whole skin needing washing like a Wicklow sheep?

CHRISTY [*looking round with satisfaction*]. It's a nice room, and if it's not humbugging me you are, I'm thinking that I'll surely stay.

JIMMY [*jumps up*]. Now, by the grace of God, herself will be safe this night, with a man killed his father holding danger from the door, and let you come on, Michael James, or they'll have the best stuff drunk at the wake.

MICHAEL [*going to the door with men*]. And begging your pardon, mister, what name will we call you, for we'd like to know?

CHRISTY. Christopher Mahon.

MICHAEL. Well, God bless you, Christy, and a good rest till we meet again when the sun'll be rising to the noon of day.

CHRISTY. God bless you all.

MEN. God bless you.

[*They go out, except* SHAWN, *who lingers at the door.*]

SHAWN [*to* PEGEEN]. Are you wanting me to stop along with you and keep you from harm?

PEGEEN [*gruffly*]. Didn't you say you were fearing Father Reilly?

SHAWN. There'd be no harm staying now, I'm thinking, and himself in it too.

PEGEEN. You wouldn't stay when there was need for you, and let you step off nimble this time when there's none.

SHAWN. Didn't I say it was Father Reilly . . .

PEGEEN. Go on, then, to Father Reilly [*in a jeering tone*], and let him put you in the holy brotherhoods, and leave that lad to me.

SHAWN. If I meet the Widow Quin . . .

PEGEEN. Go on, I'm saying, and don't be waking this place with your noise. [*She hustles him out and bolts door.*] That lad would wear the spirits from the saints of peace. [*Bustles about, then takes off her apron and pins it up in the window as a blind,* CHRISTY *watching her timidly. Then she comes to him and speaks with bland good-humour.*] Let you stretch out now by the fire, young fellow. You should be destroyed travelling.

CHRISTY [*shyly again, drawing off his boots*]. I'm tired surely, walking wild eleven days, and waking fearful in the night.

[*He holds up one of his feet, feeling his blisters, and looking at them with compassion.*]

PEGEEN [*standing beside him, watching him with delight*]. You should have had great people in your family, I'm thinking, with the little, small feet you have, and you with a kind of a quality name, the like of what you'd find on the great powers and potentates of France and Spain.

CHRISTY [*with pride*]. We were great, surely, with wide and windy acres of rich Munster land.

PEGEEN. Wasn't I telling you, and you a fine handsome young fellow with a noble brow?

CHRISTY [*with a flash of delighted surprise*]. Is it me?

PEGEEN. Aye. Did you never hear that from the young girls where you come from in the west or south?

CHRISTY [*with venom*]. I did not, then. Oh, they're bloody liars in the naked parish where I grew a man.

PEGEEN. If they are itself, you've heard it these days, I'm thinking, and you walking the world telling out your story to young girls or old.

CHRISTY. I've told my story no place till this night, Pegeen Mike, and it's foolish I was here, maybe, to be talking free; but you're decent people, I'm thinking, and yourself a kindly woman, the way I wasn't fearing you at all.

PEGEEN [*filling a sack with straw*]. You've said the like of that, maybe, in every cot and cabin where you've met a young girl on your way.

CHRISTY [*going over to her, gradually raising his voice*]. I've said it nowhere till this night, I'm telling you; for I've seen none the like of you the eleven long days I am walking the world, looking over a low ditch or a high ditch on my north or south, into stony, scattered fields, or scribes of bog, where you'd see young, limber girls, and fine, prancing women making laughter with the men.

PEGEEN. If you weren't destroyed travelling, you'd have as much talk and streeleen, I'm thinking, as Owen Roe

O'Sullivan or the poets of the Dingle Bay; and I've heard all times it's the poets are your like – fine, fiery fellows with great rages when their temper's roused.

CHRISTY [*drawing a little nearer to her*]. You've a power of rings, God bless you, and would there be any offence if I was asking are you single now?

PEGEEN. What would I want wedding so young?

CHRISTY [*with relief*]. We're alike, so.

PEGEEN [*she puts sack on settle and beats it up*]. I never killed my father. I'd be afeard to do that, except I was the like of yourself with blind rages tearing me within, for I'm thinking you should have had great tussling when the end was come.

CHRISTY [*expanding with delight at the first confidential talk he has ever had with a woman*]. We had not then. It was a hard woman was come over the hill; and if he was always a crusty kind when he'd a hard woman setting him on, not the divil himself or his four fathers could put up with him at all.

PEGEEN [*with curiosity*]. And isn't it a great wonder that one wasn't fearing you?

CHRISTY [*very confidentially*]. Up to the day I killed my father, there wasn't a person in Ireland knew the kind I was, and I there drinking, waking, eating, sleeping, a quiet, simple poor fellow with no man giving me heed.

PEGEEN [*getting a quilt out of cupboard and putting it on the sack*]. It was the girls were giving you heed, maybe, and I'm thinking it's most conceit you'd have to be gaming with their like.

CHRISTY [*shaking his head, with simplicity*]. Not the girls itself, and I won't tell you a lie. There wasn't anyone heeding me in that place saving only the dumb beasts of the field. [*He sits down at fire.*]

Repressed / frustrated childhood.

PEGEEN [*with disappointment*]. And I thinking you should
have been living the like of a king of Norway or the
eastern world.

[*She comes and sits beside him after placing bread and mug of
milk on the table.*]

CHRISTY [*laughing piteously*]. The like of a king, is it? And
I after toiling, moiling, digging, dodging from the dawn
till dusk; with never a sight of joy or sport saving only
when I'd be abroad in the dark night poaching rabbits on
hills, for I was a divil to poach, God forgive me, [*very
naïvely*] and I near got six months for going with a dung
fork and stabbing a fish.

PEGEEN. And it's that you'd call sport, is it, to be abroad
in the darkness with yourself alone?

CHRISTY. I did, God help me, and there I'd be as happy
as the sunshine of St Martin's Day, watching the light
passing the north or the patches of fog, till I'd hear a
rabbit starting to screech and I'd go running in the furze.
Then, when I'd my full share, I'd come walking down
where you'd see the ducks and geese stretched sleeping
on the highway of the road, and before I'd pass the dung-
hill, I'd hear himself snoring out – a loud, lonesome
snore he'd be making all times, the while he was sleeping; and he a man'd be raging all times, the while he was
waking, like a gaudy officer you'd hear cursing and
damning and swearing oaths.

PEGEEN. Providence and Mercy, spare us all!

CHRISTY. It's that you'd say surely if you seen him and he
after drinking for weeks, rising up in the red dawn, or
before it maybe, and going out into the yard as naked as
an ash-tree in the moon of May, and shying clods against
the visage of the stars till he'd put the fear of death into
the banbhs and the screeching sows.

PEGEEN. I'd be well-nigh afeard of that lad myself, I'm thinking. And there was no one in it but the two of you alone?

CHRISTY. The divil a one, though he'd sons and daughters walking all great states and territories of the world, and not a one of them, to this day, but would say their seven curses on him, and they rousing up to let a cough or sneeze, maybe, in the deadness of the night.

PEGEEN [*nodding her head*]. Well, you should have been a queer lot. I never cursed my father the like of that, though I'm twenty and more years of age.

CHRISTY. Then you'd have cursed mine, I'm telling you, and he a man never gave peace to any, saving when he'd get two months or three, or be locked in the asylums for battering peelers or assaulting men [*with depression*], the way it was a bitter life he led me till I did up a Tuesday and halve his skull.

PEGEEN [*putting her hand on his shoulder*]. Well, you'll have peace in this place, Christy Mahon, and none to trouble you, and it's near time a fine lad like you should have your good share of the earth.

CHRISTY. It's time surely, and I a seemly fellow with great strength in me and bravery of . . . [*Some one knocks.*]

CHRISTY [*clinging to* PEGEEN]. Oh, glory! it's late for knocking, and this last while I'm in terror of the peelers, and the walking dead. [*Knocking again.*]

PEGEEN. Who's there?

VOICE [*outside*]. Me.

PEGEEN. Who's me?

VOICE. The Widow Quin.

PEGEEN [*jumping up and giving him the bread and milk*]. Go on now with your supper, and let on to be sleepy, for if

she found you were such a warrant to talk, she'd be
stringing gabble till the dawn of day.

[*He takes bread and sits shyly with his back to the door.*]

PEGEEN [*opening door, with temper*]. What ails you, or what
is it you're wanting at this hour of the night?

WIDOW QUIN [*coming in a step and peering at* CHRISTY].
I'm after meeting Shawn Keogh and Father Reilly below,
who told me of your curiosity man, and they fearing by
this time he was maybe roaring, romping on your hands
with drink.

PEGEEN [*pointing to* CHRISTY]. Look now is he roaring,
and he stretched out drowsy with his supper and his mug
of milk. Walk down and tell that to Father Reilly and to
Shaneen Keogh.

WIDOW QUIN [*coming forward*]. I'll not see them again,
for I've their word to lead that lad forward for to lodge
with me.

PEGEEN [*in blank amazement*]. This night is it?

WIDOW QUIN [*going over*]. This night. 'It isn't fitting,'
says the priesteen, 'to have his likeness lodging with an
orphaned girl.' [*To* CHRISTY.] God save you, mister!

CHRISTY [*shyly*]. God save you kindly!

WIDOW QUIN [*looking at him with half-amused curiosity*].
Well, aren't you a little smiling fellow? It should have
been great and bitter torments did rouse your spirits to a
deed of blood.

CHRISTY [*doubtfully*]. It should, maybe.

WIDOW QUIN. It's more than 'maybe' I'm saying, and
it'd soften my heart to see you sitting so simple with
your cup and cake, and you fitter to be saying your
catechism than slaying your da.

PEGEEN [*at counter, washing glasses*]. There's talking when
any'd see he's fit to be holding his head high with the

wonders of the world. Walk on from this, for I'll not have him tormented, and he destroyed travelling since Tuesday was a week.

WIDOW QUIN [*peaceably*]. We'll be walking surely when his supper's done, and you'll find we're great company, young fellow, when it's of the like of you and me you'd hear the penny poets singing in an August Fair.

CHRISTY [*innocently*]. Did you kill your father?

PEGEEN [*contemptuously*]. She did not. She hit himself with a worn pick, and the rusted poison did corrode his blood the way he never overed it, and died after. That was a sneaky kind of murder did win small glory with the boys itself.

[*She crosses to* CHRISTY's *left.*]

WIDOW QUIN [*with good-humour*]. If it didn't, maybe all knows a widow woman has buried her children and destroyed her man is a wiser comrade for a young lad than a girl, the like of you, who'd go helter-skeltering after any man would let you a wink upon the road.

PEGEEN [*breaking out into wild rage*]. And you'll say that, Widow Quin, and you gasping with the rage you had racing the hill beyond to look on his face.

WIDOW QUIN [*laughing derisively*]. Me, is it? Well, Father Reilly has cuteness to divide you now. [*She pulls* CHRISTY *up.*] There's great temptation in a man did slay his da, and we'd best be going, young fellow; so rise up and come with me.

PEGEEN [*seizing his arm*]. He'll not stir. He's pot-boy in this place, and I'll not have him stolen off and kidnapped while himself's abroad.

WIDOW QUIN. It'd be a crazy pot-boy'd lodge him in the shebeen where he works by day, so you'd have a right to come on, young fellow, till you see my little houseen, a perch off on the rising hill.

PEGEEN. Wait till morning, Christy Mahon. Wait till you lay eyes on her leaky thatch is growing more pasture for her buck goat than her square of fields, and she without a tramp itself to keep in order her place at all.

WIDOW QUIN. When you see me contriving in my little gardens, Christy Mahon, you'll swear the Lord God formed me to be living lone, and that there isn't my match in Mayo for thatching, or mowing, or shearing a sheep.

PEGEEN [*with noisy scorn*]. It's true the Lord God formed you to contrive indeed. Doesn't the world know you reared a black ram at your own breast, so that the Lord Bishop of Connaught felt the elements of a Christian, and he eating it after in a kidney stew? Doesn't the world know you've been seen shaving the foxy skipper from France for a threepenny-bit and a sop of grass tobacco would wring the liver from a mountain goat you'd meet leaping the hills?

WIDOW QUIN [*with amusement*]. Do you hear her now, young fellow? Do you hear the way she'll be rating at your own self when a week is by?

PEGEEN [*to* CHRISTY]. Don't heed her. Tell her to go on into her pigsty and not plague us here.

WIDOW QUIN. I'm going; but he'll come with me.

PEGEEN [*shaking him*]. Are you dumb, young fellow?

CHRISTY [*timidly to* WIDOW QUIN]. God increase you; but I'm pot-boy in this place, and it's here I liefer stay.

PEGEEN [*triumphantly*]. Now you have heard him, and go on from this.

WIDOW QUIN [*looking round the room*]. It's lonesome this

hour crossing the hill, and if he won't come along with me, I'd have a right maybe to stop this night with yourselves. Let me stretch out on the settle, Pegeen Mike; and himself can lie by the hearth.

PEGEEN [*short and fiercely*]. Faith, I won't. Quit off or I will send you now.

WIDOW QUIN [*gathering her shawl up*]. Well, it's a terror to be aged a score. [*To* CHRISTY.] God bless you now, young fellow, and let you be wary, or there's right torment will await you here if you go romancing with her like, and she waiting only, as they bade me say, on a sheepskin parchment to be wed with Shawn Keogh of Killakeen.

CHRISTY [*going to* PEGEEN *as she bolts door*]. What's that she's after saying?

PEGEEN. Lies and blather, you've no call to mind. Well, isn't Shawn Keogh an impudent fellow to send up spying on me? Wait till I lay hands on him. Let him wait, I'm saying.

CHRISTY. And you're not wedding him at all?

PEGEEN. I wouldn't wed him if a bishop came walking for to join us here.

CHRISTY. That God in glory may be thanked for that.

PEGEEN. There's your bed now. I've put a quilt upon you I'm after quilting a while since with my own two hands, and you'd best stretch out now for your sleep, and may God give you a good rest till I call you in the morning when the cocks will crow.

CHRISTY [*as she goes to inner room*]. May God and Mary and St Patrick bless you and reward you for your kindly talk. [*She shuts the door behind her. He settles his bed slowly, feeling the quilt with immense satisfaction.*] Well, it's a clean bed and soft with it, and it's great luck and company I've

162

won me in the end of time – two fine women fighting for the likes of me – till I'm thinking this night wasn't I a foolish fellow not to kill my father in the years gone by.

CURTAIN

Killing one's father put side by side with a dog without licence etc. Morality mixed.

Romantic Treatment :

Love and aspiration towards untrammelled infinity which is doomed to disappointment. Symbol of humdrum destiny is Shawn or Michael James in "the Shadow of the Glen."

founded on a lie.

Final adjustment is his attitude to his father. Play ∴ story of realisation of a character.

ACT TWO

Scene as before. Brilliant morning light. CHRISTY, *looking bright and cheerful, is cleaning a girl's boots.*

CHRISTY [*to himself, counting jugs on dresser*]. Half a hundred beyond. Ten there. A score that's above. Eighty jugs. Six cups and a broken one. Two plates. A power of glasses. Bottles, a schoolmaster'd be hard set to count, and enough in them, I'm thinking, to drunken all the wealth and wisdom of the county Clare. [*He puts down the boot carefully.*] There's her boots now, nice and decent for her evening use, and isn't it grand brushes she has? [*He puts them down and goes by degrees to the looking-glass.*] Well, this'd be a fine place to be my whole life talking out with swearing Christians, in place of my old dogs and cat; and I stalking around, smoking my pipe and drinking my fill, and never a day's work but drawing a cork an odd time, or wiping a glass or rinsing out a shiny tumbler for a decent man. [*He takes the looking-glass from the wall and puts it on the back of a chair; then sits down in front of it and begins washing his face.*] Didn't I know rightly, I was handsome, though it was the divil's own mirror we had beyond, would twist a squint across an angel's brow; and I'll be growing fine from this day, the way I'll have a soft lovely skin on me and won't be the like of the clumsy young fellows do be ploughing all times in the earth and dung. [*He starts.*] Is she coming again? [*He looks out.*] Stranger girls. God help me, where'll I hide myself away and my long neck naked to the world? [*He looks out.*] I'd best go to the room maybe till I'm dressed again.

[*He gathers up his coat and the looking-glass, and runs into the inner room. The door is pushed open, and* SUSAN BRADY *looks in, and knocks on door.*

SUSAN. There's nobody in it. [*Knocks again.*]

NELLY [*pushing her in and following her, with* HONOR BLAKE *and* SARA TANSEY]. It'd be early for them both to be out walking the hill.

SUSAN. I'm thinking Shawn Keogh was making game of us, and there's no such man in it at all.

HONOR [*pointing to straw and quilt*]. Look at that. He's been sleeping there in the night. Well, it'll be a hard case if he's gone off now, the way we'll never set our eyes on a man killed his father, and we after rising early and destroying ourselves running fast on the hill.

NELLY. Are you thinking them's his boots?

SARA [*taking them up*]. If they are, there should be his father's track on them. Did you never read in the papers the way murdered men do bleed and drip?

SUSAN. Is that blood there, Sara Tansey?

SARA [*smelling it*]. That's bog water, I'm thinking; but it's his own they are, surely, for I never seen the like of them for whitey mud, and red mud, and turf on them, and the fine sands of the sea. That man's been walking, I'm telling you.

[*She goes down right, putting on one of his boots.*]

SUSAN [*going to window*]. Maybe he's stolen off to Belmullet with the boots of Michael James, and you'd have a right so to follow after him, Sara Tansey, and you the one yoked the ass cart and drove ten miles to set your eyes on the man bit the yellow lady's nostril on the northern shore. [*She looks out.*]

SARA [*running to window, with one boot on*]. Don't be talking, and we fooled to-day. [*Putting on the other boot.*] There's a pair do fit me well and I'll be keeping them for walking to the priest, when you'd be ashamed this place, going up winter and summer with nothing worth while to confess at all.

HONOR [*who has been listening at door*]. Whisht! there's some one inside the room. [*She pushes door a chink open.*] It's a man.

[*SARA kicks off boots and puts them where they were. They all stand in a line looking through chink.*]

SARA. I'll call him. Mister! Mister! [*He puts in his head.*] Is Pegeen within?

CHRISTY [*coming in as meek as a mouse, with the looking-glass held behind his back*]. She's above on the cnuceen, seeking the nanny goats, the way she'd have a sup of goats' milk for to colour my tea.

SARA. And asking your pardon, is it you's the man killed his father?

CHRISTY [*sidling toward the nail where the glass was hanging*]. I am, God help me!

SARA [*taking eggs she has brought*]. Then my thousand welcomes to you, and I've run up with a brace of duck's eggs for your food to-day. Pegeen's ducks is no use, but these are the real rich sort. Hold out your hand and you'll see it's no lie I'm telling you.

CHRISTY [*coming forward shyly, and holding out his left hand*]. They're a great and weighty size.

SUSAN. And I run up with a pat of butter, for it'd be a poor thing to have you eating your spuds dry, and you after running a great way since you did destroy your da.

CHRISTY. Thank you kindly.

HONOR. And I brought you a little cut of a cake, for you should have a thin stomach on you, and you that length walking the world.

NELLY. And I brought you a little laying pullet – boiled and all she is – was crushed at the fall of night by the curate's car. Feel the fat of that breast, mister.

CHRISTY. It's bursting, surely.

[*He feels it with the back of his hand, in which he holds the presents.*]

SARA. Will you pinch it? Is your right hand too sacred for to use at all? [*She slips round behind him.*] It's a glass he has. Well, I never seen to this day a man with a looking-glass held to his back. Them that kills their fathers is a vain lot surely.

[GIRLS *giggle.*]

CHRISTY [*smiling innocently and piling presents on glass*]. I'm very thankful to you all to-day. . . .

WIDOW QUIN [*coming in quickly, at door*]. Sara Tansey, Susan Brady, Honor Blake! What in glory has you here at this hour of day?

GIRLS [*giggling*]. That's the man killed his father.

WIDOW QUIN [*coming to them*]. I know well it's the man; and I'm after putting him down in the sports below for racing, leaping, pitching, and the Lord knows what.

SARA [*exuberantly*]. That's right, Widow Quin. I'll bet my dowry that he'll lick the world.

WIDOW QUIN. If you will, you'd have a right to have him fresh and nourished in place of nursing a feast. [*Taking presents.*] Are you fasting or fed, young fellow?

CHRISTY. Fasting, if you please.

WIDOW QUIN [*loudly*]. Well, you're the lot. Stir up now and give him his breakfast. [*To* CHRISTY.] Come here to me [*she puts him on bench beside her while the* GIRLS *make tea and get his breakfast*], and let you tell us your story before Pegeen will come, in place of grinning your ears off like the moon of May.

CHRISTY [*beginning to be pleased*]. It's a long story; you'd be destroyed listening.

WIDOW QUIN. Don't be letting on to be shy, a fine, gamey, treacherous lad the like of you. Was it in your house beyond you cracked his skull?

CHRISTY [*shy but flattered*]. It was not. We were digging spuds in his cold, sloping, stony, divil's patch of a field.

WIDOW QUIN. And you went asking money of him, or making talk of getting a wife would drive him from his farm?

CHRISTY. I did not, then; but there I was, digging and digging, and 'You squinting idiot,' says he, 'let you walk down now and tell the priest you'll wed the Widow Casey in a score of days.'

WIDOW QUIN. And what kind was she?

CHRISTY [*with horror*]. A walking terror from beyond the hills, and she two score and five years, and two hundredweights and five pounds in the weighing scales, with a limping leg on her, and a blinded eye, and she a woman of noted misbehaviour with the old and young.

GIRLS [*clustering round him, serving him*]. Glory be.

WIDOW QUIN. And what did he want driving you to wed with her?

[*She takes a bit of the chicken.*]

CHRISTY [*eating with growing satisfaction*]. He was letting on I was wanting a protector from the harshness of the world, and he without a thought the whole while but how he'd have her hut to live in and her gold to drink.

WIDOW QUIN. There's maybe worse than a dry hearth and a widow woman and your glass at night. So you hit him then?

CHRISTY [*getting almost excited*]. I did not. 'I won't wed her,' says I, 'when all know she did suckle me for six weeks when I came into the world, and she a hag this day with a tongue on her has the crows and seabirds scattered, the way they wouldn't cast a shadow on her garden with the dread of her curse.'

WIDOW QUIN [*teasingly*]. That one should be right company.

SARA [*eagerly*]. Don't mind her. Did you kill him then?

CHRISTY. 'She's too good for the like of you,' says he, 'and go on now or I'll flatten you out like a crawling beast has passed under a dray.' 'You will not if I can help it,' says I. 'Go on,' says he, 'or I'll have the divil making garters of your limbs to-night.' 'You will not if I can help it,' says I.

[*He sits up brandishing his mug.*]

SARA. You were right surely.

CHRISTY [*impressively*]. With that the sun came out between the cloud and the hill, and it shining green in my face. 'God have mercy on your soul,' says he, lifting a scythe. 'Or on your own,' says I, raising the loy.

SUSAN. That's a grand story.

HONOR. He tells it lovely.

CHRISTY [*flattered and confident, waving bone*]. He gave a drive with the scythe, and I gave a lep to the east. Then I turned around with my back to the north, and I hit a blow on the ridge of his skull, laid him stretched out, and he split to the knob of his gullet.

[*He raises the chicken bone to his Adam's apple.*]

GIRLS [*together*]. Well, you're a marvel! Oh, God bless you! You're the lad, surely!

SUSAN. I'm thinking the Lord God sent him this road to make a second husband to the Widow Quin, and she with a great yearning to be wedded, though all dread her here. Lift him on her knee, Sara Tansey.

WIDOW QUIN. Don't tease him.

SARA [*going over to dresser and counter very quickly, and getting two glasses and porter*]. You're heroes, surely, and let you drink a supeen with your arms linked like the outlandish lovers in the sailor's song. [*She links their arms and gives them the glasses.*] There now. Drink a health to the wonders of the western world, the pirates, preachers, poteen-makers, with the jobbing jockies; parching peelers, and the juries fill their stomachs selling judgements of the English law.

[*Brandishing the bottle.*]

WIDOW QUIN. That's a right toast, Sara Tansey. Now, Christy.

[*They drink with their arms linked, he drinking with his left hand, she with her right. As they are drinking, PEGEEN MIKE comes in with a milk-can and stands aghast. They all spring away from CHRISTY. He goes down left. WIDOW QUIN remains seated.*]

PEGEEN [*angrily, to SARA*]. What is it you're wanting?

SARA [*twisting her apron*]. An ounce of tobacco.

PEGEEN. Have you tuppence?

SARA. I've forgotten my purse.

PEGEEN. Then you'd best be getting it and not be fooling us here. [*To the WIDOW QUIN, with more elaborate scorn.*] And what is it you're wanting, Widow Quin?

WIDOW QUIN [*insolently*]. A penn'orth of starch.

PEGEEN [*breaking out*]. And you without a white shift or a shirt in your whole family since the drying of the flood. I've no starch for the like of you, and let you walk on now to Killamuck.

WIDOW QUIN [*turning to CHRISTY, as she goes out with the GIRLS*]. Well, you're mighty huffy this day, Pegeen

Mike, and you, young fellow, let you not forget the
sports and racing when the noon is by. [*They go out.*]

PEGEEN [*imperiously*]. Fling out that rubbish and put them
cups away. [CHRISTY *tidies away in great haste.*] Shove in
the bench by the wall. [*He does so.*] And hang that glass
on the nail. What disturbed it at all ?

CHRISTY [*very meekly*]. I was making myself decent only,
and this a fine country for young lovely girls.

PEGEEN [*sharply*]. Whisht your talking of girls. [*Goes to
counter on right.*]

CHRISTY. Wouldn't any wish to be decent in a place . . .

PEGEEN. Whisht, I'm saying.

CHRISTY [*looks at her face for a moment with great misgivings,
then as a last effort takes up a loy, and goes towards her, with
feigned assurance*]. It was with a loy the like of that I killed
my father.

PEGEEN [*still sharply*]. You've told me that story six times
since the dawn of day.

CHRISTY [*reproachfully*]. It's a queer thing you wouldn't
care to be hearing it and them girls after walking four
miles to be listening to me now.

PEGEEN [*turning round astonished*]. Four miles ?

CHRISTY [*apologetically*]. Didn't himself say there were
only bona fides living in the place ?

PEGEEN. It's bona fides by the road they are, but that lot
came over the river lepping the stones. It's not three
perches when you go like that, and I was down this morning looking on the papers the post-boy does have in his
bag. [*With meaning and emphasis.*] For there was great
news this day, Christopher Mahon.

[*She goes into room on left.*]

CHRISTY [*suspiciously*]. Is it news of my murder ?

PEGEEN [*inside*]. Murder, indeed.

CHRISTY [*loudly*]. A murdered da?

PEGEEN [*coming in again and crossing right*]. There was not, but a story filled half a page of the hanging of a man. Ah, that should be a fearful end, young fellow, and it worst of all for a man destroyed his da; for the like of him would get small mercies, and when it's dead he is they'd put him in a narrow grave, with cheap sacking wrapping him round, and pour down quicklime on his head, the way you'd see a woman pouring any frish-frash from a cup.

CHRISTY [*very miserably*]. Oh, God help me. Are you thinking I'm safe? You were saying at the fall of night I was shut of jeopardy and I here with yourselves.

PEGEEN [*severely*]. You'll be shut of jeopardy no place if you go talking with a pack of wild girls the like of them do be walking abroad with the peelers, talking whispers at the fall of night.

CHRISTY [*with terror*]. And you're thinking they'd tell?

PEGEEN [*with mock sympathy*]. Who knows, God help you?

CHRISTY [*loudly*]. What joy would they have to bring hanging to the likes of me?

PEGEEN. It's queer joys they have, and who knows the thing they'd do, if it'd make the green stones cry itself to think of you swaying and swiggling at the butt of a rope, and you with a fine, stout neck, God bless you! the way you'd be a half an hour, in great anguish, getting your death.

CHRISTY [*getting his boots and putting them on*]. If there's that terror of them, it'd be best, maybe, I went on wandering like Esau or Cain and Abel on the sides of Neifin or the Erris plain.

PEGEEN [*beginning to play with him*]. It would, maybe, for I've heard the Circuit Judges this place is a heartless crew.

CHRISTY [*bitterly*]. It's more than Judges this place is a heartless crew. [*Looking up at her*]. And isn't it a poor thing to be starting again, and I a lonesome fellow will be looking out on women and girls the way the needy fallen spirits do be looking on the Lord?

PEGEEN. What call have you to be that lonesome when there's poor girls walking Mayo in their thousands now?

CHRISTY [*grimly*]. It's well you know what call I have. It's well you know it's a lonesome thing to be passing small towns with the lights shining sideways when the night is down, or going in strange places with a dog noising before you and a dog noising behind, or drawn to the cities where you'd hear a voice kissing and talking deep love in every shadow of the ditch, and you passing on with an empty, hungry stomach failing from your heart.

PEGEEN. I'm thinking you're an odd man, Christy Mahon. The oddest walking fellow I ever set my eyes on to this hour to-day.

CHRISTY. What would any be but odd men and they living lonesome in the world?

PEGEEN. I'm not odd, and I'm my whole life with my father only.

CHRISTY [*with infinite admiration*]. How would a lovely, handsome woman the like of you be lonesome when all men should be thronging around to hear the sweetness of your voice, and the little infant children should be pestering your steps, I'm thinking, and you walking the roads.

PEGEEN. I'm hard set to know what way a coaxing fellow the like of yourself should be lonesome either.

CHRISTY. Coaxing.

PEGEEN. Would you have me think a man never talked with the girls would have the words you've spoken to-day? It's only letting on you are to be lonesome, the way you'd get around me now.

CHRISTY. I wish to God I was letting on; but I was lonesome all times, and born lonesome, I'm thinking, as the moon of dawn.

[*Going to door.*]

PEGEEN [*puzzled by his talk*]. Well, it's a story I'm not understanding at all why you'd be worse than another, Christy Mahon, and you a fine lad with the great savagery to destroy your da.

CHRISTY. It's little I'm understanding myself, saving only that my heart's scalded this day, and I going off stretching out the earth between us, the way I'll not be waking near you another dawn of the year till the two of us do arise to hope or judgement with the saints of God, and now I'd best be going with my wattle in my hand, for hanging is a poor thing [*turning to go*], and it's little welcome only is left me in this house to-day.

PEGEEN [*sharply*]. Christy. [*He turns round.*] Come here to me. [*He goes towards her.*] Lay down that switch and throw some sods on the fire. You're pot-boy in this place, and I'll not have you mitch off from us now.

CHRISTY. You were saying I'd be hanged if I stay.

PEGEEN [*quite kindly at last*]. I'm after going down and reading the fearful crimes of Ireland for two weeks or three, and there wasn't a word of your murder. [*Getting up and going over to the counter.*] They've likely not found the body. You're safe so with ourselves.

CHRISTY [*astonished, slowly*]. It's making game of me you were [*following her with fearful joy*], and I can stay so, working at your side, and I not lonesome from this mortal day.

PEGEEN. What's to hinder you staying, except the widow woman or the young girls would inveigle you off?

CHRISTY [*with rapture*]. And I'll have your words from this day filling my ears, and that look is come upon you meeting my two eyes, and I watching you loafing around in the warm sun, or rinsing your ankles when the night is come.

PEGEEN [*kindly, but a little embarrassed*]. I'm thinking you'll be a loyal young lad to have working around, and if you vexed me a while since with your leaguing with the girls, I wouldn't give a thraneen for a lad hadn't a mighty spirit in him and a gamey heart.

[SHAWN KEOGH *runs in carrying a cleeve on his back, followed by the* WIDOW QUIN.]

SHAWN [*to* PEGEEN]. I was passing below, and I seen your mountainy sheep eating cabbages in Jimmy's field. Run up or they'll be bursting, surely.

PEGEEN. Oh, God mend them!

[*She puts a shawl over her head and runs out.*]

CHRISTY [*looking from one to the other. Still in high spirits*]. I'd best go to her aid maybe. I'm handy with ewes.

WIDOW QUIN [*closing the door*]. She can do that much, and there is Shaneen has long speeches for to tell you now.

[*She sits down with an amused smile.*]

SHAWN [*taking something from his pocket and offering it to* CHRISTY]. Do you see that, mister?

CHRISTY [*looking at it*]. The half of a ticket to the Western States!

SHAWN [*trembling with anxiety*]. I'll give it to you and my new hat [*pulling it out of hamper*]; and my breeches with

the double seat [*pulling it out*]; and my new coat is woven
from the blackest shearings for three miles around [*giving
him the coat*]; I'll give you the whole of them, and my
blessing, and the blessing of Father Reilly itself, maybe,
if you'll quit from this and leave us in the peace we had
till last night at the fall of dark.

CHRISTY [*with a new arrogance*]. And for what is it you're
wanting to get shut of me?

SHAWN [*looking to the* WIDOW *for help*]. I'm a poor scholar
with middling faculties to coin a lie, so I'll tell you the
truth, Christy Mahon. I'm wedding with Pegeen beyond,
and I don't think well of having a clever, fearless man the
like of you dwelling in her house.

CHRISTY [*almost pugnaciously*]. And you'd be using bribery
for to banish me?

SHAWN [*in an imploring voice*]. Let you not take it badly,
mister honey; isn't beyond the best place for you, where
you'll have golden chains and shiny coats and you riding
upon hunters with the ladies of the land.

[*He makes an eager sign to the* WIDOW QUIN *to come to
help him.*]

WIDOW QUIN [*coming over*]. It's true for him, and you'd
best quit off and not have that poor girl setting her mind
on you, for there's Shaneen thinks she wouldn't suit you,
though all is saying that she'll wed you now.

[CHRISTY *beams with delight.*]

SHAWN [*in terrified earnest*]. She wouldn't suit you, and she
with the divil's own temper the way you'd be strangling
one another in a score of days. [*He makes the movement of
strangling with his hands.*] It's the like of me only that she's
fit for; a quiet simple fellow wouldn't raise a hand upon
her if she scratched itself.

WIDOW QUIN [*putting* SHAWN'S *hat on* CHRISTY]. Fit

them clothes on you anyhow, young fellow, and he'd maybe loan them to you for the sports. [*Pushing him towards inner door.*] Fit them on and you can give your answer when you have them tried.

CHRISTY [*beaming, delighted with the clothes*]. I will then. I'd like herself to see me in them tweeds and hat.

[*He goes into room and shuts the door.*]

SHAWN [*in great anxiety*]. He'd like herself to see them. He'll not leave us, Widow Quin. He's a score of divils in him the way it's well-nigh certain he will wed Pegeen.

WIDOW QUIN [*jeeringly*]. It's true all girls are fond of courage and do hate the like of you.

SHAWN [*walking about in desperation*]. Oh, Widow Quin, what'll I be doing now? I'd inform again him, but he'd burst from Kilmainham and he'd be sure and certain to destroy me. If I wasn't so God-fearing, I'd near have courage to come behind him and run a pike into his side. Oh, it's a hard case to be an orphan and not to have your father that you're used to, and you'd easy kill and make yourself a hero in the sight of all. [*Coming up to her.*] Oh, Widow Quin, will you find me some contrivance when I've promised you a ewe?

WIDOW QUIN. A ewe's a small thing, but what would you give me if I did wed him and did save you so?

SHAWN [*with astonishment*]. You?

WIDOW QUIN. Aye. Would you give me the red cow you have and the mountainy ram, and the right of way across your rye path, and a load of dung at Michaelmas, and turbary upon the western hill?

SHAWN [*radiant with hope*]. I would, surely, and I'd give you the wedding-ring I have, and the loan of a new suit, the way you'd have him decent on the wedding-day. I'd give you two kids for your dinner, and a gallon of poteen, and I'd call the piper on the long car to your wedding from Crossmolina or from Ballina. I'd give you . . .

WIDOW QUIN. That'll do, so, and let you whisht, for he's coming now again.

[CHRISTY *comes in very natty in the new clothes.* WIDOW QUIN *goes to him admiringly.*]

WIDOW QUIN. If you seen yourself now, I'm thinking you'd be too proud to speak to at all, and it'd be a pity surely to have your like sailing from Mayo to the western world.

CHRISTY [*as proud as a peacock*]. I'm not going. If this is a poor place itself, I'll make myself contented to be lodging here.

[WIDOW QUIN *makes a sign to* SHAWN *to leave them.*]

SHAWN. Well, I'm going measuring the racecourse while the tide is low, so I'll leave you the garments and my blessing for the sports to-day. God bless you!

[*He wriggles out.*]

WIDOW QUIN [*admiring* CHRISTY]. Well, you're mighty spruce, young fellow. Sit down now while you're quiet till you talk with me.

CHRISTY [*swaggering*]. I'm going abroad on the hillside for to seek Pegeen.

WIDOW QUIN. You'll have time and plenty for to seek Pegeen, and you heard me saying at the fall of night the two of us should be great company.

CHRISTY. From this out I'll have no want of company when all sorts is bringing me their food and clothing [*he swaggers to the door, tightening his belt*], the way they'd set their eyes upon a gallant orphan cleft his father with one blow to the breeches belt. [*He opens door, then staggers back.*] Saints of glory! Holy angels from the throne of light!

WIDOW QUIN [*going over*]. What ails you?

CHRISTY. It's the walking spirit of my murdered da!

WIDOW QUIN [*looking out*]. Is it that tramper?

CHRISTY [*wildly*]. Where'll I hide my poor body from that ghost of hell?

[*The door is pushed open, and old* MAHON *appears on threshold.* CHRISTY *darts in behind door.*]

WIDOW QUIN [*in great amusement*]. God save you, my poor man.

MAHON [*gruffly*]. Did you see a young lad passing this way in the early morning or the fall of night?

WIDOW QUIN. You're a queer kind to walk in not saluting at all.

MAHON. Did you see the young lad?

WIDOW QUIN [*stiffly*]. What kind was he?

MAHON. An ugly young streeler with a murderous gob on him, and a little switch in his hand. I met a tramper seen him coming this way at the fall of night.

WIDOW QUIN. There's harvest hundreds do be passing these days for the Sligo boat. For what is it you're wanting him, my poor man?

MAHON. I want to destroy him for breaking the head on me with the clout of a loy. [*He takes off a big hat, and shows his head in a mass of bandages and plaster, with some pride.*] It was he did that, and amn't I a great wonder to think I've traced him ten days with that rent in my crown?

WIDOW QUIN [*taking his head in both hands and examining it with extreme delight*]. That was a great blow. And who hit you? A robber maybe?

MAHON. It was my own son hit me, and he the divil a robber, or anything else, but a dirty, stuttering lout.

WIDOW QUIN [*letting go his skull and wiping her hands in her apron*]. You'd best be wary of a mortified scalp, I think they call it, lepping around with that wound in the splendour of the sun. It was a bad blow, surely, and you should have vexed him fearful to make him strike that gash in his da.

MAHON. Is it me?

WIDOW QUIN [*amusing herself*]. Aye. And isn't it a great shame when the old and hardened do torment the young?

MAHON [*raging*]. Torment him is it? And I after holding out with the patience of a martyred saint till there's nothing but destruction on, and I'm driven out in my old age with none to aid me.

WIDOW QUIN [*greatly amused*]. It's a sacred wonder the way that wickedness will spoil a man.

MAHON. My wickedness, is it? Amn't I after saying it is himself has me destroyed, and he a lier on walls, a talker of folly, a man you'd see stretched the half of the day in the brown ferns with his belly to the sun.

WIDOW QUIN. Not working at all?

MAHON. The divil a work, or if he did itself, you'd see him raising up a haystack like the stalk of a rush, or driving our last cow till he broke her leg at the hip, and when he wasn't at that he'd be fooling over little birds he had – finches and felts – or making mugs at his own self in the bit of a glass we had hung on the wall.

WIDOW QUIN [*looking at* CHRISTY]. What way was he so foolish? It was running wild after the girls maybe?

MAHON [*with a shout of derision*]. Running wild, is it? If he seen a red petticoat coming swinging over the hill, he'd be off to hide in the sticks, and you'd see him shooting out his sheep's eyes between the little twigs and the leaves, and his two ears rising like a hare looking out through a gap. Girls, indeed!

WIDOW QUIN. It was drink maybe?

MAHON. And he a poor fellow would get drunk on the smell of a pint. He'd a queer rotten stomach, I'm telling you, and when I gave him three pulls from my pipe a while since, he was taken with contortions till I had to send him in the ass-cart to the females' nurse.

WIDOW QUIN [*clasping her hands*]. Well, I never, till this day, heard tell of a man the like of that!

MAHON. I'd take a mighty oath you didn't, surely, and wasn't he the laughing joke of every female woman where four baronies meet, the way the girls would stop their weeding if they seen him coming the road to let a roar at him, and call him the looney of Mahon's.

WIDOW QUIN. I'd give the world and all to see the like of him. What kind was he?

MAHON. A small, low fellow.

WIDOW QUIN. And dark?

MAHON. Dark and dirty.

WIDOW QUIN [*considering*]. I'm thinking I seen him.

MAHON [*eagerly*]. An ugly young blackguard.

WIDOW QUIN. A hideous, fearful villain, and the spit of you.

MAHON. What way is he fled?

WIDOW QUIN. Gone over the hills to catch a coasting steamer to the north or south.

MAHON. Could I pull up on him now?

WIDOW QUIN. If you'll cross the sands below where the tide is out, you'll be in it as soon as himself, for he had to go round ten miles by the top of the bay. [*She points to the door.*] Strike down by the head beyond and then follow on the roadway to the north and east.

[MAHON *goes abruptly.*]

WIDOW QUIN [*shouting after him*]. Let you give him a good vengeance when you come up with him, but don't put yourself in the power of the law, for it'd be a poor thing to see a judge in his black cap reading out his sentence on a civil warrior the like of you. [*She swings the door to and looks at* CHRISTY, *who is cowering in terror, for a moment, then she bursts into a laugh.*] Well, you're the walking Playboy of the Western World, and that's the poor man you had divided to his breeches belt.

CHRISTY [*looking out; then, to her*]. What'll Pegeen say when she hears that story? What'll she be saying to me now?

WIDOW QUIN. She'll knock the head of you, I'm thinking, and drive you from the door. God help her to be taking you for a wonder, and you a little schemer making up a story you destroyed your da.

CHRISTY [*turning to the door, nearly speechless with rage, half to himself*]. To be letting on he was dead, and coming back to his life, and following after me like an old weasel tracing a rat, and coming in here laying desolation between my own self and the fine women of Ireland, and he a kind of carcase that you'd fling upon the sea. . . .

WIDOW QUIN [*more soberly*]. There's talking for a man's one only son.

CHRISTY [*breaking out*]. His one son, is it? May I meet him with one tooth and it aching, and one eye to be seeing seven and seventy divils in the twists of the road, and one old timber leg on him to limp into the scalding grave. [*Looking out.*] There he is now crossing the strands, and that the Lord God would send a high wave to wash him from the world.

WIDOW QUIN [*scandalized*]. Have you no shame? [*Putting her hand on his shoulder and turning him round.*] What ails you? Near crying, is it?

CHRISTY [*in despair and grief*]. Amn't I after seeing the love-

light of the star of knowledge shining from her brow,
and hearing words would put you thinking on the holy
Brigid speaking to the infant saints, and now she'll be
turning again, and speaking hard words to me, like an
old woman with a spavindy ass she'd have, urging on a
hill.

WIDOW QUIN. There's poetry talk for a girl you'd see
itching and scratching, and she with a stale stink of
poteen on her from selling in the shop.

CHRISTY [*impatiently*]. It's her like is fitted to be handling
merchandise in the heavens above, and what'll I be doing
now, I ask you, and I a kind of wonder was jilted by the
heavens when a day was by.

[*There is a distant noise of* GIRLS' *voices.* WIDOW QUIN
looks from window and comes to him, hurriedly.]

WIDOW QUIN. You'll be doing like myself, I'm thinking,
when I did destroy my man, for I'm above many's the
day, odd times in great spirits, abroad in the sunshine,
darning a stocking or stitching a shift; and odd times
again looking out on the schooners, hookers, trawlers is
sailing the sea, and I thinking on the gallant hairy fellows
are drifting beyond, and myself long years living alone.

CHRISTY [*interested*]. You're like me, so.

WIDOW QUIN. I am your like, and it's for that I'm taking
a fancy to you, and I with my little houseen above where
there'd be myself to tend you, and none to ask were you
a murderer or what at all.

CHRISTY. And what would I be doing if I left Pegeen?

WIDOW QUIN. I've nice jobs you could be doing – gathering shells to make a white-wash for our hut within,
building up a little goose-house, or stretching a new skin
on an old curagh I have, and if my hut is far from all sides,
it's there you'll meet the wisest old men, I tell you, at

the corner of my wheel, and it's there yourself and me will have great times whispering and hugging. . . .

VOICES [*outside, calling far away*]. Christy! Christy Mahon! Christy!

CHRISTY. Is it Pegeen Mike?

WIDOW QUIN. It's the young girls, I'm thinking, coming to bring you to the sports below, and what is it you'll have me to tell them now?

CHRISTY. Aid me for to win Pegeen. It's herself only that I'm seeking now. [WIDOW QUIN *gets up and goes to window.*] Aid me for to win her, and I'll be asking God to stretch a hand to you in the hour of death, and lead you short cuts through the Meadows of Ease, and up the floor of Heaven to the Footstool of the Virgin's Son.

WIDOW QUIN. There's praying!

VOICES [*nearer*]. Christy! Christy Mahon!

CHRISTY [*with agitation*]. They're coming. Will you swear to aid and save me, for the love of Christ?

WIDOW QUIN [*looks at him for a moment*]. If I aid you, will you swear to give me a right of way I want, and a mountainy ram, and a load of dung at Michaelmas, the time that you'll be master here?

CHRISTY. I will, by the elements and stars of night.

WIDOW QUIN. Then we'll not say a word of the old fellow, the way Pegeen won't know your story till the end of time.

CHRISTY. And if he chances to return again?

WIDOW QUIN. We'll swear he's a maniac and not your da. I could take an oath I seen him raving on the sands to-day.

[GIRLS *run in.*]

SUSAN. Come on to the sports below. Pegeen says you're to come.

SARA TANSEY. The lepping's beginning, and we've a jockey's suit to fit upon you for the mule race on the sands below.

HONOR. Come on, will you?

CHRISTY. I will then if Pegeen's beyond.

SARA. She's in the boreen making game of Shaneen Keogh.

CHRISTY. Then I'll be going to her now.

[*He runs out, followed by the* GIRLS.]

WIDOW QUIN. Well, if the worst comes in the end of all, it'll be great game to see there's none to pity him but a widow woman, the like of me, has buried her children and destroyed her man.

[*She goes out.*]

CURTAIN

ACT THREE

Scene as before. Later in the day. JIMMY *comes in, slightly drunk.*

JIMMY [*calls*]. Pegeen! [*Crosses to inner door.*] Pegeen Mike! [*Comes back again into the room.*] Pegeen! [PHILLY *comes in in the same state – To* PHILLY.] Did you see herself?

PHILLY. I did not; but I sent Shawn Keogh with the ass-cart for to bear him home. [*Trying cupboards, which are locked.*] Well, isn't he a nasty man to get into such staggers at a morning wake; and isn't herself the divil's daughter for locking, and she so fussy after that young gaffer, you might take your death with drouth and none to heed you?

JIMMY. It's little wonder she'd be fussy, and he after bringing bankrupt ruin on the roulette man, and the trick-o'-the-loop man, and breaking the nose of the cock-shot-man, and winning all in the sports below, racing, lepping, dancing, and the Lord knows what! He's right luck, I'm telling you.

PHILLY. If he has, he'll be rightly hobbled yet, and he not able to say ten words without making a brag of the way he killed his father, and the great blow he hit with the loy.

JIMMY. A man can't hang by his own informing, and his father should be rotten by now.

[OLD MAHON *passes window slowly.*]

PHILLY. Supposing a man's digging spuds in that field with a long spade, and supposing he flings up the two halves of that skull, what'll be said then in the papers and the courts of law?

JIMMY. They'd say it was an old Dane, maybe, was drowned in the flood. [OLD MAHON *comes in and sits down near door listening.*] Did you never hear tell of the skulls they have in the city of Dublin, ranged out like blue jugs in a cabin of Connaught?

PHILLY. And you believe that?

JIMMY [*pugnaciously*]. Didn't a lad see them and he after coming from harvesting in the Liverpool boat? 'They have them there,' says he, 'making a show of the great people there was one time walking the world. White skulls and black skulls and yellow skulls, and some with full teeth, and some haven't only but one.'

PHILLY. It was no lie, maybe, for when I was a young lad there was a graveyard beyond the house with the remnants of a man who had thighs as long as your arm. He was a horrid man, I'm telling you, and there was many a fine Sunday I'd put him together for fun, and he with shiny bones, you wouldn't meet the like of these days in the cities of the world.

MAHON [*getting up*]. You wouldn't, is it? Lay your eyes on that skull, and tell me where and when there was another the like of it, is splintered only from the blow of a loy.

PHILLY. Glory be to God! And who hit you at all?

MAHON [*triumphantly*]. It was my own son hit me. Would you believe that?

JIMMY. Well, there's wonders hidden in the heart of man!

PHILLY [*suspiciously*]. And what way was it done?

MAHON [*wandering about the room*]. I'm after walking hundreds and long scores of miles, winning clean beds and the fill of my belly four times in the day, and I doing nothing but telling stories of that naked truth. [*He comes to them a little aggressively.*] Give me a supeen and I'll tell you now.

[WIDOW QUIN *comes in and stands aghast behind him. He is facing* JIMMY *and* PHILLY, *who are on the left.*]

JIMMY. Ask herself beyond. She's the stuff hidden in her shawl.

WIDOW QUIN [*coming to* MAHON *quickly*]. You here, is it? You didn't go far at all?

MAHON. I seen the coasting steamer passing, and I got a drouth upon me and a cramping leg, so I said, 'The divil go along with him,' and turned again. [*Looking under her shawl.*] And let you give me a supeen, for I'm destroyed travelling since Tuesday was a week.

WIDOW QUIN [*getting a glass, in a cajoling tone*]. Sit down then by the fire and take your ease for a space. You've a right to be destroyed indeed, with your walking, and fighting, and facing the sun [*giving him poteen from a stone jar she has brought in*]. There now is a drink for you, and may it be to your happiness and length of life.

MAHON [*taking glass greedily, and sitting down by fire*]. God increase you!

WIDOW QUIN [*taking men to the right stealthily*]. Do you know what? That man's raving from his wound to-day, for I met him a while since telling a rambling tale of a tinker had him destroyed. Then he heard of Christy's deed, and he up and says it was his son had cracked his skull. Oh, isn't madness a fright, for he'll go killing some one yet, and he thinking it's the man has struck him so?

JIMMY [*entirely convinced*]. It's a fright surely. I knew a party was kicked in the head by a red mare, and he went killing horses a great while, till he eat the insides of a clock and died after.

PHILLY [*with suspicion*]. Did he see Christy?

WIDOW QUIN. He didn't. [*With a warning gesture.*] Let you not be putting him in mind of him, or you'll be likely summoned if there's murder done. [*Looking round at* MAHON.] Whisht! He's listening. Wait now till you hear me taking him easy and unravelling all. [*She goes to* MAHON.] And what way are you feeling, mister? Are you in contentment now?

MAHON [*slightly emotional from his drink*]. I'm poorly only, for it's a hard story the way I'm left to-day, when it was I did tend him from his hour of birth, and he a dunce never reached his second book, the way he'd come from school, many's the day, with his legs lamed under him, and he blackened with his beatings like a tinker's ass. It's a hard story, I'm saying, the way some do have their next and nighest raising up a hand of murder on them, and some is lonesome getting their death with lamentation in the dead of night.

WIDOW QUIN [*not knowing what to say*]. To hear you talking so quiet, who'd know you were the same fellow we seen pass to-day?

MAHON. I'm the same surely. The wrack and ruin of three-score years; and it's a terror to live that length, I tell you, and to have your sons going to the dogs against you, and you wore out scolding them, and skelping them, and God knows what.

PHILLY [*to* JIMMY]. He's not raving. [*To* WIDOW QUIN.] Will you ask him what kind was his son?

WIDOW QUIN [*to* MAHON, *with a peculiar look*]. Was your son that hit you a lad of one year and a score maybe, a great hand at racing and lepping and licking the world?

MAHON [*turning on her with a roar of rage*]. Didn't you hear me say he was the fool of men, the way from this out he'll know the orphan's lot, with old and young making game of him, and they swearing, raging, kicking at him like a mangy cur.

[*A great burst of cheering outside, some way off.*]

MAHON [*putting his hands to his ears*]. What in the name of God do they want roaring below?

WIDOW QUIN [*with the shade of a smile*]. They're cheering a young lad, the champion Playboy of the Western World.

[*More cheering.*]

MAHON [*going to window*]. It'd split my heart to hear them, and I with pulses in my brain-pan for a week gone by. Is it racing they are?

JIMMY [*looking from door*]. It is, then. They are mounting him for the mule race will be run upon the sands. That's the playboy on the winkered mule.

MAHON [*puzzled*]. That lad, is it? If you said it was a fool he was, I'd have laid a mighty oath he was the likeness of my wandering son. [*Uneasily, putting his hand to his head.*] Faith, I'm thinking I'll go walking for to view the race.

WIDOW QUIN [*stopping him, sharply*]. You will not. You'd best take the road to Belmullet, and not be dilly-dallying in this place where there isn't a spot you could sleep.

PHILLY [*coming forward*]. Don't mind her. Mount there on the bench and you'll have a view of the whole. They're hurrying before the tide will rise, and it'd be near over if you went down the pathway through the crags below.

MAHON [*mounts on bench, WIDOW QUIN beside him*]. That's a right view again the edge of the sea. They're coming now from the point. He's leading. Who is he at all?

WIDOW QUIN. He's the champion of the world, I tell

you, and there isn't a hap'orth isn't falling lucky to his hands to-day.

PHILLY [*looking out, interested in the race*]. Look at that. They're pressing him now.

JIMMY. He'll win it yet.

PHILLY. Take your time, Jimmy Farrell. It's too soon to say.

WIDOW QUIN [*shouting*]. Watch him taking the gate. There's riding.

JIMMY [*cheering*]. More power to the young lad!

MAHON. He's passing the third.

JIMMY. He'll lick them yet.

WIDOW QUIN. He'd lick them if he was running races with a score itself.

MAHON. Look at the mule he has, kicking the stars.

WIDOW QUIN. There was a lep! [*Catching hold of* MAHON *in her excitement.*] He's fallen? He's mounted again! Faith, he's passing them all!

JIMMY. Look at him skelping her!

PHILLY. And the mountain girls hooshing him on!

JIMMY. It's the last turn! The post's cleared for them now!

MAHON. Look at the narrow place. He'll be into the bogs! [*With a yell.*] Good rider! He's through it again!

JIMMY. He neck and neck!

MAHON. Good boy to him! Flames, but he's in! [*Great cheering, in which all join.*]

MAHON [*with hesitation*]. What's that? They're raising him up. They're coming this way. [*With a roar of rage and astonishment.*] It's Christy, by the stars of God! I'd know his way of spitting and he astride the moon.

[*He jumps down and makes a run for the door, but* WIDOW QUIN *catches him and pulls him back.*]

WIDOW QUIN. Stay quiet, will you? That's not your son. [*To* JIMMY.] Stop him, or you'll get a month for the abetting of manslaughter and be fined as well.

JIMMY. I'll hold him.

MAHON [*struggling*]. Let me out! Let me out, the lot of you, till I have my vengeance on his head to-day.

WIDOW QUIN [*shaking him, vehemently*]. That's not your son. That's a man is going to make a marriage with the daughter of this house, a place with fine trade, with a licence, and with poteen too.

MAHON [*amazed*]. That man marrying a decent and a moneyed girl! It is mad yous are? Is it in a crazy-house for females that I'm landed now?

WIDOW QUIN. It's mad yourself is with the blow upon your head. That lad is the wonder of the western world.

MAHON. I seen it's my son.

WIDOW QUIN. You seen that you're mad. [*Cheering outside.*] Do you hear them cheering him in the zig-zags of the road? Aren't you after saying that your son's a fool, and how would they be cheering a true idiot born?

MAHON [*getting distressed*]. It's maybe out of reason that that man's himself. [*Cheering again.*] There's none surely will go cheering him. Oh, I'm raving with a madness that would fright the world! [*He sits down with his hand to his head.*] There was one time I seen ten scarlet divils letting on they'd cork my spirit in a gallon can; and one time I seen rats as big as badgers sucking the lifeblood from the butt of my lug; but I never till this day confused that dribbling idiot with a likely man. I'm destroyed surely.

WIDOW QUIN. And who'd wonder when it's your brain-pan that is gaping now?

MAHON. Then the blight of the sacred drouth upon my-

self and him, for I never went mad to this day, and I not
three weeks with the Limerick girls drinking myself
silly and parlatic from the dusk to dawn. [*To* WIDOW
QUIN, *suddenly*.] Is my visage astray?

WIDOW QUIN. It is, then. You're a sniggering maniac, a
child could see.

MAHON [*getting up more cheerfully*]. Then I'd best be going
to the union beyond, and there'll be a welcome before
me, I tell you [*with great pride*], and I a terrible and fearful
case, the way that there I was one time, screeching in a
straightened waistcoat, with seven doctors writing out
my sayings in a printed book. Would you believe that?

WIDOW QUIN. If you're a wonder itself, you'd best be
hasty, for them lads caught a maniac one time and pelted
the poor creature till he ran out, raving and foaming, and
was drowned in the sea.

MAHON [*with philosophy*]. It's true mankind is the divil
when your head's astray. Let me out now and I'll slip
down the boreen, and not see them so.

WIDOW QUIN [*showing him out*]. That's it. Run to the
right, and not a one will see.

[*He runs off.*]

PHILLY [*wisely*]. You're at some gaming, Widow Quin;
but I'll walk after him and give him his dinner and a time
to rest, and I'll see then if he's raving or as sane as you.

WIDOW QUIN [*annoyed*]. If you go near that lad, let you
be wary of your head, I'm saying. Didn't you hear him
telling he was crazed at times?

PHILLY. I heard him telling a power; and I'm thinking
we'll have right sport before night will fall. [*He goes out.*]

JIMMY. Well, Philly's a conceited and foolish man. How
could that madman have his senses and his brain-pan slit?
I'll go after them and see him turn on Philly now.

[*He goes;* WIDOW QUIN *hides poteen behind counter. Then hubbub outside.*]

VOICES. There you are! Good jumper! Grand lepper! Darlint boy! He's the racer! Bear him on, will you!

[CHRISTY *comes in, in jockey's dress, with* PEGEEN MIKE, SARA, *and other* GIRLS *and* MEN.]

PEGEEN [*to crowd*]. Go on now and don't destroy him and he drenching with sweat. Go along, I'm saying, and have your tug-of-warring till he's dried his skin.

CROWD. Here's his prizes! A bagpipes! A fiddle was played by a poet in the years gone by! A flat and three-thorned blackthorn would lick the scholars out of Dublin town!

CHRISTY [*taking prizes from the* MEN]. Thank you kindly, the lot of you. But you'd say it was little only I did this day if you'd seen me a while since striking my one single blow.

TOWN CRIER [*outside ringing a bell*]. Take notice, last event of this day! Tug-of-warring on the green below! Come on, the lot of you! Great achievements for all Mayo men!

PEGEEN. Go on and leave him for to rest and dry. Go on, I tell you, for he'll do no more.

[*She hustles crowd out;* WIDOW QUIN *following them.*]

MEN [*going*]. Come on, then. Good luck for the while!

PEGEEN [*radiantly, wiping his face with her shawl*]. Well, you're the lad, and you'll have great times from this out when you could win that wealth of prizes, and you sweating in the heat of noon!

CHRISTY [*looking at her with delight*]. I'll have great times if I win the crowning prize I'm seeking now, and that's your promise that you'll wed me in a fortnight, when our banns is called.

PEGEEN [*backing away from him*]. You've right daring to go ask me that, when all knows you'll be starting to some girl in your own townland, when your father's rotten in four months, or five.

CHRISTY [*indignantly*]. Starting from you, is it? [*He follows her.*] I will not, then, and when the airs is warming, in four months or five, it's then yourself and me should be pacing Neifin in the dews of night, the times sweet smells do be rising, and you'd see a little, shiny new moon, maybe, sinking on the hills.

PEGEEN [*looking at him playfully*]. And it's that kind of a poacher's love you'd make, Christy Mahon, on the sides of Neifin, when the night is down?

CHRISTY. It's little you'll think if my love's a poacher's, or an earl's itself, when you'll feel my two hands stretched around you, and I squeezing kisses on your puckered lips, till I'd feel a kind of pity for the Lord God is all ages sitting lonesome in His golden chair.

PEGEEN. That'll be right fun, Christy Mahon, and any girl would walk her heart out before she'd meet a young man was your like for eloquence, or talk at all.

CHRISTY [*encouraged*]. Let you wait, to hear me talking, till we're astray in Erris, when Good Friday's by, drinking a sup from a well, and making mighty kisses with our wetted mouths, or gaming in a gap of sunshine, with yourself stretched back unto your necklace, in the flowers of the earth.

PEGEEN [*in a low voice, moved by his tone*]. I'd be nice so, is it?

CHRISTY [*with rapture*]. If the mitred bishops seen you that time, they'd be the like of the holy prophets, I'm thinking, do be straining the bars of Paradise to lay eyes on the

Lady Helen of Troy, and she abroad, pacing back and forward, with a nosegay in her golden shawl.

PEGEEN [*with real tenderness*]. And what is it I have, Christy Mahon, to make me fitting entertainment for the like of you, that has such poet's talking, and such bravery of heart.

CHRISTY [*in a low voice*]. Isn't there the light of seven heavens in your heart alone, the way you'll be an angel's lamp to me from this out, and I abroad in the darkness, spearing salmons in the Owen or the Carrowmore?

PEGEEN. If I was your wife I'd be along with you those nights, Christy Mahon, the way you'd see I was a great hand at coaxing bailiffs, or coining funny nicknames for the stars of night.

CHRISTY. You, is it? Taking your death in the hailstones, or in the fogs of dawn.

PEGEEN. Yourself and me would shelter easy in a narrow bush [*with a qualm of dread*]; but we're only talking, maybe, for this would be a poor, thatched place to hold a fine lad is the like of you.

CHRISTY [*putting his arm round her*]. If I wasn't a good Christian, it's on my naked knees I'd be saying my prayers and paters to every jackstraw you have roofing your head, and every stony pebble is paving the laneway to your door.

PEGEEN [*radiantly*]. If that's the truth I'll be burning candles from this out to the miracles of God that have brought you from the south to-day, and I with my gowns bought ready, the way that I can wed you, and not wait at all.

CHRISTY. It's miracles, and that's the truth. Me there toiling a long while, and walking a long while, not knowing at all I was drawing all times nearer to this holy day.

PEGEEN. And myself, a girl, was tempted often to go sailing the seas till I'd marry a Jew-man, with ten kegs of gold, and I not knowing at all there was the like of you drawing nearer, like the stars of God.

CHRISTY. And to think I'm long years hearing women talking that talk, to all bloody fools, and this the first time I've heard the like of your voice talking sweetly for my own delight.

PEGEEN. And to think it's me is talking sweetly, Christy Mahon, and I the fright of seven townlands for my biting tongue. Well, the heart's a wonder; and, I'm thinking, there won't be our like in Mayo, for gallant lovers, from this hour to-day. [*Drunken singing is heard outside.*] There's my father coming from the wake, and when he's had his sleep we'll tell him, for he's peaceful then.

[*They separate.*]

MICHAEL [*singing outside*]:

> The jailer and the turnkey
> They quickly ran us down,
> And brought us back as prisoners
> Once more to Cavan town.

[*He comes in supported by* SHAWN.]

> There we lay bewailing
> All in a prison bound. . . .

[*He sees* CHRISTY. *Goes and shakes him drunkenly by the hand, while* PEGEEN *and* SHAWN *talk on the left.*]

MICHAEL [*to* CHRISTY]. The blessing of God and the holy angels on your head, young fellow, I hear tell you're after winning all in the sports below; and wasn't it a shame I didn't bear you along with me to Kate Cassidy's wake, a fine, stout lad, the like of you, for you'd never see the match of it for flows of drink, the way when we sunk her bones at noonday in her narrow grave, there were five men, aye, and six men, stretched out retching speechless on the holy stones.

CHRISTY [*uneasily, watching* PEGEEN]. Is that the truth?

MICHAEL. It is, then; and aren't you a louty schemer to go burying your poor father unbeknownst when you'd a right to throw him on the crupper of a Kerry mule and drive him westwards, like holy Joseph in the days gone by, the way we could have given him a decent burial, and not have him rotting beyond, and not a Christian drinking a smart drop to the glory of his soul?

CHRISTY [*gruffly*]. It's well enough he's lying, for the likes of him.

MICHAEL [*slapping him on the back*]. Well, aren't you a hardened slayer? It'll be a poor thing for the household man where you go sniffing for a female wife; and [*pointing to* SHAWN] look beyond at that shy and decent Christian I have chosen for my daughter's hand, and I after getting the gilded dispensation this day for to wed them now.

CHRISTY. And you'll be wedding them this day, is it?

MICHAEL [*drawing himself up*]. Aye. Are you thinking, if I'm drunk itself, I'd leave my daughter living single with a little frisky rascal is the like of you?

PEGEEN [*breaking away from* SHAWN]. Is it the truth the dispensation's come?

MICHAEL [*triumphantly*]. Father Reilly's after reading it in gallous Latin, and 'It's come in the nick of time,' says he; 'so I'll wed them in a hurry, dreading that young gaffer who'd capsize the stars.'

PEGEEN [*fiercely*]. He's missed his nick of time, for it's that lad, Christy Mahon, that I'm wedding now.

MICHAEL [*loudly, with horror*]. You'd be making him a son

198

to me, and he wet and crusted with his father's blood?

PEGEEN. Aye. Wouldn't it be a bitter thing for a girl to go marrying the like of Shaneen, and he a middling kind of a scarecrow, with no savagery or fine words in him at all?

MICHAEL [*gasping and sinking on a chair*]. Oh, aren't you a heathen daughter to go shaking the fat of my heart, and I swamped and drownded with the weight of drink? Would you have them turning on me the way that I'd be roaring to the dawn of day with the wind upon my heart? Have you not a word to aid me, Shaneen? Are you not jealous at all?

SHAWN [*in great misery*]. I'd be afeard to be jealous of a man did slay his da!

PEGEEN. Well, it'd be a poor thing to go marrying your like. I'm seeing there's a world of peril for an orphan girl, and isn't it a great blessing I didn't wed you before himself came walking from the west or south?

SHAWN. It's a queer story you'd go picking a dirty tramp up from the highways of the world.

PEGEEN [*playfully*]. And you think you're a likely beau to go straying along with the shiny Sundays of the opening year, when it's sooner on a bullock's liver you'd put a poor girl thinking than on the lily or the rose?

SHAWN. And have you no mind of my weight of passion, and the holy dispensation, and the drift of heifers I'm giving, and the golden ring?

PEGEEN. I'm thinking you're too fine for the like of me, Shawn Keogh of Killakeen, and let you go off till you'd find a radiant lady with droves of bullocks on the plains of Meath, and herself bedizened in the diamond jewelleries of Pharaoh's ma. That'd be your match, Shaneen. So God save you now!

[*She retreats behind* CHRISTY.]

SHAWN. Won't you hear me telling you . . . ?

CHRISTY [*with ferocity*]. Take yourself from this, young
fellow, or I'll maybe add a murder to my deeds to-day.

MICHAEL [*springing up with a shriek*]. Murder is it? Is it
mad yous are? Would you go making murder in this
place, and it piled with poteen for our drink to-night?
Go on to the foreshore if it's fighting you want, where
the rising tide will wash all traces from the memory of
man.

[*Pushing* SHAWN *towards* CHRISTY.]

SHAWN [*shaking himself free, and getting behind* MICHAEL].
I'll not fight him, Michael James. I'd liefer live a
bachelor, simmering in passions to the end of time, than
face a lepping savage the like of him has descended from
the Lord knows where. Strike him yourself, Michael
James, or you'll lose my drift of heifers and my blue bull
from Sneem.

MICHAEL. Is it me fight him, when it's father-slaying he's
bred to now? [*Pushing* SHAWN.] Go on, you fool, and
fight him now.

SHAWN [*coming forward a little*]. Will I strike him with my
hand?

MICHAEL. Take the loy is on your western side.

SHAWN. I'd be afeard of the gallows if I struck with that.

CHRISTY [*taking up the loy*]. Then I'll make you face the
gallows or quit off from this. [SHAWN *flies out of the door*.]

CHRISTY. Well, fine weather be after him [*going to*
MICHAEL, *coaxingly*], and I'm thinking you wouldn't
wish to have that quaking blackguard in your house at
all. Let you give us your blessing and hear her swear her
faith to me, for I'm mounted on the spring-tide of the
stars of luck, the way it'll be good for any to have me in
the house.

PEGEEN [*at the other side of* MICHAEL]. Bless us now, for I
swear to God I'll wed him, and I'll not renege.

MICHAEL [*standing up in the centre, holding on to both of
them*]. It's the will of God, I'm thinking, that all should
win an easy or a cruel end, and it's the will of God that
all should rear up lengthy families for the nurture of the
earth. What's a single man, I ask you, eating a bit in one
house and drinking a sup in another, and he with no place
of his own, like an old braying jackass strayed upon the
rocks? [*To* CHRISTY.] It's many would be in dread to
bring your like into their house for to end them, maybe,
with a sudden end; but I'm a decent man of Ireland, and
I'd liefer face the grave untimely and I seeing a score of
grandsons growing up little gallant swearers by the name
of God, than go peopling my bedside with puny weeds
the like of what you'd breed, I'm thinking, out of
Shaneen Keogh. [*He joins their hands.*] A daring fellow is
the jewel of the world, and a man did split his father's
middle with a single clout should have the bravery of ten,
so may God and Mary and St Patrick bless you, and
increase you from this mortal day.

CHRISTY *and* PEGEEN. Amen, O Lord!

[*Hubbub outside.* OLD MAHON *rushes in, followed by all
the crowd, and* WIDOW QUIN. *He makes a rush at* CHRISTY,
knocks him down, and begins to beat him.]

PEGEEN [*dragging back his arm*]. Stop that, will you? Who
are you at all?

MAHON. His father, God forgive me!

PEGEEN [*drawing back*]. Is it rose from the dead?

MAHON. Do you think I look so easy quenched with the
tap of a loy?

[*Beats* CHRISTY *again.*]

PEGEEN [*glaring at* CHRISTY]. And it's lies you told,

letting on you had him slitted, and you nothing at all.

CHRISTY [*catching* MAHON'S *stick*]. He's not my father. He's a raving maniac would scare the world. [*Pointing to* WIDOW QUIN.] Herself knows it is true.

CROWD. You're fooling Pegeen! The Widow Quin seen him this day, and you likely knew! You're a liar!

CHRISTY [*dumbfounded*]. It's himself was a liar, lying stretched out with an open head on him, letting on he was dead.

MAHON. Weren't you off racing the hills before I got my breath with the start I had seeing you turn on me at all?

PEGEEN. And to think of the coaxing glory we had given him, and he after doing nothing but hitting a soft blow and chasing northward in a sweat of fear. Quit off from this.

CHRISTY [*piteously*]. You've seen my doings this day, and let you save me from the old man; for why would you be in such a scorch of haste to spur me to destruction now?

PEGEEN. It's there your treachery is spurring me, till I'm hard set to think you're the one I'm after lacing in my heart-strings half an hour gone by. [*To* MAHON.] Take him on from this, for I think bad the world should see me raging for a Munster liar, and the fool of men.

MAHON. Rise up now to retribution, and come on with me.

CROWD [*jeeringly*]. There's the playboy! There's the lad thought he'd rule the roost in Mayo! Slate him now, mister.

CHRISTY [*getting up in shy terror*]. What is it drives you to torment me here, when I'd asked the thunders of the might of God to blast me if I ever did hurt to any saving only that one single blow.

MAHON [*loudly*]. If you didn't, you're a poor good-for-nothing, and isn't it by the like of you the sins of the whole world are committed?

CHRISTY [*raising his hands*]. In the name of the Almighty God . . .

MAHON. Leave troubling the Lord God. Would you have Him sending down droughts, and fevers, and the old hen and the cholera morbus?

CHRISTY [*to* WIDOW QUIN]. Will you come between us and protect me now?

WIDOW QUIN. I've tried a lot, God help me, and my share is done.

CHRISTY [*looking round in desperation*]. And I must go back into my torment is it, or run off like a vagabond straying through the unions with the dust of August making mudstains in the gullet of my throat; or the winds of March blowing on me till I'd take an oath I felt them making whistles of my ribs within?

SARA. Ask Pegeen to aid you. Her like does often change.

CHRISTY. I will not, then, for there's torment in the splendour of her like, and she a girl any moon of midnight would take pride to meet, facing southwards on the heaths of Keel. But what did I want crawling forward to scorch my understanding at her flaming brow?

PEGEEN [*to* MAHON, *vehemently, fearing she will break into tears*]. Take him on from this or I'll set the young lads to destroy him here.

MAHON [*going to him, shaking his stick*]. Come on now if you wouldn't have the company to see you skelped.

PEGEEN [*half-laughing, through her tears*]. That's it, now the world will see him pandied, and he an ugly liar was playing off the hero, and the fright of men.

CHRISTY [*to* MAHON, *very sharply*]. Leave me go!

CROWD. That's it. Now, Christy. If them two set fighting, it will lick the world.

MAHON [*making a grab at* CHRISTY]. Come here to me.

CHRISTY [*more threateningly*]. Leave me go, I'm saying.

MAHON. I will, maybe, when your legs is limping, and your back is blue.

CROWD. Keep it up, the two of you. I'll back the old one. Now the playboy.

CHRISTY [*in low and intense voice*]. Shut your yelling, for if you're after making a mighty man of me this day by the power of a lie, you're setting me now to think if it's a poor thing to be lonesome it's worse, maybe, go mixing with the fools of earth.

[MAHON *makes a movement towards him.*]

CHRISTY [*almost shouting*]. Keep off . . . lest I do show a blow unto the lot of you would set the guardian angels winking in the clouds above.

[*He swings round with a sudden rapid movement and picks up a loy.*]

CROWD [*half-frightened, half-amused*]. He's going mad! Mind yourselves! Run from the idiot!

CHRISTY. If I am an idiot, I'm after hearing my voice this day saying words would raise the top-knot on a poet in a merchant's town. I've won your racing, and your lepping, and . . .

MAHON. Shut your gullet and come on with me.

CHRISTY. I'm going, but I'll stretch you first.

[*He runs at old* MAHON *with the loy, chases him out of the door, followed by crowd and* WIDOW QUIN. *There is a great noise outside, then a yell, and dead silence for a moment.* CHRISTY *comes in, half-dazed, and goes to fire.*]

WIDOW QUIN [*coming in hurriedly, and going to him*].

They're turning again you. Come on, or you'll be hanged, indeed.

CHRISTY. I'm thinking, from this out, Pegeen'll be giving me praises, the same as in the hours gone by.

WIDOW QUIN [*impatiently*]. Come by the back-door. I'd think bad to have you stifled on the gallows tree.

CHRISTY [*indignantly*]. I will not, then. What good'd be my lifetime if I left Pegeen?

WIDOW QUIN. Come on, and you'll be no worse than you were last night; and you with a double murder this time to be telling to the girls.

CHRISTY. I'll not leave Pegeen Mike.

WIDOW QUIN [*impatiently*]. Isn't there the match of her in every parish public, from Binghamstown unto the plain of Meath? Come on, I tell you, and I'll find you finer sweethearts at each waning moon.

CHRISTY. It's Pegeen I'm seeking only, and what'd I care if you brought me a drift of chosen females, standing in their shifts itself, maybe, from this place to the eastern world?

SARA [*runs in, pulling off one of her petticoats*]. They're going to hang him. [*Holding out petticoat and shawl.*] Fit these upon him, and let him run off to the east.

WIDOW QUIN. He's raving now; but we'll fit them on him, and I'll take him in the ferry to the Achill boat.

CHRISTY [*struggling feebly*]. Leave me go, will you? when I'm thinking of my luck to-day, for she will wed me surely, and I a proven hero in the end of all.

[*They try to fasten petticoat round him.*]

WIDOW QUIN. Take his left hand, and we'll pull him now. Come on, young fellow.

CHRISTY [*suddenly starting up*]. You'll be taking me from

her? You're jealous, is it, of her wedding me? Go on from this.

[*He snatches up a stool, and threatens them with it.*]

WIDOW QUIN [*going*]. It's in the madhouse they should put him, not in jail, at all. We'll go by the back-door to call the doctor, and we'll save him so.

[*She goes out, with* SARA, *through inner room.* MEN *crowd in the doorway.* CHRISTY *sits down again by the fire.*]

MICHAEL [*in a terrified whisper*]. Is the old lad killed surely?

PHILLY. I'm after feeling the last gasps quitting his heart.

[*They peer in at* CHRISTY.]

MICHAEL [*with a rope*]. Look at the way he is. Twist a hangman's knot on it, and slip it over his head, while he's not minding at all.

PHILLY. Let you take it, Shaneen. You're the soberest of all that's here.

SHAWN. Is it me to go near him, and he the wickedest and worst with me? Let you take it, Pegeen Mike.

PEGEEN. Come on, so.

[*She goes forward with the others, and they drop the double hitch over his head.*]

CHRISTY. What ails you?

SHAWN [*triumphantly, as they pull the rope tight on his arms*]. Come on to the peelers, till they stretch you now.

CHRISTY. Me!

MICHAEL. If we took pity on you the Lord God would, maybe, bring us ruin from the law to-day, so you'd best come easy, for hanging is an easy and a speedy end.

CHRISTY. I'll not stir. [*To* PEGEEN.] And what is it you'll say to me, and I after doing it this time in the face of all?

PEGEEN. I'll say, a strange man is a marvel, with his

206

mighty talk; but what's a squabble in your back-yard, and the blow of a loy, have taught me that there's a great gap between a gallous story and a dirty deed. [*To* MEN.] Take him on from this, or the lot of us will be likely put on trial for his deed to-day.

CHRISTY [*with horror in his voice*]. And it's yourself will send me off, to have a horny-fingered hangman hitching his bloody slipknots at the butt of my ear.

MEN [*pulling rope*]. Come on, will you?
[*He is pulled down on the floor.*]

CHRISTY [*twisting his legs round the table*]. Cut the rope, Pegeen, and I'll quit the lot of you, and live from this out, like the madmen of Keel, eating muck and green weeds on the faces of the cliffs.

PEGEEN. And leave us to hang, is it, for a saucy liar, the like of you? [*To* MEN.] Take him on, out from this.

SHAWN. Pull a twist on his neck, and squeeze him so.

PHILLY. Twist yourself. Sure he cannot hurt you, if you keep your distance from his teeth alone.

SHAWN. I'm afeard of him. [*To* PEGEEN.] Lift a lighted sod, will you, and scorch his leg.

PEGEEN [*blowing the fire with a bellows*]. Leave go now, young fellow, or I'll scorch your shins.

CHRISTY. You're blowing for to torture me. [*His voice rising and growing stronger.*] That's your kind, is it? Then let the lot of you be wary, for, if I've to face the gallows, I'll have a gay march down, I tell you, and shed the blood of some of you before I die.

SHAWN [*in terror*]. Keep a good hold, Philly. Be wary, for the love of God. For I'm thinking he would liefest wreak his pains on me.

CHRISTY [*almost gaily*]. If I do lay my hands on you, it's the way you'll be at the fall of night, hanging as a scarecrow for the fowls of hell. Ah, you'll have a gallous jaunt, I'm saying, coaching out through Limbo with my father's ghost.

SHAWN [to PEGEEN]. Make haste, will you? Oh, isn't he a holy terror, and isn't it true for Father Reilly, that all drink's a curse that has the lot of you so shaky and uncertain now?

CHRISTY. If I can wring a neck among you, I'll have a royal judgement looking on the trembling jury in the courts of law. And won't there be crying out in Mayo the day I'm stretched upon the rope, with ladies in their silks and satins snivelling in their lacy kerchiefs, and they rhyming songs and ballads on the terror of my fate?

[He squirms round on the floor and bites SHAWN's leg.]

SHAWN [shrieking]. My leg's bit on me. He's the like of a mad dog, I'm thinking, the way that I will surely die.

CHRISTY [delighted with himself]. You will, then, the way you can shake out hell's flags of welcome for my coming in two weeks or three, for I'm thinking Satan hasn't many have killed their da in Kerry, and in Mayo too.

[OLD MAHON comes in behind on all fours and looks on unnoticed.]

MEN [to PEGEEN]. Bring the sod, will you?

PEGEEN [coming over]. God help him so. [Burns his leg.]

CHRISTY [kicking and screaming]. Oh, glory be to God!

[He kicks loose from the table, and they all drag him towards the door.]

JIMMY [seeing old MAHON]. Will you look what's come in?
[They all drop CHRISTY and run left.]

CHRISTY [scrambling on his knees face to face with old MAHON]. Are you coming to be killed a third time, or what ails you now?

MAHON. For what is it they have you tied?

CHRISTY. They're taking me to the peelers to have me hanged for slaying you.

MICHAEL [*apologetically*]. It is the will of God that all should guard their little cabins from the treachery of law, and what would my daughter be doing if I was ruined or was hanged itself?

MAHON [*grimly, loosening* CHRISTY]. It's little I care if you put a bag on her back, and went picking cockles till the hour of death; but my son and myself will be going our own way, and we'll have great times from this out telling stories of the villainy of Mayo, and the fools is here. [*To* CHRISTY, *who is freed.*] Come on now.

CHRISTY. Go with you, is it? I will then, like a gallant captain with his heathen slave. Go on now and I'll see you from this day stewing my oatmeal and washing my spuds, for I'm master of all fights from now. [*Pushing* MAHON.] Go on, I'm saying.

MAHON. Is it me?

CHRISTY. Not a word out of you. Go on from this.

MAHON [*walking out and looking back at* CHRISTY *over his shoulder*]. Glory be to God! [*With a broad smile.*] I am crazy again. [*Goes.*]

CHRISTY. Ten thousand blessings upon all that's here, for you've turned me a likely gaffer in the end of all, the way I'll go romancing through a romping lifetime from this hour to the dawning of the judgement day. [*He goes out.*]

MICHAEL. By the will of God, we'll have peace now for our drinks. Will you draw the porter, Pegeen?

SHAWN [*going up to her*]. It's a miracle Father Reilly can wed us in the end of all, and we'll have none to trouble us when his vicious bite is healed.

PEGEEN [*hitting him a box on the ear*]. Quit my sight. [*Putting her shawl over her head and breaking out into wild lamentations.*] Oh, my grief, I've lost him surely. I've lost the only Playboy of the Western World.

CURTAIN

Deirdre of the Sorrows

Also Fate here.

PERSONS IN THE PLAY

LAVARCHAM, *Deirdre's nurse*

OLD WOMAN, *Lavarcham's servant*

OWEN, *Conchubor's attendant and spy*

CONCHUBOR, *High King of Ulster*

FERGUS, *Conchubor's friend*

DEIRDRE

NAISI, *Deirdre's lover*

AINNLE, *Naisi's brother*

ARDAN, *Naisi's brother*

TWO SOLDIERS

SCENE — *Act I, Lavarcham's house in Slieve Fuadh. Act II, Alban. Early morning in the beginning of winter. Outside the tent of Deirdre and Naisi. Act III, Tent below Emain Macha*

Truth of the nature of existence :— it is because one bids farewell to life that one grasps it to the full.

Deirdre of the Sorrows

·

ACT ONE

LAVARCHAM'S *house on Slieve Fuadh. There is a door to inner room on the left, and a door to open air on the right. Window at back and a frame with a half-finished piece of tapestry. There are also a large press and heavy oak chest near the back wall. The place is neat and clean but bare.* LAVARCHAM, *woman of fifty, is working at tapestry frame.* OLD WOMAN *comes in from left.*

OLD WOMAN. She hasn't come yet, is it, and it falling to the night?

LAVARCHAM. She has not. . . . [*Concealing her anxiety.*] It's dark with the clouds are coming from the west and south, but it isn't later than the common.

OLD WOMAN. It's later, surely, and I hear tell the Sons of Usna, Naisi and his brothers, are above chasing hares for two days or three, and the same awhile since when the moon was full.

LAVARCHAM [*more anxiously*]. The gods send they don't set eyes on her – [*with a sign of helplessness*] yet if they do itself, it wasn't my wish brought them or could send them away.

OLD WOMAN [*reprovingly*]. If it wasn't you'd do well to keep a check on her, and she turning a woman that was meant to be a queen.

LAVARCHAM. Who'd check her like was made to have her pleasure only, the way if there were no warnings told

about her you'd see troubles coming when an old king
is taking her, and she without a thought but for her
beauty and to be straying the hills.

OLD WOMAN. The gods help the lot of us. . . . Shouldn't
she be well pleased getting the like of Conchubor, and
he middling settled in his years itself? I don't know what
he wanted putting her this wild place to be breaking her
in, or putting myself to be roasting her supper and she
with no patience for her food at all. [*She looks out.*]

LAVARCHAM. Is she coming from the glen?

OLD WOMAN. She is not. But whisht – there's two men
leaving the furze – [*crying out*] it's Conchubor and Fergus
along with him. Conchubor'll be in a blue stew this
night and herself abroad.

LAVARCHAM [*settling room hastily*]. Are they close by?

OLD WOMAN. Crossing the stream, and there's herself on
the hillside with a load of twigs. Will I run out and put
her in order before they'll set eyes on her at all?

LAVARCHAM. You will not. Would you have him see you,
and he a man would be jealous of a hawk would fly between her and the rising sun. [*She looks out.*] Go up to the
hearth and be as busy as if you hadn't seen them at all.

OLD WOMAN [*sitting down to polish vessel*]. There'll be
trouble this night, for he should be in his tempers from
the way he's stepping out, and he swinging his hands.

LAVARCHAM [*wearied with the whole matter*]. It'd be best of
all, maybe, if he got in tempers with herself, and made
an end quickly, for I'm in a poor way between the pair
of them [*going back to tapestry frame*]. There they are now
at the door.

[CONCHUBOR *and* FERGUS *come in.*]

CONCHUBOR *and* FERGUS. The gods save you.

LAVARCHAM [*getting up and curtseying*]. The gods save and

keep you kindly, and stand between you and all harm for ever.

CONCHUBOR [*looking around*]. Where is Deirdre?

LAVARCHAM [*trying to speak with indifference*]. Abroad upon Slieve Fuadh. She does be all times straying around picking flowers or nuts, or sticks itself; but so long as she's gathering new life I've a right not to heed her, I'm thinking, and she taking her will.

[FERGUS *talks to* OLD WOMAN.]

CONCHUBOR [*stiffly*]. A night with thunder coming is no night to be abroad.

LAVARCHAM [*more uneasily*]. She's used to every track and pathway, and the lightning itself wouldn't let down its flame to singe the beauty of her like.

FERGUS [*cheerfully*]. She's right, Conchubor, and let you sit down and take your ease [*he takes a wallet from under his cloak*], and I'll count out what we've brought, and put it in the presses within.

[*He goes into the inner room with the* OLD WOMAN.]

CONCHUBOR [*sitting down and looking about*]. Where are the mats and hangings and the silver skillets I sent up for Deirdre?

LAVARCHAM. The mats and hangings are in this press, Conchubor. She wouldn't wish to be soiling them, she said, running out and in with mud and grasses on her feet, and it raining since the night of Samhain. The silver skillets and the golden cups we have beyond locked in the chest.

CONCHUBOR. Bring them out and use them from this day.

LAVARCHAM. We'll do it, Conchubor.

CONCHUBOR [*getting up and going to frame*]. Is this hers?

LAVARCHAM [*pleased to speak of it*]. It is, Conchubor. All

say there isn't her match at fancying figures and throwing purple upon crimson, and she edging them all times with her greens and gold.

CONCHUBOR [*a little uneasily*]. Is she keeping wise and busy since I passed before, and growing ready for her life in Emain ?

LAVARCHAM [*dryly*]. That is a question will give small pleasure to yourself or me. [*Making up her mind to speak out.*] If it's the truth I'll tell you, she's growing too wise to marry a big king and she a score only. Let you not be taking it bad, Conchubor, but you'll get little good seeing her this night, for with all my talking it's wilfuller she's growing these two months or three.

CONCHUBOR [*severely, but relieved things are no worse*]. Isn't it a poor thing you're doing so little to school her to meet what is to come ?

LAVARCHAM. I'm after serving you two score of years, and I'll tell you this night, Conchubor, she's little call to mind an old woman when she has the birds to school her, and the pools in the rivers where she goes bathing in the sun. I'll tell you if you seen her that time, with her white skin, and her red lips, and the blue water and the ferns about her, you'd know, maybe, and you greedy itself, it wasn't for your like she was born at all.

CONCHUBOR. It's little I heed for what she was born; she'll be my comrade, surely.

[*He examines her workbox.*]

LAVARCHAM [*sinking into sadness again*]. I'm in dread so they were right saying she'd bring destruction on the world, for it's a poor thing when you see a settled man putting the love he has for a young child, and the love he has for a full woman, on a girl the like of her; and it's a poor thing, Conchubor, to see a High King, the way you

216

are this day, prying after her needles and numbering her lines of thread.

CONCHUBOR [*getting up*]. Let you not be talking too far and you old itself. [*Walks across room and back.*] Does she know the troubles are foretold?

LAVARCHAM [*in the tone of the earlier talk*]. I'm after telling her one time and another, but I'd do as well speaking to a lamb of ten weeks and it racing the hills. . . . It's not the dread of death or troubles that would tame her like.

CONCHUBOR [*he looks out*]. She's coming now, and let you walk in and keep Fergus till I speak with her a while.

LAVARCHAM [*going left*]. If I'm after vexing you itself, it'd be best you weren't taking her hasty or scolding her at all.

CONCHUBOR [*very stiffly*]. I've no call to. I'm well pleased she's light and airy.

LAVARCHAM [*offended at his tone*]. Well pleased is it? [*With a snort of irony.*] It's a queer thing the way the likes of me do be telling the truth, and the wise are lying all times.

[*She goes into room on left.* CONCHUBOR *arranges himself before a mirror for a moment, then goes a little to the left and waits.* DEIRDRE *comes in poorly dressed, with a little bag and a bundle of twigs in her arms. She is astonished for a moment when she sees* CONCHUBOR; *then she makes a curtsey to him, and goes to the hearth without any embarrassment.*]

CONCHUBOR. The gods save you, Deirdre. I have come up bringing you rings and jewels from Emain Macha.

DEIRDRE. The gods save you.

CONCHUBOR. What have you brought from the hills?

DEIRDRE [*quite self-possessed*]. A bag of nuts, and twigs for our fires at the dawn of day.

CONCHUBOR [*showing annoyance in spite of himself*]. And

it's that way you're picking up the manners will fit you
to be Queen of Ulster?

DEIRDRE [*made a little defiant by his tone*]. I have no wish to
be a queen.

CONCHUBOR [*almost sneeringly*]. You'd wish to be dressing
in your duns and grey, and you herding your geese or
driving your calves to their shed – like the common lot
scattered in the glens.

DEIRDRE [*very defiant*]. I would not, Conchubor. [*She goes
to tapestry and begins to work.*] A girl born the way I'm
born is more likely to wish for a mate who'd be her likeness. . . . A man with his hair like the raven, maybe, and
his skin like the snow and his lips like blood spilt on it.

CONCHUBOR [*sees his mistake, and after a moment takes a
flattering tone, looking at her work*]. Whatever you wish,
there's no queen but would be well pleased to have your
skill at choosing colours and making pictures on the
cloth. [*Looking closely.*] What is it you're figuring?

DEIRDRE [*deliberately*]. Three young men and they chasing
in the green gap of a wood.

CONCHUBOR [*now almost pleading*]. It's soon you'll have
dogs with silver chains to be chasing in the woods of
Emain, for I have white hounds rearing up for you, and
grey horses, that I've chosen from the finest in Ulster and
Britain and Gaul.

DEIRDRE [*unmoved as before*]. I've heard tell, in Ulster and
Britain and Gaul, Naisi and his brothers have no match
and they chasing in the woods.

CONCHUBOR [*very gravely*]. Isn't it a strange thing you'd
be talking of Naisi and his brothers, or figuring them
either, when you know the things that are foretold about
themselves and you? Yet you've little knowledge, and
I'd do wrong taking it bad when it'll be my share from

this out to keep you in the way you'll have little call to trouble for knowledge, or its want either.

DEIRDRE. Yourself should be wise, surely.

CONCHUBOR. The like of me has a store of knowledge that's a weight and terror. It's for that we do choose out the like of yourself that are young and glad only. . . . I'm thinking you are gay and lively each day in the year?

DEIRDRE. I don't know if that's true, Conchubor. There are lonesome days and bad nights in this place like another.

CONCHUBOR. You should have as few sad days, I'm thinking, as I have glad and good ones.

DEIRDRE. What is it has you that way ever coming this place, when you'd hear the old woman saying a good child's as happy as a king?

CONCHUBOR. How would I be happy seeing age coming on me each year, when the dry leaves are blowing back and forward at the gate of Emain? And yet this last while I'm saying out, when I see the furze breaking and the daws sitting two and two on ash-trees by the duns of Emain, Deirdre's a year nearer her full age when she'll be my mate and comrade, and then I'm glad surely.

DEIRDRE [*almost to herself*]. I will not be your mate in Emain.

CONCHUBOR [*not heeding her*]. It's there you'll be proud and happy and you'll learn that, if young men are great hunters, yet it's with the like of myself you'll find a knowledge of what is priceless in your own like. What we all need is a place is safe and splendid, and it's that you'll get in Emain in two days or three.

DEIRDRE [*aghast*]. Two days!

CONCHUBOR. I have the rooms ready, and in a little

while you'll be brought down there, to be my queen and
queen of the five parts of Ireland.

DEIRDRE [*standing up frightened and pleading*]. I'd liefer
stay this place, Conchubor. . . . Leave me this place,
where I'm well used to the tracks and pathways and the
people of the glens. . . . It's for this life I'm born, surely.

CONCHUBOR. You'll be happier and greater with myself
in Emain. It is I will be your comrade and will stand between you and the great troubles are foretold.

DEIRDRE. I will not be your queen in Emain when it's my
pleasure to be having my freedom on the edges of the
hills.

CONCHUBOR. It's my wish to have you quickly; I'm sick
and weary thinking of the day you'll be brought down to
me, and seeing you walking into my big, empty halls. I've
made all sure to have you, and yet all said there's a fear
in the back of my mind I'd miss you and have great
troubles in the end. It's for that, Deirdre, I'm praying
that you'll come quickly; and you may take the word of
a man has no lies, you'll not find, with any other, the
like of what I'm bringing you in wildness and confusion
in my own mind.

DEIRDRE. I cannot go, Conchubor.

CONCHUBOR [*taking a triumphant tone*]. It is my pleasure
to have you, and I a man is waiting a long while on the
throne of Ulster. Wouldn't you liefer be my comrade,
growing up the like of Emer and Maeve, than to be in
this place and you a child always?

DEIRDRE. You don't know me and you'd have little joy
taking me, Conchubor. . . . I'm a long while watching
the days getting a great speed passing me by. I'm too
long taking my will, and it's that way I'll be living
always.

CONCHUBOR [*dryly*]. Call Fergus to come with me. This is your last night upon Slieve Fuadh.

DEIRDRE [*now pleadingly*]. Leave me a short space longer, Conchubor. Isn't it a poor thing I should be hastened away, when all these troubles are foretold? Leave me a year, Conchubor; it isn't much I'm asking.

CONCHUBOR. It's much to have me two score and two weeks waiting for your voice in Emain, and you in this place growing lonesome and shy. I'm a ripe man and in great love, and yet, Deirdre, I'm the King of Ulster. [*He gets up.*] I'll call Fergus, and we'll make Emain ready in the morning.

[*He goes towards door on left.*]

DEIRDRE [*clinging to him*]. Do not call him, Conchubor. . . . Promise me a year of quiet. . . . It's one year I'm asking only.

CONCHUBOR. You'd be asking a year next year, and the years that follow. [*Calling.*] Fergus! Fergus! [*To DEIRDRE.*] Young girls are slow always; it is their lovers that must say the word. [*Calling.*] Fergus!

[DEIRDRE *springs away from him as* FERGUS *comes in with* LAVARCHAM *and the* OLD WOMAN.]

CONCHUBOR [*to* FERGUS]. There is a storm coming, and we'd best be going to our people when the night is young.

FERGUS [*cheerfully*]. The gods shield you, Deirdre. [*To CONCHUBOR.*] We're late already, and it's no work the High King to be slipping on stepping-stones and hilly pathways when the floods are rising with the rain.

[*He helps* CONCHUBOR *into his cloak.*]

CONCHUBOR [*glad that he has made his decision — to* LAVARCHAM]. Keep your rules a few days longer, and

you'll be brought down to Emain, you and Deirdre with
you.

LAVARCHAM [*obediently*]. Your rules are kept always.

CONCHUBOR. The gods shield you.

[*He goes out with* FERGUS. OLD WOMAN *bolts door.*]

LAVARCHAM [*looking at* DEIRDRE, *who has covered her
face*]. Wasn't I saying you'd do it? You've brought your
marriage a sight nearer not heeding those are wiser than
yourself.

DEIRDRE [*with agitation*]. It wasn't I did it. Will you take
me from this place, Lavarcham, and keep me safe in the
hills?

LAVARCHAM. He'd have us tracked in the half of a day,
and then you'd be his queen in spite of you, and I and
mine would be destroyed for ever.

DEIRDRE [*terrified with the reality that is before her*]. Are
there none can go against Conchubor?

LAVARCHAM. Maeve of Connaught only, and those that
are her like.

DEIRDRE. Would Fergus go against him?

LAVARCHAM. He would, maybe, and his temper roused.

DEIRDRE [*in a lower voice with sudden excitement*]. Would
Naisi and his brothers?

LAVARCHAM [*impatiently*]. Let you not be dwelling on
Naisi and his brothers. . . . In the end of all there is none
can go against Conchubor, and it's folly that we're talking, for if any went against Conchubor it's sorrows he'd
earn and the shortening of his day of life.

[*She turns away, and* DEIRDRE *stands up stiff with excitement and goes and looks out of the window.*]

DEIRDRE. Are the stepping-stones flooding, Lavarcham?
Will the night be stormy in the hills?

LAVARCHAM [*looking at her curiously*]. The stepping-stones

are flooding, surely, and the night will be the worst, I'm thinking, we've seen these years gone by.

DEIRDRE [*tearing open the press and pulling out clothes and tapestries*]. Lay these mats and hangings by the windows, and at the tables for our feet, and take out the skillets of silver, and the golden cups we have, and our two flasks of wine.

LAVARCHAM. What ails you?

DEIRDRE [*gathering up a dress*]. Lay them out quickly, Lavarcham, we've no call dawdling this night. Lay them out quickly; I'm going into the room to put on the rich dresses and jewels have been sent from Emain.

LAVARCHAM. Putting on dresses at this hour, and it dark and drenching with the weight of rain! Are you away in your head!

DEIRDRE [*gathering her things together with an outburst of excitement*]. I will dress like Emer in Dundealgan, or Maeve in her house in Connaught. If Conchubor'll make me a queen, I'll have the right of a queen who is a master, taking her own choice and making a stir to the edges of the seas. . . . Lay out your mats and hangings where I can stand this night and look about me. Lay out the skins of the rams of Connaught and of the goats of the west. I will not be a child or plaything; I'll put on my robes that are the richest, for I will not be brought down to Emain as Cuchulain brings his horse to the yoke, or Conall Cearneach puts his shield upon his arm; and maybe from this day I will turn the men of Ireland like a wind blowing on the heath.

[*She goes into room.* LAVARCHAM *and* OLD WOMAN *look at each other, then the* OLD WOMAN *goes over, looks in at* DEIRDRE *through chink of the door, and then closes it carefully.*]

OLD WOMAN [*in a frightened whisper*]. She's thrown off the

rags she had about her, and there she is in her skin; she's putting her hair in shiny twists. Is she raving, Lavarcham, or has she a good right turning to a queen like Maeve?

LAVARCHAM [*putting up hanging very anxiously*]. It's more than raving's in her mind, or I'm the more astray; and yet she's as good a right as another, maybe, having her pleasure, though she'd spoil the world.

OLD WOMAN [*helping her*]. Be quick before she'll come back. . . . Who'd have thought we'd run before her, and she so quiet till to-night. Will the High King get the better of her, Lavarcham? If I was Conchubor, I wouldn't marry with her like at all.

LAVARCHAM. Hang that by the window. That should please her, surely. When all's said, it's her like will be the master till the end of time.

OLD WOMAN [*at the window*]. There's a mountain of blackness in the sky, and the greatest rain falling has been these long years on the earth. The gods help Conchubor. He'll be a sorry man this night, reaching his dun, and he with all his spirits, thinking to himself he'll be putting his arms around her in two days or three.

LAVARCHAM. It's more than Conchubor'll be sick and sorry, I'm thinking, before this story is told to the end.

[*Loud knocking on door at the right.*]

LAVARCHAM [*startled*]. Who is that?

NAISI [*outside*]. Naisi, and his brothers.

LAVARCHAM. We are lonely women. What is it you're wanting in the blackness of the night?

NAISI. We met a young girl in the woods who told us we might shelter this place if the rivers rose on the pathways and the floods gathered from the butt of the hills.

[OLD WOMAN *clasps her hands in horror.*]

LAVARCHAM [*with great alarm*]. You cannot come in. . . .
There is no one let in here, and no young girl with us.

NAISI. Let us in from the great storm. Let us in and we
will go further when the cloud will rise.

LAVARCHAM. Go round east to the shed and you'll have
shelter. You cannot come in.

NAISI [*knocking loudly*]. Open the door or we will burst it.
[*The door is shaken.*]

OLD WOMAN [*in a timid whisper*]. Let them in, and keep
Deirdre in her room to-night.

AINNLE and ARDAN [*outside*]. Open! Open!

LAVARCHAM [*to* OLD WOMAN]. Go in and keep her.

OLD WOMAN. I couldn't keep her. I've no hold on her.
Go in yourself and I will free the door.

LAVARCHAM. I must stay and turn them out. [*She pulls her
hair and cloak over her face.*] Go in and keep her.

OLD WOMAN. The gods help us.

[*She runs into the inner room.*]

VOICES. Open!

LAVARCHAM [*opening the door*]. Come in then and ill-luck
if you'll have it so.

[NAISI and AINNLE and ARDAN *come in and look round
with astonishment.*]

NAISI. It's a rich man has this place, and no herd at all.

LAVARCHAM [*sitting down with her head half covered*]. It is
not, and you'd best be going quickly.

NAISI [*hilariously, shaking rain from his clothes*]. When we've
had the pick of luck finding princely comfort in the darkness of the night! Some rich man of Ulster should come
here and he chasing in the woods. May we drink? [*He
takes up flask.*] Whose wine is this that we may drink his
health?

LAVARCHAM. It's no one's that you've call to know.

225

NAISI. Your own health then and length of life. [*Pouring out wine for the three. They drink.*]

LAVARCHAM [*very crossly*]. You're great boys taking a welcome where it isn't given, and asking questions where you've no call to. . . . If you'd a quiet place settled up to be playing yourself, maybe, with a gentle queen, what'd you think of young men prying around and carrying tales? When I was a bit of a girl the big men of Ulster had better manners, and they the like of your three selves, in the top folly of youth. That'll be a story to tell out in Tara that Naisi is a tippler and stealer, and Ainnle the drawer of a stranger's cork.

NAISI [*quite cheerfully, sitting down beside her*]. At your age you should know there are nights when a king like Conchubor would spit upon his arm ring, and queens will stick their tongues out at the rising moon. We're that way this night, and it's not wine we're asking only. Where is the young girl told us we might shelter here?

LAVARCHAM. Asking me you'd be? . . . We're decent people, and I wouldn't put you tracking a young girl, not if you gave me the gold clasp you have hanging on your coat.

NAISI [*giving it to her*]. Where is she?

LAVARCHAM [*in confidential whisper, putting her hand on his arm*]. Let you walk back into the hills and turn up by the second cnuceen where there are three together. You'll see a path running on the rocks and then you'll hear the dogs barking in the houses, and their noise will guide you till you come to a bit of cabin at the foot of an ash-tree. It's there there is a young and flighty girl that I'm thinking is the one you've seen.

NAISI [*hilariously*]. Here's health, then, to herself and you!

ARDAN. Here's to the years when you were young as she!

AINNLE [*in a frightened whisper*]. Naisi!

[NAISI *looks up and* AINNLE *beckons to him. He goes over and* AINNLE *points to something on the golden mug he holds in his hand.*]

NAISI [*looking at it in astonishment*]. This is the High King's . . . I see his mark on the rim. Does Conchubor come lodging here?

LAVARCHAM [*jumping up with extreme annoyance*]. Who says it's Conchubor's? How dare young fools the like of you – [*speaking with vehement insolence*] come prying around, running the world into troubles for some slip of a girl? What brings you this place straying from Emain? [*Very bitterly.*] Though you think, maybe, young men can do their fill of foolery and there is none to blame them.

NAISI [*very soberly*]. Is the rain easing?

ARDAN. The clouds are breaking. . . . I can see Orion in the gap of the glen.

NAISI [*still cheerfully*]. Open the door and we'll go forward to the little cabin between the ash-tree and the rocks. Lift the bolt and pull it.

[DEIRDRE *comes in on left royally dressed and very beautiful. She stands for a moment, and then as the door opens she calls softly.*]

DEIRDRE. Naisi! Do not leave me, Naisi. I am Deirdre of the Sorrows.

NAISI [*transfixed with amazement*]. And it is you who go around in the woods making the thrushes bear a grudge against the heavens for the sweetness of your voice singing.

DEIRDRE. It is with me you've spoken surely. [*To* LAVARCHAM *and* OLD WOMAN.] Take Ainnle and Ardan, these two princes, into the little hut where we eat, and serve them with what is best and sweetest. I have many things for Naisi only.

LAVARCHAM [*overawed by her tone*]. I will do it, and I ask their pardon. I have fooled them here.

DEIRDRE [*to* AINNLE *and* ARDAN]. Do not take it badly that I am asking you to walk into our hut for a little. You will have a supper that is cooked by the cook of Conchubor, and Lavarcham will tell you stories of Maeve and Nessa and Rogh.

AINNLE. We'll ask Lavarcham to tell us stories of yourself, and with that we'll be well pleased to be doing your wish.

[*They all go out except* DEIRDRE *and* NAISI.]

DEIRDRE [*sitting in the high chair in the centre*]. Come to this stool, Naisi [*pointing to the stool*]. If it's low itself the High King would sooner be on it this night than on the throne of Emain Macha.

NAISI [*sitting down*]. You are Fedlimid's daughter that Conchubor has walled up from all the men of Ulster.

DEIRDRE. Do many know what is foretold, that Deirdre will be the ruin of the Sons of Usna, and have a little grave by herself, and a story will be told for ever?

NAISI. It's a long while men have been talking of Deirdre, the child who had all gifts, and the beauty that has no equal; there are many know it, and there are kings would give a great price to be in my place this night and you grown to a queen.

DEIRDRE. It isn't many I'd call, Naisi. . . . I was in the woods at the full moon and I heard a voice singing. Then I gathered up my skirts, and I ran on a little path I have to the verge of a rock, and I saw you pass by underneath, in your crimson cloak, singing a song, and you standing

out beyond your brothers are called the Flower of
Ireland.

NAISI. It's for that you called us in the dusk?

DEIRDRE [*in a low voice*]. Since that, Naisi, I have been one
time the like of a ewe looking for a lamb that had been
taken away from her, and one time seeing new gold on
the stars, and a new face on the moon, and all times
dreading Emain.

NAISI [*pulling himself together and beginning to draw back a
little*]. Yet it should be a lonesome thing to be in this
place and you born for great company.

DEIRDRE [*softly*]. This night I have the best company in
the whole world.

NAISI [*still a little formally*]. It is I who have the best company, for when you're queen in Emain you will have
none to be your match or fellow.

DEIRDRE. I will not be queen in Emain.

NAISI. Conchubor has made an oath you will, surely.

DEIRDRE. It's for that maybe I'm called Deirdre, the girl
of many sorrows . . . for it's a sweet life you and I could
have, Naisi. . . . It should be a sweet thing to have what
is best and richest, if it's for a short space only.

NAISI [*very distressed*]. And we've a short space only to be
triumphant and brave.

DEIRDRE. You must not go, Naisi, and leave me to the
High King, a man is ageing in his dun, with his crowds
round him, and his silver and gold. [*More quickly.*] I will
not live to be shut up in Emain, and wouldn't we do well
paying, Naisi, with silence and a near death. [*She stands
up and walks away from him.*] I'm a long while in the woods
with my own self, and I'm in little dread of death, and
it earned with riches would make the sun red with envy,
and he going up the heavens; and the moon pale and

lonesome, and she wasting away. [*She comes to him and puts her hands on his shoulders.*] Isn't it a small thing is foretold about the ruin of ourselves, Naisi, when all men have age coming and great ruin in the end?

NAISI. Yet it's a poor thing it's I should bring you to a tale of blood and broken bodies, and the filth of the grave. . . . Wouldn't we do well to wait, Deirdre, and I each twilight meeting you on the sides of the hills?

DEIRDRE [*despondently*]. His messengers are coming.

NAISI. Messengers are coming?

DEIRDRE. To-morrow morning or the next, surely.

NAISI. Then we'll go away. It isn't I will give your like to Conchubor, not if the grave was dug to be my lodging when a week was by. [*He looks out.*] The stars are out, Deirdre, and let you come with me quickly, for it is the stars will be our lamps many nights and we abroad in Alban, and taking our journeys among the little islands in the sea. There has never been the like of the joy we'll have, Deirdre, you and I, having our fill of love at the evening and the morning till the sun is high.

DEIRDRE. And yet I'm in dread leaving this place, where I have lived always. Won't I be lonesome and I thinking on the little hills beyond, and the apple-trees, do be budding in the springtime by the post of the door? [*A little shaken by what has passed.*] Won't I be in great dread to bring you to destruction, Naisi, and you so happy and young?

NAISI. Are you thinking I'd go on living after this night, Deirdre, and you with Conchubor in Emain? Are you thinking I'd go out after hares when I've had your lips in my sight?

[LAVARCHAM *comes in as they cling to each other.*]

LAVARCHAM. Are you raving, Deirdre? Are you choosing this night to destroy the world?

DEIRDRE [*very deliberately*]. It's Conchubor has chosen this night calling me to Emain. [*To* NAISI.] Bring in Ainnle and Ardan, and take me from this place, where I'm in dread from this out of the footsteps of a hare passing. [*He goes.*]

DEIRDRE [*clinging to* LAVARCHAM]. Do not take it bad I'm going, Lavarcham. It's you have been a good friend and given me great freedom and joy, and I living on Slieve Fuadh; and maybe you'll be well pleased one day saying you have nursed Deirdre.

LAVARCHAM [*moved*]. It isn't I'll be well pleased and I far away from you. Isn't it a hard thing you're doing, but who can help it? Birds go mating in the spring of the year, and ewes at the leaves falling, but a young girl must have her lover in all the course of the sun and moon.

DEIRDRE. Will you go to Emain in the morning?

LAVARCHAM. I will not. I'll go to Brandon in the south; and in the course of a piece, maybe, I'll be sailing back and forward on the seas to be looking on your face and the little ways you have that none can equal.

[NAISI *comes back with* AINNLE *and* ARDAN *and* OLD WOMAN.]

DEIRDRE [*taking* NAISI's *hand*]. My two brothers, I am going with Naisi to Alban and the north to face the troubles are foretold. Will you take word to Conchubor in Emain?

AINNLE. We will go with you.

ARDAN. We will be your servants and your huntsmen, Deirdre.

DEIRDRE. It isn't one brother only of you three is brave

and courteous. Will you wed us, Lavarcham? You have
the words and customs.

LAVARCHAM. I will not, then. What would I want meddling in the ruin you will earn?

NAISI. Let Ainnle wed us. . . . He has been with wise men
and he knows their ways.

AINNLE [*joining their hands*]. By the sun and moon and the
whole earth, I wed Deirdre to Naisi. [*He steps back and
holds up his hands.*] May the air bless you, and water and
the wind, the sea, and all the hours of the sun and moon.

CURTAIN

*Alban. Early morning in the beginning of winter. A wood outside
the tent of* DEIRDRE *and* NAISI. LAVARCHAM *comes in
muffled in a cloak.*

LAVARCHAM [*calling*]. Deirdre. . . . Deirdre. . . .

DEIRDRE [*coming from tent*]. My welcome, Lavarcham. . . .
Whose curagh is rowing from Ulster? I saw the oars
through the tops of the trees, and I thought it was you
were coming towards us.

LAVARCHAM. I came in the shower was before dawn.

DEIRDRE. And who is coming?

LAVARCHAM [*mournfully*]. Let you not be startled or taking
it bad, Deirdre. It's Fergus bringing messages of peace
from Conchubor to take Naisi and his brother back to
Emain.

[*Sitting down.*]

DEIRDRE [*lightly*]. Naisi and his brothers are well pleased
with this place; and what would take them back to
Conchubor in Ulster?

LAVARCHAM. Their like would go any place where they'd
see death standing. [*With more agitation.*] I'm in dread
Conchubor wants to have yourself and to kill Naisi,
and that that'll be the ruin of the Sons of Usna. I'm
silly, maybe, to be dreading the like, but those have
a great love for yourself have a right to be in dread
always.

DEIRDRE [*more anxiously*]. Emain should be no safe place
for myself and Naisi. And isn't it a hard thing they'll
leave us no peace, Lavarcham, and we so quiet in the
woods?

LAVARCHAM [*impressively*]. It's a hard thing, surely; but let you take my word and swear Naisi, by the earth, and the sun over it, and the four quarters of the moon, he'll not go back to Emain – for good faith or bad faith – the time Conchubor's keeping the high throne of Ireland. . . . It's that would save you, surely.

DEIRDRE [*without hope*]. There's little power in oaths to stop what's coming, and little power in what I'd do, Lavarcham, to change the story of Conchubor and Naisi and the things old men foretold.

LAVARCHAM [*aggressively*]. Was there little power in what you did the night you dressed in your finery and ran Naisi off along with you, in spite of Conchubor and the big nobles did dread the blackness of your luck? It was power enough you had that night to bring distress and anguish; and now I'm pointing you a way to save Naisi, you'll not stir stick or straw to aid me.

DEIRDRE [*a little haughtily*]. Let you not raise your voice against me, Lavarcham, if you have will itself to guard Naisi.

LAVARCHAM [*breaking out in anger*]. Naisi is it? I didn't care if the crows were stripping his thigh-bones at the dawn of day. It's to stop your own despair and wailing, and you waking up in a cold bed, without the man you have your heart on, I am raging now. [*Starting up with temper.*] Yet there is more men than Naisi in it; and maybe I was a big fool thinking his dangers, and this day, would fill you up with dread.

DEIRDRE [*sharply*]. Let you end: such talking is a fool's only, when it's well you know if a thing harmed Naisi it isn't I would live after him. [*With distress.*] It's well you know it's this day I'm dreading seven years, and I fine nights watching the heifers walking to the haggard with long shadows on the grass; [*with emotion*] or the time I've been stretched in the sunshine, when I've heard Ainnle and Ardan stepping lightly, and they saying: Was there ever the like of Deirdre for a happy and sleepy queen?

LAVARCHAM [*not fully pacified*]. And yet you'll go, and welcome is it, if Naisi chooses?

DEIRDRE. I've dread going or staying, Lavarcham. It's lonesome this place, having happiness like ours, till I'm asking each day will this day match yesterday, and will to-morrow take a good place beside the same day in the year's that gone, and wondering all times is it a game worth playing, living on until you're dried and old, and our joy is gone for ever.

LAVARCHAM. If it's that ails you, I tell you there's little hurt getting old, though young girl and poets do be storming at the shapes of age. [*Passionately.*] There's little hurt getting old, saving when you're looking back, the way I'm looking this day, and seeing the young you have a love for breaking up their hearts with folly. [*Going to* DEIRDRE.] Take my word and stop Naisi, and the day'll come you'll have more joy having the senses of an old woman and you with your little grandsons shrieking round you, than I'd have this night putting on the red mouth and the white arms you have, to go walking lonesome byeways with a gamey king.

DEIRDRE. It's little joy of a young woman, or an old woman, I'll have from this day, surely. But what use is in our talking when there's Naisi on the foreshore, and Fergus with him?

LAVARCHAM [*despairingly*]. I'm late so with my warnings, for Fergus'd talk the moon over to take a new path in the sky. [*With reproach.*] You'll not stop him this day, and isn't it a strange story you were a plague and torment, since you were that height, to those did hang their life-times on your voice. [*Overcome with trouble; gathering her cloak about her.*] Don't think bad of my crying. I'm not the like of many and I'd see a score of naked corpses and not heed them at all, but I'm destroyed seeing yourself in your hour of joy when the end is coming surely.

[OWEN *comes in quickly, rather ragged, bows to* DEIRDRE.]

OWEN [*to* LAVARCHAM]. Fergus's men are calling you. You were seen on the path, and he and Naisi want you for their talk below.

LAVARCHAM [*looking at him with dislike*]. Yourself's an ill-lucky thing to meet a morning is the like of this. Yet if you are a spy itself I'll go and give my word that's wanting surely. [*Goes out.*]

OWEN [*to* DEIRDRE]. So I've found you alone, and I after waiting three weeks getting ague and asthma in the chill of the bogs, till I saw Naisi caught with Fergus.

DEIRDRE. I've heard news of Fergus; what brought you from Ulster?

OWEN [*who has been searching, finds a loaf and sits down eating greedily, and cutting it with a large knife*]. The full moon, I'm thinking, and it squeezing the crack in my skull. Was there ever a man crossed nine waves after a fool's wife and he not away in his head?

DEIRDRE [*absently*]. It should be a long time since you left Emain, where there's civility in speech with queens.

OWEN. It's a long while, surely. It's three weeks I am losing my manners beside the Saxon bull-frogs at the head of the bog. Three weeks is a long space, and yet you're seven years spancelled with Naisi and the pair.

DEIRDRE [*beginning to fold up her silks and jewels*]. Three

weeks of your days might be long, surely, yet seven years
are a short space for the like of Naisi and myself.

OWEN [*derisively*]. If they're a short space there aren't
many the like of you. Wasn't there a queen in Tara had
to walk out every morning till she'd meet a stranger and
see the flame of courtship leaping up within his eye?
Tell me now [*leaning towards her*], are you well pleased
that length with the same man snorting next you at the
dawn of day?

DEIRDRE [*very quietly*]. Am I well pleased seven years seeing
the same sun throwing light across the branches at the
dawn of day? It's a heart-break to the wise that it's for a
short space we have the same things only. [*With contempt.*] Yet the earth itself is a silly place, maybe, when a
man's a fool and talker.

OWEN [*sharply*]. Well, go, take your choice. Stay here and
rot with Naisi or go to Conchubor in Emain. Conchubor's a wrinkled fool with a swelling belly on him,
and eyes falling downward from his shining crown;
Naisi should be stale and weary. Yet there are many
roads, Deirdre, and I tell you I'd liefer be bleaching in a
bog-hole than living on without a touch of kindness from
your eyes and voice. It's a poor thing to be so lonesome
you'd squeeze kisses on a cur dog's nose.

DEIRDRE. Are there no women like yourself could be
your friends in Emain?

OWEN [*vehemently*]. There are none like you, Deirdre. It's
for that I'm asking are you going back this night with
Fergus?

DEIRDRE. I will go where Naisi chooses.

OWEN [*with a burst of rage*]. It's Naisi, Naisi, is it? Then, I
tell you, you'll have great sport one day seeing Naisi
getting a harshness in his two sheep's eyes and he looking

on yourself. Would you credit it, my father used to be in the broom and heather kissing Lavarcham, with a little bird chirping out above their heads, and now she'd scare a raven from a carcase on a hill. [*With a sad cry that brings dignity into his voice.*] Queens get old, Deirdre, with their white and long arms going from them, and their backs hooping. I tell you it's a poor thing to see a queen's nose reaching down to scrape her chin.

DEIRDRE [*looking out, a little uneasy*]. Naisi and Fergus are coming on the path.

OWEN. I'll go so, for if I had you seven years I'd be jealous of the midges and the dust is in the air. [*Muffles himself in his cloak; with a sort of warning in his voice.*] I'll give you a riddle, Deirdre: Why isn't my father as ugly and old as Conchubor? You've no answer? . . . It's because Naisi killed him. [*With curious expression.*] Think of that and you awake at night, hearing Naisi snoring, or the night you hear strange stories of the things I'm doing in Alban or in Ulster either.

[*He goes out, and in a moment* NAISI *and* FERGUS *come in on the other side.*]

NAISI [*gaily*]. Fergus has brought messages of peace from Conchubor.

DEIRDRE [*greeting* FERGUS]. He is welcome. Let you rest, Fergus, you should be hot and thirsty after mounting the rocks.

FERGUS. It's a sunny nook you've found in Alban; yet any man would be well pleased mounting higher rocks to fetch yourself and Naisi back to Emain.

DEIRDRE [*with keenness*]. They've answered? They would go?

FERGUS [*benignly*]. They have not, but when I was a young man we'd have given a lifetime to be in Ireland a score of weeks; and to this day the old men have nothing so heavy as knowing it's in a short while they'll lose the high skies are over Ireland, and the lonesome mornings with birds crying on the bogs. Let you come this day, for there's no place but Ireland where the Gael can have peace always.

NAISI [*gruffly*]. It's true, surely. Yet we're better this place while Conchubor's in Emain Macha.

FERGUS [*giving him parchments*]. There are your sureties and Conchubor's seal. [*To* DEIRDRE.] I am your surety with Conchubor. You'll not be young always, and it's time you were making yourselves ready for the years will come, building up a homely dun beside the seas of Ireland, and getting in your children from the princes' wives. It's little joy wandering till age is on you and your youth is gone away, so you'd best come this night, for you'd have great pleasure putting out your foot and saying, 'I am in Ireland, surely.'

DEIRDRE. It isn't pleasure I'd have while Conchubor is king in Emain.

FERGUS [*almost annoyed*]. Would you doubt the seals of Conal Cearneach and the kings of Meath? [*He gets parchments from his cloak and gives them to* NAISI. *More gently.*] It's easy being fearful and you alone in the woods, yet it would be a poor thing if a timid woman [*taunting her a little*] could turn away the Sons of Usna from the life of kings. Let you be thinking on the years to come, Deirdre, and the way you'd have a right to see Naisi a high and white-haired justice beside some king of Emain. Wouldn't it be a poor story if a queen the like of you should have no thought but to be scraping up her hours dallying in the sunshine with the sons of kings?

DEIRDRE [*turning away a little haughtily*]. I leave the choice to Naisi. [*Turning back towards* FERGUS.] Yet you'd do well, Fergus, to go on your own way, for the sake of your own years, so you'll not be saying till your hour of death, maybe, it was yourself brought Naisi and his brothers to a grave was scooped by treachery. [*Goes into tent.*]

FERGUS. It is a poor thing to see a queen so lonesome and afraid. [*He watches till he is sure* DEIRDRE *cannot hear him.*] Listen now to what I'm saying. You'd do well to come back to men and women are your match and comrades, and not be lingering until the day that you'll grow weary, and hurt Deirdre showing her the hardness will grow up within your eyes. . . . You're here years and plenty to know it's truth I'm saying.

[DEIRDRE *comes out of tent with a horn of wine, she catches the beginning of* NAISI's *speech and stops with stony wonder.*]

NAISI [*very thoughtfully*]. I'll not tell you a lie. There have been days a while past when I've been throwing a line for salmon or watching for the run of hares, that I've a dread upon me a day'd come I'd weary of her voice, [*very slowly*] and Deirdre'd see I'd wearied.

FERGUS [*sympathetic but triumphant*]. I knew it, Naisi. . . . And take my word, Deirdre's seen your dread and she'll have no peace from this out in the woods.

NAISI [*with confidence*]. She's not seen it. . . . Deirdre's no thought of getting old or wearied; it's that puts wonder in her ways, and she with spirits would keep bravery and laughter in a town with plague.

[DEIRDRE *drops the horn of wine and crouches down where she is.*]

FERGUS. That humour'll leave her. But we've no call going too far, with one word borrowing another. Will you come this night to Emain Macha?

NAISI. I'll not go, Fergus. I've had dreams of getting old

and weary, and losing my delight in Deirdre; but my dreams were dreams only. What are Conchubor's seals and all your talk of Emain and the fools of Meath beside one evening in Glen Masain? We'll stay this place till our lives and time are worn out. It's that word you may take in your curagh to Conchubor in Emain.

FERGUS [*gathering up his parchments*]. And you won't go, surely?

NAISI. I will not. . . . I've had dread, I tell you, dread winter and summer, and the autumn and the springtime, even when there's a bird in every bush making his own stir till the fall of night; but this talk's brought me ease, and I see we're as happy as the leaves on the young trees, and we'll be so ever and always, though we'd live the age of the eagle and the salmon and the crow of Britain.

FERGUS [*with anger*]. Where are your brothers? My message is for them also.

NAISI. You'll see them above chasing otters by the stream.

FERGUS [*bitterly*]. It isn't much I was mistaken, thinking you were hunters only.

[*He goes,* NAISI *turns towards tent, and sees* DEIRDRE *crouching down with her cloak round her face.* DEIRDRE *comes out.*]

NAISI. You've heard my words to Fergus? [*She does not answer. A pause. He puts his arm round her.*] Leave troubling, and we'll go this night to Glen da Ruadh, where the salmon will be running with the tide.

[*Crosses and sits down.*]

DEIRDRE [*in a very low voice*]. With the tide in a little while we will be journeying again, or it is our own blood maybe will be running away. [*She turns and clings to him.*] The dawn and evening are a little while, the winter and the summer pass quickly, and what way would you and I, Naisi, have joy for ever?

NAISI. We'll have the joy is highest till our age is come, for it isn't Fergus's talk of great deeds could take us back to Emain.

DEIRDRE. It isn't to great deeds you're going but to near troubles, and the shortening of your days the time that they are bright and sunny; and isn't it a poor thing that I, Deirdre, could not hold you away?

NAISI. I've said we'd stay in Alban always.

DEIRDRE. There's no place to stay always. . . . It's a long time we've had, pressing the lips together, going up and down, resting in our arms, Naisi, waking with the smell of June in the tops of the grasses, and listening to the birds in the branches that are highest. . . . It's a long time we've had, but the end has come, surely.

NAISI. Would you have us go to Emain, though if any ask the reason we do not know it, and we journeying as the thrushes come from the north, or young birds fly out on a dark sea?

DEIRDRE. There's reason all times for an end that's come. And I'm well pleased, Naisi, we're going forward in the winter the time the sun has a low place, and the moon has her mastery in a dark sky, for it's you and I are well lodged our last day, where there is a light behind the clear trees, and the berries on the thorns are a red wall.

NAISI. If our time in this place is ended, come away without Ainnle and Ardan to the woods of the east, for it's right to be away from all people when two lovers have their love only. Come away and we'll be safe always.

DEIRDRE [*broken-hearted*]. There's no safe place, Naisi, on the ridge of the world. . . . And it's in the quiet woods

I've seen them digging our grave, throwing out the clay on leaves are bright and withered.

NAISI [*still more eagerly*]. Come away, Deirdre, and it's little we'll think of safety or the grave beyond it, and we resting in a little corner between the daytime and the long night.

DEIRDRE [*clearly and gravely*]. It's this hour we're between the daytime and a night where there is sleep for ever, and isn't it a better thing to be following on to a near death, than to be bending the head down, and dragging with the feet, and seeing one day a blight showing upon love where it is sweet and tender?

NAISI [*his voice broken with distraction*]. If a near death is coming what will be my trouble losing the earth and the stars over it, and you, Deirdre, are their flame and bright crown? Come away into the safety of the woods.

DEIRDRE [*shaking her head slowly*]. There are as many ways to wither love as there are stars in a night of Samhain; but there is no way to keep life, or love with it, a short space only. . . . It's for that there's nothing lonesome like a love is watching out the time most lovers do be sleeping. . . . It's for that we're setting out for Emain Macha when the tide turns on the sand.

NAISI [*giving in*]. You're right, maybe. It should be a poor thing to see great lovers and they sleepy and old.

DEIRDRE [*with a more tender intensity*]. We're seven years without roughness or growing weary; seven years so sweet and shining, the gods would be hard set to give us seven days the like of them. It's for that we're going to Emain, where there'll be a rest for ever, or a place for forgetting, in great crowds and they making a stir.

NAISI [*very softly*]. We'll go, surely, in place of keeping a watch on a love had no match and it wasting away. [*They*

cling to each other for a moment, then NAISI *looks up.*]
There are Fergus and Lavarcham and my two brothers.

[DEIRDRE *goes.* NAISI *sits with his head bowed.* OWEN *runs in stealthily, comes behind* NAISI *and seizes him round the arms.* NAISI *shakes him off and whips out his sword.*]

OWEN [*screaming with derisive laughter and showing his empty hands*]. Ah, Naisi, wasn't it well I didn't kill you that time? There was a fright you got! I've been watching Fergus above – don't be frightened – and I've come down to see him getting the cold shoulder, and going off alone.

[FERGUS *and others come in. They are all subdued like men at a queen's wake.*]

NAISI [*putting up his sword*]. There he is. [*Goes to* FERGUS]. We are going back when the tide turns, I and Deirdre with yourself.

ALL. Going back!

AINNLE. And you'll end your life with Deirdre, though she has no match for keeping spirits in a little company is far away by itself?

ARDAN. It's seven years myself and Ainnle have been servants and bachelors for yourself and Deirdre. Why will you take her back to Conchubor?

NAISI. I have done what Deirdre wishes and has chosen.

FERGUS. You've made a choice wise men will be glad of in the five ends of Ireland.

OWEN. Wise men is it, and they going back to Conchubor? I could stop them only Naisi put in his sword among my father's ribs, and when a man's done that he'll not credit your oath. Going to Conchubor! I could tell of plots and tricks, and spies were well paid for their play. [*He throws up a bag of gold.*] Are you paid, Fergus?

[*He scatters gold pieces over* FERGUS.]

FERGUS. He is raving. . . . Seize him.

OWEN [*flying between them*]. You won't. Let the lot of you be off to Emain, but I'll be off before you. . . . Dead men, dead men! Men who'll die for Deirdre's beauty; I'll be before you in the grave!

[*Runs out with his knife in his hand. They all run after him except* LAVARCHAM, *who looks out and then clasps her hands.* DEIRDRE *comes out to her in a dark cloak.*]

DEIRDRE. What has happened?

LAVARCHAM. It's Owen's gone raging mad, and he's after splitting his gullet beyond at the butt of the stone. There was ill luck this day in his eye. And he knew a power if he'd said it all.

[NAISI *comes back quickly, followed by the others.*]

AINNLE [*coming in very excited*]. That man knew plots of Conchubor's. We'll not go to Emain, where Conchubor may love her and have hatred for yourself.

FERGUS. Would you mind a fool and raver?

AINNLE. It's many times there's more sense in madmen than the wise. We will not obey Conchubor.

NAISI. I and Deirdre have chosen; we will go back with Fergus.

ARDAN. We will not go back. We will burn your curaghs by the sea.

FERGUS. My sons and I will guard them.

AINNLE. We will blow the horn of Usna and our friends will come to aid us.

NAISI. It is my friends will come.

AINNLE. Your friends will bind your hands, and you out of your wits.

[DEIRDRE *comes forward quickly and comes between* AINNLE *and* NAISI.]

DEIRDRE [*in a low voice*]. For seven years the Sons of Usna have not raised their voices in a quarrel.

AINNLE. We will not take you to Emain.

ARDAN. It is Conchubor has broken our peace.

AINNLE [*to* DEIRDRE]. Stop Naisi going. What way would
we live if Conchubor should take you from us ?

DEIRDRE. There is no one could take me from you. I have
chosen to go back with Fergus. Will you quarrel with
me, Ainnle, though I have been your queen these seven
years in Alban ?

AINNLE [*subsiding suddenly*]. Naisi has no call to take you.

ARDAN. Why are you going ?

DEIRDRE [*to both of them and the others*]. It is my wish. . . .
It may be I will not have Naisi growing an old man in
Alban with an old woman at his side, and young girls
pointing out and saying, 'That is Deirdre and Naisi had
great beauty in their youth.' It may be we do well putting
a sharp end to the day is brave and glorious, as our fathers
put a sharp end to the days of the kings of Ireland; or
that I'm wishing to set my foot on Slieve Fuadh, where I
was running one time and leaping the streams, [*to*
LAVARCHAM] and that I'd be well pleased to see our
little apple-trees, Lavarcham, behind our cabin on the
hill; or that I've learned, Fergus, it's a lonesome thing
to be away from Ireland always.

AINNLE [*giving in*]. There is no place but will be lonesome
to us from this out, and we thinking on our seven years
in Alban.

DEIRDRE [*to* NAISI]. It's in this place we'd be lonesome
in the end. . . . Take down Fergus to the sea. He has
been a guest had a hard welcome and he bringing messages of peace.

FERGUS. We will make your curagh ready and it fitted for
the voyage of a king.

[*He goes with* NAISI.]

DEIRDRE. Take your spears, Ainnle and Ardan, and go
down before me, and take your horse-boys to be carrying
my cloaks are on the threshold.

AINNLE [*obeying*]. It's with a poor heart we'll carry your
things this day we have carried merrily so often, and we
hungry and cold. [*They gather up things and go out.*]

DEIRDRE [*to* LAVARCHAM]. Go you, too, Lavarcham.
You are old, and I will follow quickly.

LAVARCHAM. I'm old, surely, and the hopes I had my
pride in are broken and torn.

[*She goes out with a look of awe at* DEIRDRE.]

DEIRDRE [*clasping her hands*]. Woods of Cuan, woods of
Cuan, dear country of the east! It's seven years we've
had a life was joy only, and this day we're going west,
this day we're facing death, maybe, and death should be
a poor, untidy thing, though it's a queen that dies.

[*She goes out slowly.*]

CURTAIN

Tent below Emain, with shabby skins and benches. There is an opening at each side and at back, the latter closed. OLD WOMAN *comes in with food and fruits and arranges them on table.* CONCHUBOR *comes in on right.*

CONCHUBOR [*sharply*]. Has no one come with news for me?

OLD WOMAN. I've seen no one at all, Conchubor.

CONCHUBOR [*watches her working for a moment, then makes sure opening at back is closed*]. Go up then to Emain, you're not wanting here. [*A noise heard left.*] Who is that?

OLD WOMAN [*going left*]. It's Lavarcham coming again. She's a great wonder for jogging back and forward through the world, and I made certain she'd be off to meet them; but she's coming alone, Conchubor, my dear child Deirdre isn't with her at all.

CONCHUBOR. Go up so and leave us.

OLD WOMAN [*pleadingly*]. I'd be well pleased to set my eyes on Deirdre if she's coming this night, as we're told.

CONCHUBOR [*impatiently*]. It's not long till you'll see her. But I've matters with Lavarcham, and let you go now, I'm saying.

[*He shows her out right,* LAVARCHAM *comes in on the left.*]

LAVARCHAM [*looking round her with suspicion*]. This is a queer place to find you, and it's a queer place to be lodging Naisi and his brothers, and Deirdre with them, and the lot of us tired out with the long way we have been walking.

CONCHUBOR. You've come along with them the whole journey?

248

LAVARCHAM. I have, then, though I've no call now to be wandering that length to a wedding or a burial, or the two together. [*She sits down wearily.*] It's a poor thing the way me and you is getting old, Conchubor, and I'm thinking you yourself have no call to be loitering this place getting your death, maybe, in the cold of night.

CONCHUBOR. I'm waiting only to know is Fergus stopped in the north.

LAVARCHAM [*more sharply*]. He's stopped, surely, and that's a trick has me thinking you have it in mind to bring trouble this night on Emain and Ireland and the big world's east beyond them. [*She goes to him.*] And yet you'd do well to be going to your dun, and not putting shame on her meeting the High King, and she seamed and sweaty and in great disorder from the dust of many roads. [*Laughing derisively.*] Ah, Conchubor, my lad, beauty goes quickly in the woods, and you'd let a great gasp, I tell you, if you set your eyes this night on Deirdre.

CONCHUBOR [*fiercely*]. It's little I care if she's white and worn, for it's I did rear her from a child. I should have a good right to meet and see her always.

LAVARCHAM. A good right is it? Haven't the blind a good right to be seeing, and the lame to be dancing, and the dummies singing tunes? It's that right you have to be looking for gaiety on Deirdre's lips. [*Coaxingly.*] Come on to your dun, I'm saying, and leave her quiet for one night itself.

CONCHUBOR [*with sudden anger*]. I'll not go, when it's long enough I am above in my dun stretching east and west without a comrade, and I more needy, maybe, than the thieves of Meath. . . . You think I'm old and wise, but I tell you the wise know the old must die, and they'll

leave no chance for a thing slipping from them they've
set their blood to win.

LAVARCHAM [*nodding her head*]. If you're old and wise, it's
I'm the same, Conchubor, and I'm telling you you'll not
have her though you're ready to destroy mankind and
skin the gods to win her. There's things a king can't
have, Conchubor, and if you go rampaging this night
you'll be apt to win nothing but death for many, and a
sloppy face of trouble on your own self before the day
will come.

CONCHUBOR. It's too much talk you have. [*Goes right.*]
Where is Owen? Did you see him no place and you
coming the road?

LAVARCHAM. I seen him surely. He went spying on Naisi,
and now the worms is spying on his own inside.

CONCHUBOR [*exultingly*]. Naisi killed him?

LAVARCHAM. He did not, then. It was Owen destroyed
himself running mad because of Deirdre. Fools and kings
and scholars are all one in a story with her like, and Owen
thought he'd be a great man, being the first corpse in the
game you'll play this night in Emain.

CONCHUBOR. It's yourself should be the first corpse, but
my other messengers are coming, men from the clans
that hated Usna.

LAVARCHAM [*drawing back hopelessly*]. Then the gods have
pity on us all!

[MEN *with weapons come in.*]

CONCHUBOR [*to* SOLDIERS]. Are Ainnle and Ardan
separate from Naisi?

MEN. They are, Conchubor. We've got them off, saying
they were needed to make ready Deirdre's house.

CONCHUBOR. And Naisi and Deirdre are coming?

SOLDIER. Naisi's coming, surely, and a woman with him

is putting out the glory of the moon is rising and the sun is going down.

CONCHUBOR [*looking at* LAVARCHAM]. That's your story that she's seamed and ugly?

SOLDIER. I have more news. [*Pointing to* LAVARCHAM.] When that woman heard you were bringing Naisi this place, she sent a horse-boy to call Fergus from the north.

CONCHUBOR [*to* LAVARCHAM]. It's for that you've been playing your tricks, but what you've won is a nearer death for Naisi. [*To* SOLDIERS.] Go up and call my fighters, and take that woman up to Emain.

LAVARCHAM. I'd liefer stay this place. I've done my best, but if a bad end is coming, surely it would be a good thing maybe I was here to tend her.

CONCHUBOR [*fiercely*]. Take her to Emain; it's too many tricks she's tried this day already. [*A* SOLDIER *goes to her.*]

LAVARCHAM. Don't touch me. [*She puts her cloak round her and catches* CONCHUBOR'S *arm.*] I thought to stay your hand with my stories till Fergus would come to be beside them, the way I'd save yourself, Conchubor, and Naisi and Emain Macha; but I'll walk up now into your halls, and I'll say [*with a gesture*] it's here nettles will be growing, and beyond thistles and docks. I'll go into your high chambers, where you've been figuring yourself stretching out your neck for the kisses of a queen of women; and I'll say it's here there'll be deer stirring and goats scratching, and sheep waking and coughing when there is a great wind from the north. [*Shaking herself loose.* CONCHUBOR *makes a sign to* SOLDIERS.] I'm going, surely. In a short space I'll be sitting up with many listening to the flames crackling, and the beams breaking,

and I looking on the great blaze will be the end of Emain.
[*She goes out.*]

CONCHUBOR [*looking out*]. I see two people in the trees;
it should be Naisi and Deirdre. [*To* SOLDIER.] Let you
tell them they'll lodge here to-night.

[CONCHUBOR *goes out right.* NAISI *and* DEIRDRE *come
in on left, very weary.*]

NAISI [*to* SOLDIERS]. Is it this place he's made ready for
myself and Deirdre?

SOLDIER. The Red Branch House is being aired and swept
and you'll be called there when a space is by; till then
you'll find fruits and drink on this table, and so the gods
be with you. [*Goes out right.*]

NAISI [*looking round*]. It's a strange place he's put us camp-
ing and we come back as his friends.

DEIRDRE. He's likely making up a welcome for us, having
curtains shaken out and rich rooms put in order; and it's
right he'd have great state to meet us, and you his sister's
son.

NAISI [*gloomily*]. It's little we want with state or rich rooms
or curtains, when we're used to the ferns only and cold
streams and they making a stir.

DEIRDRE [*roaming round room*]. We want what is our right
in Emain [*looking at hangings*], and though he's riches in
store for us it's a shabby, ragged place he's put us waiting,
with frayed rugs and skins are eaten by the moths.

NAISI [*a little impatiently*]. There are few would worry over
skins and moths on this first night that we've come back
to Emain.

DEIRDRE [*brightly*]. You should be well pleased it's for
that I'd worry all times, when it's I have kept your tent
these seven years as tidy as a bee-hive or a linnet's nest.
If Conchubor'd a queen like me in Emain he'd not have

252

stretched these rags to meet us. [*She pulls hanging, and it opens.*] There's new earth on the ground and a trench dug. . . . It's a grave, Naisi, that is wide and deep.

NAISI [*goes over and pulls back curtain showing grave.*] And that'll be our home in Emain. . . . He's dug it wisely at the butt of a hill, with fallen trees to hide it. He'll want to have us killed and buried before Fergus comes.

DEIRDRE. Take me away. . . . Take me to hide in the rocks, for the night is coming quickly.

NAISI [*pulling himself together*]. I will not leave my brothers.

DEIRDRE [*vehemently*]. It's of us two he's jealous. Come away to the places where we're used to have our company. . . . Wouldn't it be a good thing to lie hid in the high ferns together? [*She pulls him left.*] I hear strange words in the trees.

NAISI. It should be the strange fighters of Conchubor. I saw them passing as we came.

DEIRDRE [*pulling him towards the right*]. Come to this side. Listen, Naisi!

NAISI. There are more of them. . . . We are shut in, and I have not Ainnle and Ardan to stand near me. Isn't it a hard thing that we three who have conquered many may not die together?

DEIRDRE [*sinking down*]. And isn't it a hard thing that you and I are this place by our opened grave; though none have lived had happiness like ours those days in Alban that went by so quick.

NAISI. It's a hard thing, surely, we've lost those days for ever; and yet it's a good thing, maybe, that all goes quick, for when I'm in that grave it's soon a day'll come you'll be too wearied to be crying out, and that day'll bring you ease.

DEIRDRE. I'll not be here to know if that is true.

NAISI. It's our three selves he'll kill to-night, and then in two months or three you'll see him walking down for courtship with yourself.

DEIRDRE. I'll not be here.

NAISI [*hard*]. You'd best keep him off, maybe, and then, when the time comes, make your way to some place west in Donegal, and it's there you'll get used to stretching out lonesome at the fall of night, and waking lonesome for the day.

DEIRDRE. Let you not be saying things are worse than death.

NAISI [*a little recklessly*]. I've one word left. If a day comes in the west that the larks are cocking their crests on the edge of the clouds, and the cuckoos making a stir, and there's a man you'd fancy, let you not be thinking that day I'd be well pleased you'd go on keening always.

DEIRDRE [*turning to look at him*]. And if it was I that died, Naisi, would you take another woman to fill up my place?

NAISI [*very mournfully*]. It's little I know, saving only that it's a hard and bitter thing leaving the earth, and a worse and harder thing leaving yourself alone and desolate to be making lamentation on its face always.

DEIRDRE. I'll die when you do, Naisi. I'd not have come from Alban but I knew I'd be along with you in Emain, and you living or dead. . . . Yet this night it's strange and distant talk you're making only.

NAISI. There's nothing, surely, the like of a new grave of open earth for putting a great space between two friends that love.

DEIRDRE. If there isn't, it's that grave when it's closed

will make us one for ever, and we two lovers have had great space without weariness or growing old or any sadness of the mind.

CONCHUBOR [*coming in on right*]. I'd bid you welcome, Naisi.

NAISI [*standing up*]. You're welcome, Conchubor, I'm well pleased you've come.

CONCHUBOR [*blandly*]. Let you not think bad of this place where I've put you till other rooms are readied.

NAISI [*breaking out*]. We know the room you've readied. We know what stirred you to send your seals and Fergus into Alban and stop him in the north, [*opening curtain and pointing to the grave*] and dig that grave before us. Now I ask what brought you here?

CONCHUBOR. I've come to look on Deirdre.

NAISI. Look on her. You're a knacky fancier, and it's well you chose the one you'd lure from Alban. Look on her, I tell you, and when you've looked I've got ten fingers will squeeze your mottled goose neck, though you're king itself.

DEIRDRE [*coming between them*]. Hush, Naisi! Maybe Conchubor'll make peace. ... Do not mind him, Conchubor; he has cause to rage.

CONCHUBOR. It's little I heed his raging, when a call would bring my fighters from the trees. ... But what do you say, Deirdre?

DEIRDRE. I'll say so near that grave we seem three lonesome people, and by a new made grave there's no man will keep brooding on a woman's lips, or on the man he hates. It's not long till your own grave will be dug in Emain, and you'd go down to it more easy if you'd let call Ainnle and Ardan, the way we'd have a supper all together, and fill that grave, and you'll be well pleased from this out, having four new friends the like of us in Emain.

CONCHUBOR [*looking at her for a moment*]. That's the first friendly word I've heard you speaking, Deirdre. A game the like of yours should be the proper thing for softening the heart and putting sweetness in the tongue; and yet this night when I hear you I've small blame left for Naisi that he stole you off from Ulster.

DEIRDRE [*to* NAISI]. Now, Naisi, answer gently, and we'll be friends to-night.

NAISI [*doggedly*]. I have no call but to be friendly. I'll answer what you will.

DEIRDRE [*taking* NAISI's *hand*]. Then you'll call Conchubor your friend and king, the man who reared me up upon Slieve Fuadh.

[*As* CONCHUBOR *is going to clasp* NAISI's *hand cries are heard behind.*]

CONCHUBOR. What noise is that?

AINNLE [*behind*]. Naisi. . . . Naisi. . . . Come to us; we are betrayed and broken.

NAISI. It's Ainnle crying out in a battle.

CONCHUBOR. I was near won this night, but death's between us now. [*He goes out.*]

DEIRDRE [*clinging to* NAISI]. There is no battle. . . . Do not leave me, Naisi.

NAISI. I must go to them.

DEIRDRE [*beseechingly*]. Do not leave me, Naisi. Let us creep up in the darkness behind the grave. If there's a battle, maybe the strange fighters will be destroyed, when Ainnle and Ardan are against them. [*Cries heard.*]

NAISI [*wildly*]. I hear Ardan crying out. Do not hold me from my brothers.

DEIRDRE. Do not leave me, Naisi. Do not leave me broken and alone.

NAISI. I cannot leave my brothers when it is I who have defied the king.

DEIRDRE. I will go with you.

NAISI. You cannot come. Do not hold me from the fight.
[*He throws her aside almost roughly.*]

DEIRDRE [*with restraint*]. Go to your brothers. For seven years you have been kindly, but the hardness of death has come between us.

NAISI [*looking at her aghast*]. And you'll have me meet death with a hard word from your lips in my ear?

DEIRDRE. We've had a dream, but this night has waked us surely. In a little while we've lived too long, Naisi, and isn't it a poor thing we should miss the safety of the grave, and we trampling its edge?

AINNLE [*behind*]. Naisi, Naisi, we are attacked and ruined!

DEIRDRE. Let you go where they are calling. [*She looks at him for an instant coldly.*] Have you no shame loitering and talking, and a cruel death facing Ainnle and Ardan in the woods?

NAISI [*frantic*]. They'll not get a death that's cruel, and they with men alone. It's women that have loved are cruel only; and if I went on living from this day I'd be putting a curse on the lot of them I'd meet walking in the east or west, putting a curse on the sun that gave them beauty, and on the madder and the stone-crop put red upon their cloaks.

DEIRDRE [*bitterly*]. I'm well pleased there's no one in this place to make a story that Naisi was a laughing-stock the night he died.

NAISI. There'd not be many'd make a story, for that

257

mockery is in your eyes this night will spot the face of Emain with a plague of pitted graves. [*He goes out.*]

CONCHUBOR [*outside*]. That is Naisi. Strike him! [*Tumult. DEIRDRE crouches down on NAISI's cloak. CONCHUBOR comes in hurriedly.*] They've met their death – the three that stole you, Deirdre, and from this out you'll be my queen in Emain.

[*A keen of men's voices is heard behind.*]

DEIRDRE [*bewildered and terrified*]. It is not I will be a queen.

CONCHUBOR. Make your lamentation a short while if you will, but it isn't long till a day'll come when you begin pitying a man is old and desolate, and High King also. . . . Let you not fear me, for it's I'm well pleased you have a store of pity for the three that were your friends in Alban.

DEIRDRE. I have pity, surely. . . . It's the way pity has me this night, when I think of Naisi, that I could set my teeth into the heart of a king.

CONCHUBOR. I know well pity's cruel, when it was my pity for my own self destroyed Naisi.

DEIRDRE [*more wildly*]. It was my words without pity gave Naisi a death will have no match until the ends of life and time. [*Breaking out into a keen.*] But who'll pity Deirdre has lost the lips of Naisi from her neck and from her cheek for ever? Who'll pity Deirdre has lost the twilight in the woods with Naisi, when beech-trees were silver and copper, and ash-trees were fine gold?

CONCHUBOR [*bewildered*]. It's I'll know the way to pity and care you, and I with a share of troubles has me thinking this night it would be a good bargain if it was I was in the grave, and Deirdre crying over me, and it was Naisi who was old and desolate.

Act Three

[*Keen heard.*]

DEIRDRE [*wild with sorrow*]. It is I who am desolate; I, Deirdre, that will not live till I am old.

CONCHUBOR. It's not long you'll be desolate, and I seven years saying, 'It's a bright day for Deirdre in the woods of Alban'; or saying again, 'What way will Deirdre be sleeping this night, and wet leaves and branches driving from the north?' Let you not break the thing I've set my life on, and you giving yourself up to your sorrow when it's joy and sorrow do burn out like straw blazing in an east wind.

DEIRDRE [*turning on him*]. Was it that way with your sorrow, when I and Naisi went northward from Slieve Fuadh and let raise our sails for Alban?

CONCHUBOR. There's one sorrow has no end surely — that's being old and lonesome. [*With extraordinary pleading.*] But you and I will have a little peace in Emain, with harps playing, and old men telling stories at the fall of the night. I've let build rooms for our two selves, Deirdre, with red gold upon the walls and ceilings that are set with bronze. There never was a queen in the east had a house the like of your house, that's waiting for yourself in Emain.

SOLDIER [*running in*]. Emain is in flames. Fergus has come back, and is setting fire to the world. Come up, Conchubor, or your state will be destroyed!

CONCHUBOR [*angry and regal again*]. Are the Sons of Usna buried?

SOLDIERS. They are in their grave, but no earth is thrown.

CONCHUBOR. Let me see them. Open the tent! [SOLDIER *opens back of tent and shows grave.*] Where are my fighters?

SOLDIER. They are gone to Emain.

CONCHUBOR [*to* DEIRDRE]. There are none to harm you. Stay here until I come again.

[*Goes out with* SOLDIER. DEIRDRE *looks round for a moment, then goes up slowly and looks into grave. She crouches down and begins swaying herself backwards and forwards, keening softly. At first her words are not heard, then they become clear*.]

DEIRDRE. It's you three will not see age or death coming – you that were my company when the fires on the hill-tops were put out and the stars were our friends only. I'll turn my thoughts back from this night, that's pitiful for want of pity, to the time it was your rods and cloaks made a little tent for me where there'd be a birch-tree making shelter and a dry stone; though from this day my own fingers will be making a tent for me, spreading out my hairs and they knotted with the rain.

[LAVARCHAM *and* OLD WOMAN *come in stealthily on right*.]

DEIRDRE [*not seeing them*]. It is I, Deirdre, will be crouching in a dark place; I, Deirdre, that was young with Naisi, and brought sorrow to his grave in Emain.

OLD WOMAN. Is that Deirdre broken down that was so light and airy?

LAVARCHAM. It is, surely, crying out over their grave. [*She goes to* DEIRDRE.]

DEIRDRE. It will be my share from this out to be making lamentation on his stone always, and I crying for a love will be the like of a star shining on a little harbour by the sea.

LAVARCHAM [*coming forward*]. Let you rise up, Deirdre, and come off while there are none to heed us, the way I'll find you shelter and some friend to guard you.

DEIRDRE. To what place would I go away from Naisi? What are the woods without Naisi or the sea shore?

LAVARCHAM [*very coaxingly*]. If it is that way you'd be, come till I find you a sunny place where you'll be a great wonder they'll call the queen of sorrows; and you'll begin taking a pride to be sitting up pausing and dreaming when the summer comes.

DEIRDRE. It was the voice of Naisi that was strong in summer – the voice of Naisi that was sweeter than pipes playing, but from this day will be dumb always.

LAVARCHAM [*to* OLD WOMAN]. She doesn't heed us at all. We'll be hard set to rouse her.

OLD WOMAN. If we don't the High King will rouse her, coming down beside her with the rage of battle in his blood, for how could Fergus stand against him?

LAVARCHAM [*touching* DEIRDRE *with her hand*]. There's a score of woman's years in store for you, and you'd best choose will you start living them beside the man you hate, or being your own mistress in the west or south?

DEIRDRE. It is not I will go on living after Ainnle and after Ardan. After Naisi I will not have a lifetime in the world.

OLD WOMAN [*with excitement*]. Look, Lavarcham! There's a light leaving the Red Branch. Conchubor and his lot will be coming quickly with a torch of bog-deal for her marriage, throwing a light on her three comrades.

DEIRDRE [*startled*]. Let us throw down clay on my three comrades. Let us cover up Naisi along with Ainnle and Ardan, they that were the pride of Emain. [*Throwing in clay.*] There is Naisi was the best of three, the choicest of the choice of many. It was a clean death was your share, Naisi; and it is not I will quit your head, when it's many a dark night among the snipe and plover that you and I were whispering together. It is not I will quit your head, Naisi, when it's many a night we saw the stars among the clear trees of Glen da Ruadh, or the moon pausing to rest her on the edges of the hills.

OLD WOMAN. Conchubor is coming, surely. I see the glare of flames throwing a light upon his cloak.

LAVARCHAM [*eagerly*]. Rise up, Deirdre, and come to Fergus, or be the High King's slave for ever!

DEIRDRE [*imperiously*]. I will not leave Naisi, who has left the whole world scorched and desolate. I will not go away when there is no light in the heavens, and no flower in the earth under them, but is saying to me that it is Naisi who is gone for ever.

CONCHUBOR [*behind*]. She is here. Stay a little back. [LAVARCHAM *and* OLD WOMAN *go into the shadow on left as* CONCHUBOR *comes in. With excitement, to* DEIRDRE.] Come forward and leave Naisi the way I've left charred timber and a smell of burning in Emain Macha, and a heap of rubbish in the storehouse of many crowns.

DEIRDRE [*more awake to what is round her*]. What are crowns and Emain Macha, when the head that gave them glory is this place, Conchubor, and it stretched upon the gravel will be my bed to-night?

CONCHUBOR. Make an end with talk of Naisi, for I've come to bring you to Dundealgan since Emain is destroyed.

[CONCHUBOR *makes a movement towards her.*]

DEIRDRE [*with a tone that stops him*]. Draw a little back from Naisi, who is young for ever. Draw a little back from the white bodies I am putting under a mound of clay and grasses that are withered – a mound will have a nook for my own self when the end is come.

CONCHUBOR [*roughly*]. Let you rise up and come along

with me in place of growing crazy with your wailings here.

DEIRDRE. It's yourself has made a crazy story, and let you go back to your arms, Conchubor, and to councils where your name is great, for in this place you are an old man and a fool only.

CONCHUBOR. If I've folly I've sense left not to lose the thing I've bought with sorrow and the deaths of many.

[*He moves towards her.*]

DEIRDRE. Do not raise a hand to touch me.

CONCHUBOR. There are other hands to touch you. My fighters are set round in among the trees.

DEIRDRE. Who'll fight the grave, Conchubor, and it opened on a dark night?

LAVARCHAM [*eagerly*]. There are steps in the wood. I hear the call of Fergus and his men.

CONCHUBOR [*furiously*]. Fergus cannot stop me. I am more powerful than he is, though I am defeated and old.

FERGUS [*comes in to* DEIRDRE; *a red glow is seen behind the grave*]. I have destroyed Emain, and now I'll guard you all times, Deirdre, though it was I, without knowledge, brought Naisi to his grave.

CONCHUBOR. It's not you will guard her, for my whole armies are gathering. Rise up, Deirdre, for you are mine surely.

FERGUS [*coming between them*]. I am come between you.

CONCHUBOR [*wildly*]. When I've killed Naisi and his brothers, is there any man that I will spare? And is it you will stand against me, Fergus, when it's seven years you've seen me getting my death with rage in Emain?

FERGUS. It's I, surely, will stand against a thief and traitor.

DEIRDRE [*stands up and sees the light from Emain*]. Draw a

little back with the squabbling of fools when I am broken up with misery. [*She turns round.*] I see the flames of Emain starting upward in the dark night; and because of me there will be weasels and wild cats crying on a lonely wall where there were queens and armies and red gold, the way there will be a story told of a ruined city and a raving king and a woman will be young for ever. [*She looks round.*] I see the trees naked and bare, and the moon shining. Little moon, little moon of Alban, it's lonesome you'll be this night, and to-morrow night, and long nights after, and you pacing the woods beyond Glen Laoi, looking every place for Deirdre and Naisi, the two lovers who slept so sweetly with each other.

FERGUS [*going to* CONCHUBOR'S *right and whispering*]. Keep back, or you will have the shame of pushing a bolt on a queen who is out of her wits.

CONCHUBOR. It is I who am out of my wits, with Emain in flames, and Deirdre raving, and my own heart gone within me.

DEIRDRE [*in a high and quiet tone*]. I have put away sorrow like a shoe that is worn out and muddy, for it is I have had a life that will be envied by great companies. It was not by a low birth I made kings uneasy, and they sitting in the halls of Emain. It was not a low thing to be chosen by Conchubor, who was wise, and Naisi had no match for bravery. It is not a small thing to be rid of grey hairs, and the loosening of the teeth. [*With a sort of triumph.*] It was the choice of lives we had in the clear woods, and in the grave we're safe, surely. . . .

CONCHUBOR. She will do herself harm.

DEIRDRE [*showing* NAISI'S *knife*]. I have a little key to unlock the prison of Naisi you'd shut upon his youth for ever. Keep back, Conchubor; for the High King who is your master has put his hands between us. [*She half turns to the grave.*] It was sorrows were foretold, but great joys were my share always; yet it is a cold place I must go to be with you, Naisi; and it's cold your arms will be this night that were warm about my neck so often. . . . It's a pitiful thing to be talking out when your ears are shut to me. It's a pitiful thing, Conchubor, you have done this night in Emain; yet a thing will be a joy and triumph to the ends of life and time.

[*She presses knife into her heart and sinks into the grave.* CON-CHUBOR *and* FERGUS *go forward. The red glow fades, leaving stage very dark.*]

FERGUS. Four white bodies are laid down together; four clear lights are quenched in Ireland. [*He throws his sword into the grave.*] There is my sword that could not shield you – my four friends that were the dearest always. The flames of Emain have gone out: Deirdre is dead and there is none to keen her. That is the fate of Deirdre and the Children of Usna, and for this night, Conchubor, our war is ended. [*He goes out.*]

LAVARCHAM. I have a little hut where you can rest, Con-chubor; there is a great dew falling.

CONCHUBOR [*with the voice of an old man*]. Take me with you. I'm hard set to see the way before me.

OLD WOMAN. This way, Conchubor.

[*They go out.*]

LAVARCHAM [*beside the grave*]. Deirdre is dead, and Naisi is dead; and if the oaks and stars could die for sorrow, it's a dark sky and a hard and naked earth we'd have this night in Emain.

CURTAIN

Note

Note

the present volume *The Tinker's Wedding* will be found after *ders to the Sea* and before *The Well of the Saints*. This seemed be the proper place for it, as it was Synge's principal work tween those two plays, and belongs, in a real sense, to the rliest part of his career as a dramatist.

It is true that the version of 1903 was superseded by that ritten early in 1906 – while Synge was at work on *The Playboy the Western World* – but the changes which he then made in , although material, and, no doubt, dramatically an improve-ent, are to be explained, in the main, by the greater free-m allowed him by external circumstances. In 1906, Synge, fact, had hopes, as he rewrote the play, that it would be oduced, in a German translation, on the stage of Berlin, and, longer influenced by any thoughts of a Dublin audience, lowed himself full liberty in handling the situation at the end the Second Act. The history of the rewriting can be gathered m his correspondence with Max Meyerfeld, the German anslator of *The Well of the Saints*, which was published in *The le Review* for July 1924.

Any changes which Synge made in the play subsequent to e spring of 1906 were of the slightest, and consisted simply toning down a passage or two which were needlessly strong. In the last of Synge's letters to Max Meyerfeld, he mentions .ving 'rewritten and improved' part of the Third Act of *The ell of the Saints* in the spring of 1908. The improved version .ll be found in the present volume. It has been taken from e Abbey Theatre's copy of the play. The changes consist incipally in the introduction of additional dialogue for the .inor characters to enliven the main action. Here and there,

elsewhere in this copy, Synge made slighter alterations, son
of which he would probably have used if he had lived
supervise a new edition of this play. But it was difficult to s.
which of these had been made simply for acting purposes,
that no other changes have been introduced in the prese
edition.

It may not be out of place to mention in this note that on
sentence in *The Playboy of the Western World* which has been t
occasion of much criticism on technical grounds – the fir
speech of the Widow Quin in Act II – did not occur in t
manuscript which Synge sent to the printers. The 'tag', as
termed it, had been in an earlier manuscript, and he restore
it in the proofs, presumably as a result of his experience of t
rehearsals.

Although the author's name appears on the title-page of t
present volume in the customary form 'John M. Synge',
seems worth pointing out that, in his lifetime, Synge nev
used this form for publication, but invariably 'J. M. Syng
The longer title was introduced by the Cuala Press in *Poems a
Translations* after his death, and has since been so genera
followed that one hesitates to revert now to his own use. '
call him 'John Synge', however, as is often done in litera
memoirs and studies, is as though one should write 'Per
Shelley', or 'George Shaw', or 'William Yeats'. The dramat
was 'John Synge' to very few people while he was alive, a
it seems strange that the circle should be enlarged after
death.

The Penguin Poets

THE PENGUIN BOOK OF CONTEMPORARY VERSE
(D12)*
Edited by Kenneth Allott

An anthology containing 127 poems by sixty-one modern poets from W. B. Yeats to Sidney Keyes.

THE CENTURIES' POETRY
Edited by D. Kilham Roberts

A comprehensive anthology in five volumes:

1. *Chaucer to Shakespeare* (D6)
2. *Donne to Dryden* (D7)
3. *Pope to Keats* (D8)
4. *Hood to Hardy* (D9)
5. *Bridges to the Present Day* (D10)

A BOOK OF ENGLISH POETRY (D5)*
Edited by G. B. Harrison

An anthology selected from the works of sixty-one English poets from Chaucer to Rossetti.

THE PENGUIN BOOK OF COMIC AND CURIOUS VERSE (D19)†
Edited by J. M. Cohen

POEMS 1951 (D18)*

The prize-winning entries for the Festival of Britain competition introduced by John Hayward.

INDIVIDUAL POETS

Wordsworth (D2) Edited by W. E. Williams
Robert Burns (D3) Edited by H. W. Meikle and W. Beattie
T. S. Eliot (D4) Selected by himself
John Donne (D13) Edited by John Hayward
Alexander Pope (D14) Edited by Douglas Grant
Edith Sitwell (D16) Selected by herself
C. Day Lewis (D17) Selected by himself

1s 6d each   *2s 6d   †3s 6d

Drama

SALOME AND OTHER PLAYS
Oscar Wilde
600

This volume contains: *Salome, A Woman of No Importance*, and *An Ideal Husband*. Salome, with its odd moonlit beauty and the luxuriance of its language, is more akin to a modern prose poem than to drama proper: while the other two are true Wildean comedies presenting serious themes in an easy, witty and fast-moving style. Readers may remember the recent screen version of *An Ideal Husband*.

A SHORT HISTORY OF ENGLISH DRAMA
B. Ifor Evans
A172

This survey of English Drama covers the whole development from the Middle Ages to modern times and will prove an indispensable guide to all students, professional or otherwise. The author's *Short History of English Literature* is also available as Pelican A72.

SEVEN FAMOUS ONE-ACT PLAYS
Edited by John Ferguson
117

One of the early Penguins, this volume has been put in print again to meet the numerous requests for its re-issue. It comprises comedy, tragedy, 'costume', fantasy, and character plays. All seven of them read as well as they act, and have, indeed, been selected as much for that quality as for their interest to dramatic societies. They are:

> *A Marriage Has Been Arranged:* ALFRED SUTRO
> *The Cloak:* CLIFFORD BAX
> *Two Gentlemen of Soho:* A. P. HERBERT
> *Campbell of Kilmohr:* J. A. FERGUSON
> *The Maker of Dreams:* OLIPHANT DOWN
> *The Dear Departed:* STANLEY HOUGHTON
> *The Monkey's Paw:* W. W. JACOBS

A second volume containing seven more one-act plays will be published later this year.